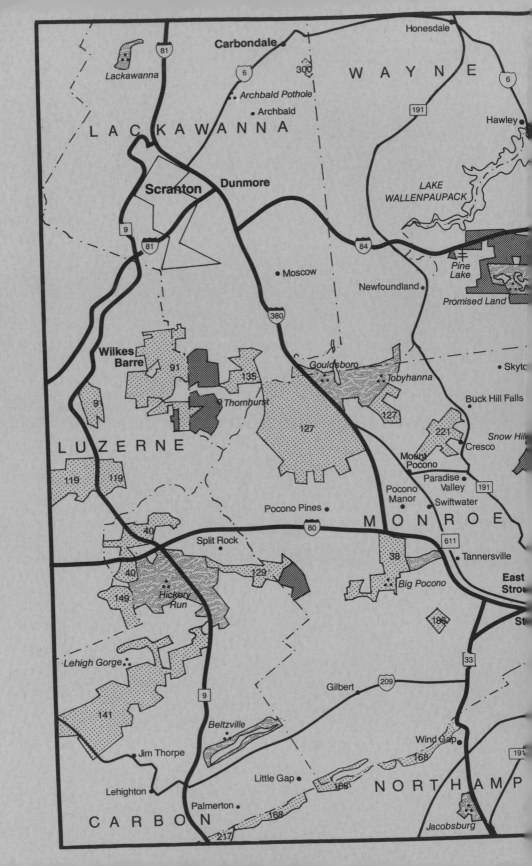

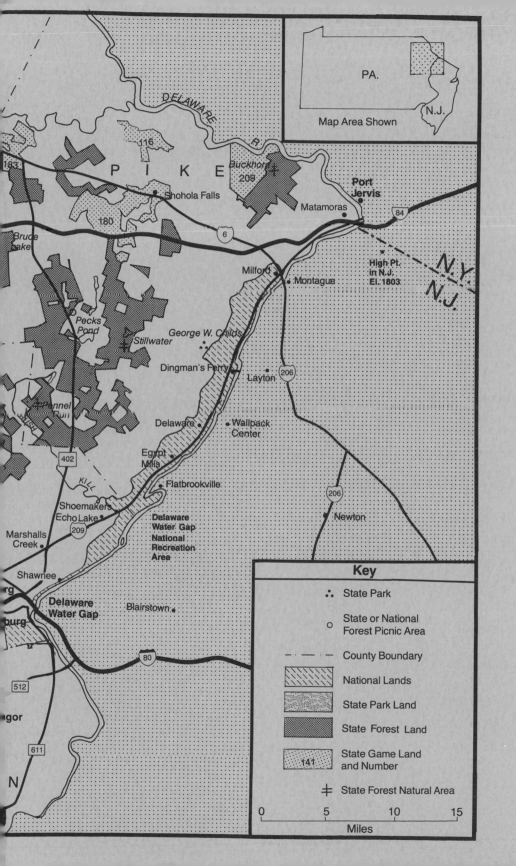

DELAWARE R

P I K E

116

Buckhorn
209

Shohola Falls

Port
Jervis

Matamoras

84

183

180

6

Bruce
Lake

Milford

Montague

High Pt.
in N.J.
El. 1803

N.Y.
N.J.

Pecks
Pond

Stillwater

George W. Childs

Dingman's Ferry

Layton

206

Tunnel
Run

Delaware

Wallpack
Center

402

Egypt
Mills

KILL

Flatbrookville

206

Shoemakers
Echo Lake

Delaware
Water Gap
National
Recreation
Area

Newton

Marshalls
Creek

209

Shawnee

Delaware
Water Gap

Blairstown

burg

80

512

gor

611

N

PA.

Map Area Shown

N.J.

Key

∴ State Park

○ State or National
Forest Picnic Area

– · – · – County Boundary

National Lands

State Park Land

State Forest Land

141 State Game Land
and Number

‡ State Forest Natural Area

0   5   10   15

Miles

THE POCONOS

THE Poconos

**CARL S. OPLINGER and
ROBERT HALMA**

Illustrations by Robert Halma

An Illustrated Natural History Guide

To Gina,

Enjoy exploring the Poconos!

Carl A. Oplinger
20 June '98

J. Robert Halma

Rutgers University Press
NEW BRUNSWICK

Third paperback printing, 1994

Copyright © 1988 by Rutgers, The State University
All Rights Reserved
Manufactured in the United States of America

Library of Congress Cataloging-in-Publication Data

Oplinger, Carl S., 1936–
    The Poconos.

    Bibliography: p.
    Includes index.
    1. Natural history—Pennsylvania—Pocono Mountains—
Guidebooks.   I. Halma, J. Robert, 1935–   .   II. Title.
QH105.P4065   1988   508.748′25   87-23442
ISBN 0-8135-1293-X
ISBN 0-8135-1294-8 (pbk.)

British Cataloging-in-Publication information available

CONTENTS

Figure

LIST OF TABLES

Table

Preface and Acknowledgments

For many individuals, the name "Poconos" brings to mind images of vacation and honeymoon resorts, golf courses and ski slopes, waterfalls and panoramic views, all within a few hours drive from eastern United States metropolitan centers. To be sure, these are a part of the Pocono scene, but to growing numbers of people, the Poconos means what it has for us for several decades—a "nearby wilderness"—a natural area of considerable beauty with an interesting geologic and ecologic history.

In recent years, many persons have rediscovered outdoor pleasures characteristic of earlier times. Hiking, cross-country skiing, canoeing, and similar activities once again flourish in the Poconos. While engaged in these pursuits, participants have had increased contact with the natural world and many have developed a curiosity about that world. We knew of no natural history guide to the Poconos and thus set out to write this volume. We hope our efforts will aid the outdoors activist, the vacationer, the amateur naturalist, or the reader who is curious about the natural history of the Poconos to "see" the Poconos in the manner suggested by Goethe who wrote, "We see what we know."

We've been assisted in the preparation of this text by Karen Reeds of Rutgers University Press. We've benefited from suggestions concerning illustrations from Ry Greene of Cedar Crest College's Art Department and Barbara Kopel of Rutgers University Press. A careful reading of the manuscript by reviewers selected by Rutgers Press was most helpful. John Pickering's review of the entire manuscript was beneficial also. Dr. Don Ryan, of Lehigh University, reviewed the geology sections. Of special note, Dr. Herbert Kraft provided extensive commentary on the portion of the text dealing with aboriginal and historic activities in the Upper Delaware River Valley. Many of his comments are incorporated into the text. Of course, the responsibility of errors of omission or commission throughout the entire text remains solely with us.

Most geology illustrations are based on material published by the *Pennsylvania Geological Survey*. Other source credits are identified with the figures.

Our typist, Linda Klosek, was superb in dealing with our numerous alterations and revisions. Financial support from Cedar Crest College and Muhlenberg College is appreciated.

Our interest and understanding of natural history and ecology owes much to others. C.O. wishes especially to thank his parents who were the first to tolerate, and, in fact, encourage an interest in snakes, frogs, and other "critters." The guidance of teachers including B. B. Owen, F. J. Trembley, W. J. Hamilton, Jr., and, especially J. E. Trainer and R. L. Schaeffer, Jr., whose friendship I was to subsequently enjoy as colleagues at Muhlenberg College, was invaluable. My daughters, Anne and Amy, allowed me to view nature through "young eyes" again, a rewarding experience. My wife, Marilee, has my sincere thanks for her constant encouragement of my teaching and research efforts.

R.H. is also appreciative of many outstanding teachers, notably, B. B. Owen, F. J. Trembley, and H. Bengelink. My family—wife Linda, son Thomas and daughter Kimberly—were supportive throughout the sometimes strained periods of "yet another night at the drafting table." My Cedar Crest College biology colleagues, and especially Marion Kayhart, kindly continued to encourage me throughout the duration of this venture.

Carl S. Oplinger
Robert Halma
Allentown, Pennsylvania
April 1987

THE POCONOS

Introduction

Several decisions had to be made as we approached the planning and writing of this book. First, we had to set geographic boundaries for our natural history survey of the Poconos. This was not an easy task—for several reasons. The Pocono Plateau is a distinct geologic feature located in Monroe and Pike counties of Pennsylvania. However, surrounding areas, of varying distances, are usually claimed by residents as the "Poconos" also. To complicate matters, residents and visitors alike usually refer to the region as the "Pocono Mountains." For our purposes, we decided to set the following boundaries: the Delaware River on the east to the Moosic Mountains on the west and from the Blue (Kittatinny) Mountain on the south to Honesdale on the north. This area—about 2000 square miles—is host to nearly ten million visitors annually and, in addition to numerous resorts, golf courses, camps, and other manmade features, possesses a diversity of natural features worthy of exploration and study.

As the above paragraph suggests, we also decided to use the English system of measurement throughout the text, although we appreciate the merits of the metric system in professional activities. We also use the Fahrenheit temperature scale. For those who wish to adopt the system employed by the scientific community, as well as most countries, the following conversions will be useful:

1 inch	= 2.54 centimeters
1 foot	= 0.30 meters
1 mile	= 1.61 kilometers
1 ounce	= 28.35 grams
1 pound	= 0.45 kilograms
1 acre	= 0.41 hectares
1 square mile	= 259 hectares

Fahrenheit to Celsius $°C = 5/9 \, (°F - 32)$

Celsius to Fahrenheit $°F = 9/5 \, (°C + 32)$

In light of our intended audience, we've avoided extensive use of scientific jargon, of which the science of ecology is not exempt. After all, as someone said, ecology is the only science that "calls a spade a geotome." We do present major ecological concepts that should add to our readers' appreciation of the intricate interrelationships of living and nonliving components of the environment.

In a similar vein, we use common names in the body of the text although we are aware of the dilemmas that arise from the use of common names. Appendix C (section I) is an alphabetic list of common names, with scientific names provided for interested readers. Readers familiar with scientific names can consult the alphabetic list of those names in Appendix C (section II). The constraints of space prohibited the inclusion of scientific names of the numerous invertebrates and extensive grasses, sedges, and most nonflowering plants discussed in various parts of the text.

To avoid the occasional and awkward "he/she" pronoun dilemma, we use only "he". Certainly, we intend no sexist bias.

We use several standard abbreviations throughout the text and figures. These are:

cs and xs	= cross section
el.	= elevation
fm.	= formation
sp.	= species
spp.	= species (plural)
fr.	= fruit
fls.	= flowers
lvs.	= leaves

Getting Started

To highlight certain ecological concepts, we've selected, as examples, sites such as state parks, state game lands, and state forests that are readily accessible to the public. Many other places in the Poconos exhibit comparable features but these areas are frequently posted against trespass. If one wishes to explore such areas, one must secure permission from the owner. In all cases, property should be respected, littering avoided, and a sincere effort made to inflict no harm to plants and animals so that others may enjoy similar experiences.

Numerous boxes, interspersed throughout the text, provide information which should serve as starting points for your explorations. If you wish to go beyond the most casual forays, make some advance preparation. This would include appropriate footgear and garments, as local terrain and weather dictate. A hand lens, binoculars, note pad, and pencil will be of value in your study. A compass, and an understanding of its use, a whistle (in case you really didn't understand how to use the compass, end up lost, and need to signal for help), and maps are advised. Sources of maps are listed in Appendix B.

It is a good rule not to venture into unfamiliar terrain alone. It is certainly unwise to go into potentially dangerous areas such as bogs, swamps, lake and river edges, etc., unaccompanied.

In addition to these general words of advice, note the following specific hazards:

Hunting season: The amateur naturalist should not venture onto state game lands and other areas during the fall hunting seasons. These times are listed in local newspapers. During these hunting pe-

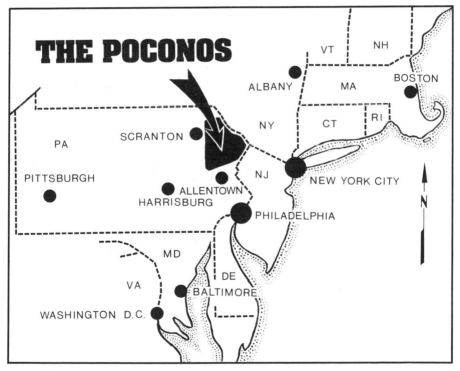

Figure I.1
The Poconos in the Mid-Atlantic Region. About 50 percent of the population of the United States lives within a six-hour drive.

riods, more protected sites near towns and villages can serve as places for nature study. Even then, it is advisable to wear bright colors and proceed with caution.

Poisonous plants: The most common poisonous plant in the Poconos is the widespread poison ivy (Figure 3.11). Its relative, poison sumac (Figure 5.22), is more toxic but restricted in distribution to swamps, bogs, and other wet places. Several other sumacs, commonly seen along roadsides and meadows (Figure 3.20), are harmless. That roadside and garden weed, the stinging nettle (Figure 6.6), will quickly reveal the reason for its common name if one brushes against it with bare skin. A number of seed-bearing plants are poisonous if eaten, as are a group of attractive, but deadly, mushrooms. The surest safeguard here is avoidance—unless positive identification by experts has been made.

Poisonous snakes: Only two poisonous snakes are found in the Poconos, the fairly common copperhead and the less common timber rattlesnake (Figure 4.11). Both species are rather reclusive and not apt to bite unless provoked. Be on the alert for these animals in most settings, especially if you scramble over rock outcroppings where your hands may be placed in unseen spots.

Insect problems: A number of common insects such as deer flies, black flies, and mosquitoes bite. Wearing long-sleeved shirts and trousers will give a measure of protection. Some type of headgear is advisable also. Insect repellent is advisable. Ticks are common in moist brushlands and wooded areas and readily attach themselves to the exposed skin or clothing of passing hikers. Since diseases are transmitted by these pests, an attached tick should receive prompt attention. Do not attempt to pull the tick off as its mouthparts are likely to remain embedded in the skin. An application of alcohol or ammonia to the tick will usually cause it to release its hold in 15 to 20 minutes.

Rabies: A number of animals carry rabies, an infectious virus that attacks the central nervous system. Avoid direct handling of dead animals, such as "road kills". It is also wise not to approach or attempt to handle any unusually friendly or strange-acting wild animal.

Continuing Explorations

We hope that readers will use this guide at home and in the field. Chapter 1, Pocono Patterns, provides an overview of present patterns that are the result of significant influences such as climate, soil, and human disturbance. A brief explanation of ecosystem dynamics is provided. The intriguing transitional location of the Poconos in the ranges of numerous plants and animals, with hints of habitats typical of more northern regions, provide numerous opportunities for exploration. Chapter 2, Geological Forces that Shaped the Poconos, follows the processes such as glaciation, erosion, and mountain-building that created the diverse Pocono landforms of today. Numerous "textbook" examples of geologic phenomena are present in the Poconos and are readily accessible.

Chapter 3, Pocono Forests, is a survey of the major forest types one will encounter in visits to the region. The dominant woody plants are highlighted, but other groups such as shrubs, ferns, and flowering plants are considered as well. Two tourist attractions, the early summer blooms of mountain laurel and rhododendron and the brilliant autumn foliage, are part of the presentation in this chapter.

Animals of Pocono Forests, Chapter 4, is an account of the somewhat elusive animal world of the Poconos. Although trees stay put, animals do not. This presents problems when attempting to provide readers a guide to potential encounters with wildlife. Nevertheless, the dominant animals are discussed and ways of recognizing their presence are noted. With some effort, skill, and luck opportunities exist to observe wildlife. The white-tailed deer and the black bear, the major large game animals in the Poconos, receive special attention.

Since aquatic habitats such as lakes, ponds, and streams are a prominent feature of the Poconos and often the destination for visitors, Chapter 5, Watercourse and Wetland Communities, deals with the natural history of these sites. Opportunities for seeing a diversity of plants and animals are enhanced by the presence of water. Again, certain sites such as bogs and swamps, though rich in wildlife, are potentially dangerous, and caution is advised when exploring such places.

Roadside Natural History, Chapter 6, suggests a pleasant way to encounter numerous Poconos plants and animals when visitors have a limited amount of time to spend in the region. The influence of edges on the diversity of wildlife is apparent to the attentive observer.

The activities of humans in the Poconos from the time of the arrival of the first native Americans through the activities of the European settlers to the varied industrial, commercial, and tourist enterprises of today are reviewed in Chapter 7, Human Activity from Native Americans to Vacationers. We wish to use this chapter not only to point out the influence that humans have had on the region but also to encourage present-day visitors to consider their impact and what they might do individually and collectively to protect and preserve those varied natural features of the region that have enticed humans to dwell in the Poconos for many centuries.

Chapter 8, the concluding chapter—Delaware Water Gap National Recreation Area—highlights this area on the eastern border of the Poconos. The presence of visitor centers with displays, maps, and informed staff—as well as the numerous, marked, well-maintained trails in varied habitats—could serve as an excellent introduction for later self-exploration of the Poconos.

Continuing Study

Since the goal of this volume is to provide the general reader with an overview of the ecology of the Poconos, we had to omit an extensive consideration of any one component. We have provided a selected list of identification manuals, field guides, and other references in the bibliography to permit readers to pursue their particular interests. Appendix A lists many agencies, societies, and other sources of information about particular aspects of the Poconos.

CHAPTER 1

Pocono Patterns

"There is much confusion between land and country. Land is the place where corn, gullies, and mortgages grow. Country is the personality of land, the collective harmony of its soil, life, and weather."
—ALDO LEOPOLD, *A Sand County Almanac*, 1949

The Delaware Water Gap in the Kittatinny Mountain serves as a gateway for the Delaware River as it flows to the Atlantic Ocean. This magnificent gorge is also considered the gateway to the Poconos. On the New Jersey side of the Gap, Mt. Tammany rises steeply from river level to a height of 1600 feet. Mt. Minsi on the Pennsylvania side has an elevation of 1460 feet.

The Delaware River forms the eastern boundary of the Poconos. The Lehigh Gap near Palmerton, where the Lehigh River flows through another gorge in the Kittatinny Mountain, marks the southwestern corner of the Pocono region. The Kittatinny Mountain, generally known locally as Blue Mountain, is positioned in a northeast to southwest plane. Kittatinny, whether a single ridge or a series of mountains—its name meant "endless hills" to the Lenape Indians—forms the southern boundary of the Pocono region. On the west, Moosic Mountains separate the Poconos from the Wyoming Valley; on the north, the Poconos slope gradually toward Honesdale. The

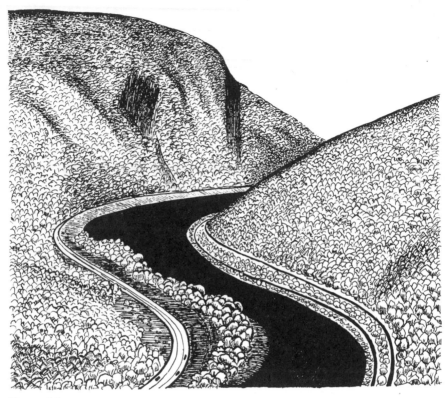

Figure 1.1
View of Delaware Water Gap. Perspective from north of the gap on the Pennsylvania side.

highland area, known as the Poconos, contains approximately 2000 square miles of extensively wooded upland interspersed with many ponds, lakes, and numerous streams with scenic waterfalls.

Geologic Patterns

Northeastern Pennsylvania is traversed by two principal physiographic provinces: the Appalachian Plateau and the Appalachian Valley and Ridge. The eastern glaciated section of the Appalachian Plateau Province extends across the northern part of northeastern

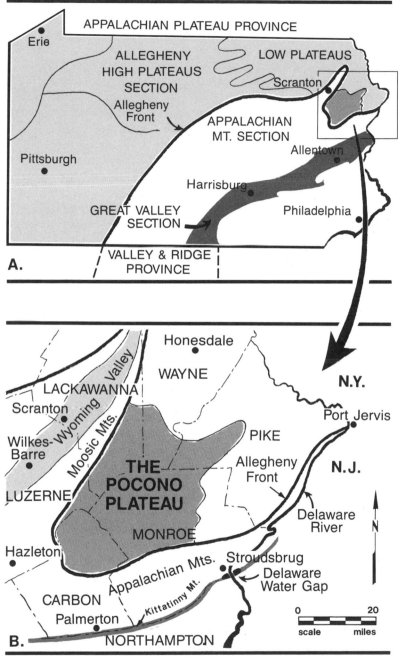

Figure 1.2
A. Physiographic provinces of Pennsylvania.
B. Detail of Pocono region.

Pennsylvania. Glaciers covered this area as recently as 15,000 years ago, profoundly influencing present Pocono patterns. The Pocono Plateau is a slightly uneven tableland ranging from 1900 to 2200 feet above sea level, underlain by nearly flat-lying sandstone and shale. East of the plateau, softer rocks have been eroded into a series of hilltops of lower elevations, 1000 to 1200 feet, separated by lakes and wetlands. On the eastern margin, the shallow, free-flowing streams, as they tumble towards the Delaware River, form the famous waterfalls that first attracted most visitors to the Poconos.

The Appalachian Mountain Section of the Valley and Ridge Province crosses the southern counties of the Pocono region: Luzerne, Carbon, and Monroe. As suggested by the name, this province is characterized by narrow ridges, which in Pennsylvania run more or less parallel in a northeast to southwest direction. A striking feature of the province is the transverse direction of the river valleys and deep water gaps, such as those of the Lehigh and Delaware, formed over eons by the rivers cutting through the ridges.

Numerous ponds and lakes dotting the Pocono region are evidence of the glaciated past. Wayne and Pike Counties share the bulk of Pennsylvania's ponds. Where glacial potholes had poor drainage, conditions were favorable for the formation of those fascinating nature preserves known as bogs.

Drainage Patterns

Most of the water of the Pocono region eventually flows into the Delaware River drainage basin. However, water from the extreme western edge of the region flows into the north branch of the Susquehanna River and its tributaries.

The Lehigh River drains most of Carbon and Monroe Counties, the western portion of the Poconos. At Easton, the Lehigh flows into the Delaware. The Delaware River, forming the eastern border of the state of Pennsylvania as well as the eastern border of the Poconos, is a modest river compared to the Colorado or Mississippi Rivers. From its headwaters in the Catskill Mountains of New York to its broad estuary south of Wilmington, the Delaware traverses only 330 miles. Yet the Delaware drains 13,000 square miles of the eastern seaboard, and its waters serve in various ways an estimated ten percent of the U. S. citizenry. The 120-mile stretch between Hancock, New York—where the east and west branches join—and the Delaware Water Gap is renowned for sport-fishing and canoeing. This relatively unspoiled stretch was designated in 1978 as a part of the National Wild and Scenic Rivers System. In the Poconos, the principal tributaries of the Delaware, from north to south, include: Equinunk Creek in Wayne County, the Lackawaxen River and Shohola Creek in Pike, Bushkill Creek in Pike and Monroe, and Pocono Creek in Monroe.

Soil Patterns

Pocono subsoils were formed from two major sources, native rock and glacial deposits. Bedrock of the region is mainly sandstone and shale. Over an extensive area of northeastern Pennsylvania, including the Poconos, there is a blanket of glacial till that may be as much as one hundred feet thick. Glacial till is a mixture of sand, clay, and boulders of various sizes. Glacial deposits may be recognized by the fact that the till does not grade downward into the underlying rock as native soils do. Boulders interspersed in the till are composed of rock materials from as far away as Canada.

Above the till is a topsoil, the product of many processes that operate to form soil in the Poconos as they do elsewhere on the planet. Solid rock will eventually start to disintegrate, as heating, cooling, thawing, and freezing weaken the rock structure. Water and air will react with minerals in the rock, further weakening the structure. Even as the rock is being broken up by these physical and chemical processes, primitive organisms such as lichens and fungi gain a foothold. Their activities continue the soil formation process. In time, mosses and ferns make their appearance. The biological community expands as small animals find dwelling places and food. Decomposition activities of microbes convert the dead plant and animal matter to inorganic compounds, adding to the increasing complexity of the forming soil.

The typical acidic topsoil of the Poconos is the product of microbial decomposition of the litter of ferns, mosses, heaths, oaks, and conifers which characterize much of the region. The cool moist climate promotes the slow rates of decomposition that enhance acidification. The thin topsoil with plant residue, the humus, in varying stages of decay, is the A horizon in what geologists term a soil profile. Beneath this dark brown topsoil lies a characteristic gray subsoil. This infertile sandy layer, the B horizon, is indicative of Podzol soils, the designation for such soils.

The thin, stony, infertile soils of the Poconos have not been hospitable to agriculture and require the addition of lime and fertilizer for the growth of the pasture grasses, hay, and silage corn needed to support the region's dairy herds.

Climatic Patterns

The elevation of the Pocono Plateau is not sufficient to produce a true mountain climate. Nevertheless, many characteristics of such a climate may be noted. Winters are long and cold, summers short and cool; these conditions produce the winter and summer vacation seasons familiar to Pocono visitors. Local variations in elevation influence air movements and produce local "frost pockets". Daily temperature fluctuations are broad, as much as 20°F (degrees Fahrenheit) in midwinter and 26°F in midsummer. The pronounced local variations in climate throughout the region can be illustrated by one observation. Tobyhanna, on the plateau, and Stroudsburg, near its base, are separated by about 20 aerial miles but have a difference in elevation of about 1470 feet. During the winter and summer months, air temperatures are 5 to 7°F cooler at Tobyhanna.

Growing seasons on the plateau are much shorter than in adjoining lowlands: in the Poconos, 115 days at Gouldsboro, 127 days at Mt. Pocono; nearby, 144 days at Stroudsburg, 176 days at Scranton. Precipitation is heavier on the plateau than in adjacent areas. Average annual precipitation is approximately 49 inches at Mt. Pocono, whereas in Scranton it is between 37 and 38 inches. Seasonal snowfall averages in excess of 50 inches in the northern part of the plateau, and the ground remains snow-covered for about three-fourths of the winter.

Vegetation Patterns

Plants and animals interact with abiotic (non-living) components of the environment—including soil characteristics, precipitation patterns, wind effects, intensity and duration of solar radiation—to produce characteristic assemblages termed ecosystems. In the broadest sense, there are two major types of ecosystems: terrestrial and aquatic.

Ecologists set apart various subdivisions (biomes) such as freshwater, estuarine, and marine aquatic ecosystems. The more numerous subdivisions of terrestrial ecosystems are desert, prairie, tundra, rainforest, and savanna.

The biome characteristic of much of the mid-Atlantic area is the temperate deciduous forest. As suggested by the name, a moderate

climate and trees that shed their leaves in autumn characterize this
biome. In the Poconos, the beech-birch-maple forest is considered the
regional or climactic vegetation pattern; that is, it is the end or climax
pattern of a series of vegetation patterns observed over time under
the weather conditions of the mid-Atlantic states. In the view of some
ecologists, it is more realistic to think of a mosaic pattern, since it is
unlikely that all communities in a given climatic region will end
up the same when physical habitats are not uniform. Other vegetation patterns observed in the Poconos may be considered local, or
edaphic (soil-related), climax patterns. These patterns are produced
as the result of special local conditions, especially soil composition,
moisture gradients, slope, and wind exposure. Principal habitat types
in the Poconos, in addition to the beech-birch-maple forest, are the
mixed oak forest, chestnut oak ridges, scrub oak barrens, hemlock-
white pine ravines, river flood plains, bogs, swamps, and marshes.

Repeated human activities such as lumbering and agriculture, an
extensive bark tanning industry more than a century ago, and now
acid rain, all have an influence on vegetation patterns. Interactions
with other organisms are significant also. Fungi caused a blight
which in a few decades of the early twentieth century killed the
American chestnut, at one time considered the most common tree in
Pennsylvania. Today, sprouts are commonly seen growing from roots
of old chestnut stumps; the sprouts occasionally grow to fifteen to
twenty feet and sometimes produce a few fruits, but the blight kills
the tree eventually. Dutch elm disease, also caused by a fungus
transmitted by bark beetles, threatens to eliminate the American elm
from parks and forests. Attack by tent caterpillars, a relatively local
phenomenon, and the more widespread gypsy moth infestations
could alter the pattern of dominant tree species over time. As indicated by Figure 1.3, climatic, physical, human, and non-human biological agents interact to produce the varied Pocono ecosystems.

Energy Flow Patterns

All ecosystems start with and are dependent upon the incredible
energy-trapping ability of green plants. Ninety-three millon miles
from our planet is a "thermonuclear or hydrogen bomb"—the sun—
where hydrogen is transmuted to helium with the release of enormous energy in the form of electromagnetic waves. Because of
Earth's distance from the sun and small size, only about one fifty-
millionth of the sun's energy output reaches Earth's outer atmosphere. Solar radiation is attenuated as it passes through the atmos-

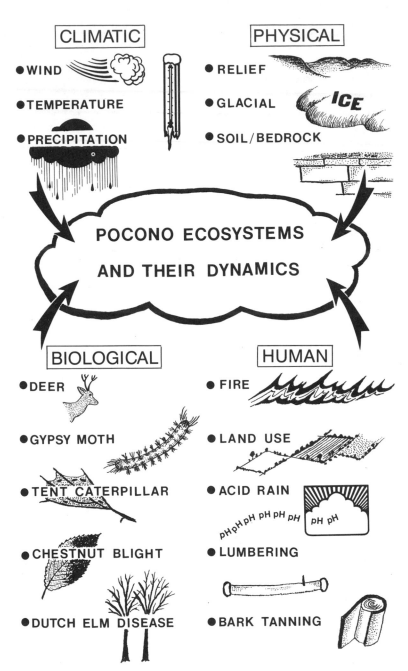

Figure 1.3
Major influences on Pocono ecosystems.

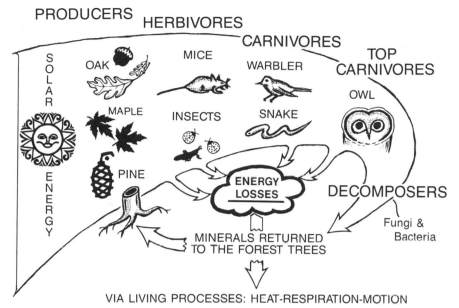

Figure 1.4
Energy flow and recycling in a generalized Pocono ecosystem.

phere; at most, 67 percent reaches the Earth's surface at noon on a clear summer day. Daily input of sunlight reaching autotrophs (organisms, primarily green plants, which produce their own food) varies according to season and weather. In mountainous areas, south-facing slopes receive more radiation than north-facing slopes—an inequality producing strikingly different microclimates with noticeably different vegetation patterns.

Only about 2 percent of the solar radiation reaching plants is trapped by means of chlorophyll. Radiant energy then converts into chemical energy as organic substances form during photosynthesis. Since plants as "living factories" continually expend energy in respiration, the remaining amount of "congealed sunlight" is the basis for almost all other life. In food chains, or more complex food webs, energy transfers occur as heterotrophs (feeders other than plants) enter the scene. At each step, a portion of the potential energy, as much as 80 to 90 percent, converts to heat. These losses dictate limits to the number of components of a food chain or web. The shorter the chain, or nearer the organism is to the beginning of the chain, the greater the energy available.

The most familiar pattern is the grazing food chain which starts with a green plant base, moves to grazing plant eaters (herbivores), and goes on to one or two levels of flesh eaters (primary and secondary carnivores). The detritus food chain is not as readily recognized. This chain starts with nonliving organic matter—dead plants or animals—that microbes such as fungi and bacteria decompose. The decomposed matter then serves as food for detritus-feeders which, in turn, serve as prey for the next trophic level.

In the beech-birch-maple biome of the Poconos, trees and other plants comprise the producer base. At the next trophic level, herbivores—ranging from ants, aphids, and caterpillars to mice, squirrels, and deer—continue the energy transfer. Animals such as snakes, weasels, and warblers are representative primary carnivores. At the top of the chain are hawks, owls, and hunters, the secondary carnivores.

An important heterotrophic component ranging throughout all trophic levels of a biome is the decomposer group: fungi and bacteria. Life depends not only on a continuous energy supply but also on a regular supply of matter. The degrading of dead plant and animal tissues, as well as wastes, provides decomposers with energy for their activities, and, importantly for the continued existence of other life, makes minerals and inorganic compounds available for recycling by plants. Nature indulged in recycling long before humans realized that it was "good for the environment".

Biogeochemical Cycles

Biogeochemical cycles involve elements and compounds moving repeatedly between abiotic and biotic components of ecosystems. Gaseous cycles—for example, those involving carbon, nitrogen, oxygen, and hydrogen—have the Earth's atmosphere or hydrosphere (oceans) as the reservoir. Much slower sedimentary cycles—involving elements such as phosphorus and iron—have the lithosphere (Earth's crust) as a reservoir.

The types, distribution, and abundance of plants and animals is greatly influenced by the available amounts of vital elements. Pocono sandstones and shales are resistant to erosion, and mineral release for them is slow, so the glacially scoured plateau provides a harsh substratum for vegetation growth. A shortage of any of the vital elements serves as a limiting factor. The highly specialized assemblage of plants in a Pocono bog results in large measure from the limited amounts of nitrogen and phosphorus salts available for their uptake.

Succession Patterns

In the Poconos, on some rocky outcrops scoured by glaciers, the presence of lichens—specialized mutualistic associations of algae and fungi—bears witness to primary succession. Over time, soil is formed from rock by the activities of lichens as well as by freezing, thawing, and other weathering. Only then can mosses and ferns assume a role in the succession process. Plants in the earliest stages of succession have short life cycles. Many are annuals. The trend toward greater longevity of species continues, as woody shrubs and, finally, trees take their place in the succession.

More frequently, what we view is secondary succession: changing patterns of vegetation, occurring where forests are cut or land once used for agriculture or pasture is abandoned. Ecologists have noted several major structural and functional trends in ecological succession: increase in species diversity, increase in structural complexity (that is, food webs rather than food chains), increase in organic matter, and tendency toward community stability.

In the Poconos, fields abandoned less than a year are quickly invaded by weed species such as foxtail grass, bracken fern, and thistles. Within a few years, the presence of numerous red cedars signals the end of the herbaceous stage. Later, species such as aspen, gray birch, pin cherry, and other shade-intolerant types will dominate. This stage is frequently observed on the Pocono Plateau. Eventually, an oak forest or, given time, the climax biome, a beech-birch-maple forest will replace this stage.

Animal Patterns

Animals—their types, distribution, and abundance—are obviously determined largely by vegetation patterns. Some ecologists have studied animal populations, especially vertebrates such as birds and mammals, in hopes of discerning patterns comparable to the more clearly defined vegetation patterns. Two factors are most important with regard to animal distribution: temperature and humidity. On this basis, faunal zones such as Canadian, Alleghenian, and Carolinean were devised; the terms relate to probable origin sites from where species dispersed. Although the terms have been largely abandoned, the zone idea is still useful.

The Poconos are an interesting faunal transition zone. For instance, higher elevations of the plateau are a breeding habitat for several species of birds typically found nesting further north, such as white-throated sparrows, hermit thrushes, and red-breasted nuthatches. Human activity may influence mammalian species distribution to a greater extent than that of birds; examples of mammals that have found new homes in the Poconos are the porcupine, rock vole, northern flying squirrel, and beaver. The boreal assemblage of plants and animals of a Pocono bog—balsam fir, larch, and black spruce together with otters and snowshoe hares—provides the most dramatic example of a transition zone. A Pocono bog may resemble parts of Maine or Canada.

CHAPTER 2

Geological Forces that Shaped the Poconos

"Public sentiment, it seems, can create mountains.... People have been referring to this area as the Pocono Mountains for so long that the description seems as immutable as—well, as a mountain."
—RON SHAFER, *Pennsylvania Naturalist*, 1980

Visitors to the Poconos are impressed by the sinuous high ridge and its gaps along the southern margin, by the numerous lakes and waterfalls, and by the escarpment (the "mountains") leading to the heart of Pocono country. These various landform features evolved over hundreds of millions of years.

The Mountains That Folded

The land mass stretching from the present site of Pittsburgh westward to the Rocky Mountains has existed since pre-Paleozoic times, more than six-hundred million years ago. To the east of this stable land mass there was once a large shallow marine basin called a geosyncline. As the internal land mass wore down, sediments gradually accumulated in this eastern basin and were subsequently transformed to sedimentary rocks. As the sediments got thicker the basin slowly subsided, and a balance of sorts was developed between subsidence and sedimentation.

After millions of years of sedimentary rock accumulation, large sections of the geosyncline were deformed by uplifting and folding as the lithospheric plates shifted positions.

Many uplifts occurred, followed by extensive freshwater erosion. During one of these freshwater erosion cycles, the famous anthracite coal beds neighboring the Poconos were fossilized from the swamp vegetation that characterized much of Pennsylvania.

At the close of the Paleozoic Era, about two hundred and eighty million years ago, the last major uplifting and folding episode concluded with the formation of a very high mountain range now called the Appalachians. Since that time, the formerly impressive range has

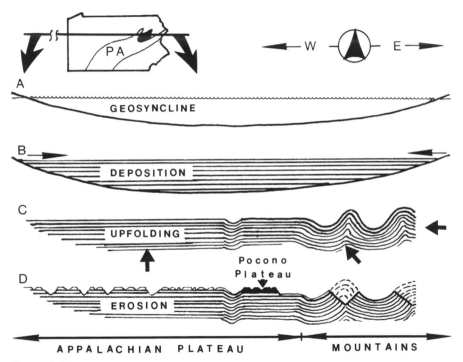

Figure 2.1
Stages in the geologic development across Pennsylvania.
A. The early formation of the geosyncline.
B. Deposition of sediments from the adjacent
   land masses and their subsequent change to
   sedimentary rock.
C. Folding from compressional and uplifting forces. The folding diminishes
   westward.
D. Erosion of the weaker rocks, particularly those that are folded, and slow
   dissection of the plateaus.

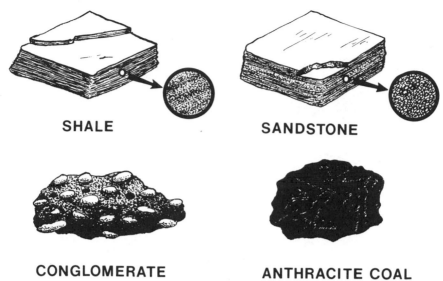

SHALE

SANDSTONE

CONGLOMERATE

ANTHRACITE COAL

Figure 2.2
Hand specimens of the common rock types of the Pocono area. Shales (or mudstones) are deposits of fine, solidified mud and clay. Sandstones, which are very resistant to weathering, are made of sand-sized particles. Conglomerates consist of deposits of gravel with variable amounts of sand and mud around the gravel. All are common sedimentary rocks in the area. Anthracite coal deposits are in the adjacent Wyoming Valley. A small formation of limestone parallels the Kittatinny Ridge to its north and the Slate Belt parallels it immediately to the south.

been worn down to the rather low profile of the present Appalachians, revealing the old sedimentary Silurian and Devonian rocks of around four hundred million years ago (see Figures 2.2 and 2.3). The more resistant rocks, such as hard sandstones and conglomerates, now form the ridges which tend northeast to southwest through much of Pennsylvania. The Kittatinny, or Blue Mountain, forms the southeastern boundary of the Keystone State's folded ridges. Places where this landmark ridge stands out are the gaps, such as Wind Gap or the Delaware Water Gap, or the Lehigh Tunnel of the Pennsylvania Turnpike. The series of ridges west of the Poconos is obvious to the traveler on the east-west part of the turnpike where it penetrates seven of the ridges with tunnels.

But what caused those gaps in the ridges? Moving water, as we know, tends to wear down a surface. Where the rock's uplifting rate exceeded the water's downcutting rate, the water was diverted to flow between the ridges, as is true of the many inter-ridge streams.

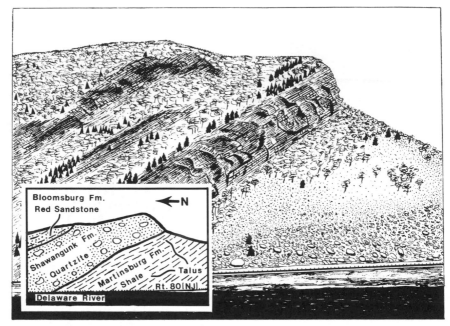

Figure 2.3
The Delaware Water Gap. It reveals tilted layers of Silurian conglomerates and sandstones of the folded Appalachians. The view is looking eastward from the Rotunda of the Delaware Water Gap National Recreation Area. The Delaware River and Route 80 (New Jersey) are in the foreground. A talus slope of rock debris tapers off to the right. Inset: sectional view through the gap with the major formations.

But the Delaware and Lehigh Rivers had sufficient power to cut down the rock faster than the uplifting rate—with the beautiful water gaps at the southern edge of the Poconos the result. An interesting exception is the case in which a river's downcutting forces won the early part of the contest but the uplifting processes prevailed in the end, forming a partial gap. Such a gap has air alone flowing through it and is appropriately called a wind gap. Figure 2.4 illustrates the gaps in the Kittatinny Ridge.

The Pocono Plateau

The uplifting and folding forces of Earth's crust were generated primarily from the east, as Figure 2.1 shows. The folding action diminished to the west, resulting in nearly horizontal rock layers that are

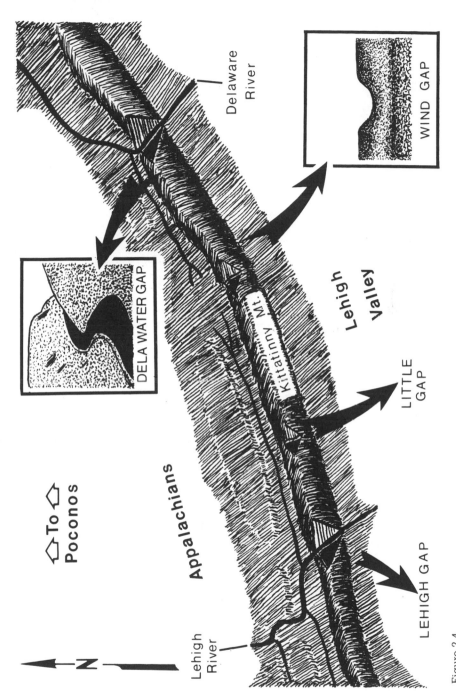

Figure 2.4
The Kittatinny Ridge and its gaps. Note how both Wind Gap and Little Gap are no longer water-cut gaps.

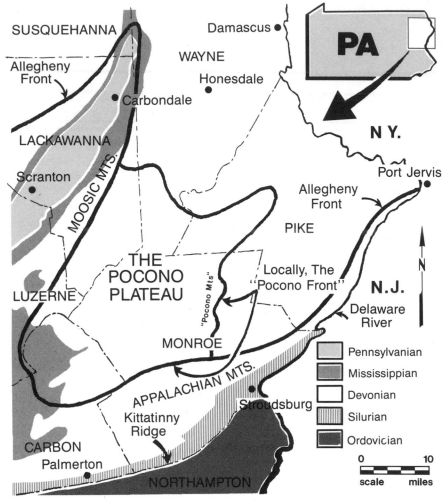

Figure 2.5
Bedrock geologic map of the Poconos area. All bedrock is of the sedimentary type of
the Paleozoic era. Approximate ages: Ordovician: 500–425 million years ago (m.y.);
Silurian, 400–425 m.y.; Devonian, 350–400 m.y.; Mississippian, 310–350 m.y.; and
Pennsylvanian, 280–310 m.y. The anthracite coal beds are in the Pennsylvanian
bedrock of the Wyoming Valley west of the Moosic Mountains.

less affected by erosion. Thus we have the High Plateaus of northwestern Pennsylvania, the Low Plateaus of northeastern Pennsylvania, and that very resistant and nearly level Pocono Plateau. (To
a geologist, a surface is nearly level if its variations in elevation
are only a few hundred feet.)

BOX 2.1

Places to See the Folded Appalachians and the Gaps

The Appalachian Mountains reach their narrowest extent in northeastern Pennsylvania (Figure 2.5). They form a band several miles north of a line between Palmerton and Stroudsburg. The most southeastern ridge of these mountains is the Blue, or Kittatinny Mountain; it is readily seen from the Lehigh Valley (from the south) or from higher points in the southern Poconos. The ridge is broken with major gaps (Figure 2.4) at the towns of Palmerton, Danielsville, Wind Gap, and Delaware Water Gap. The Appalachian Trail runs along the crest of the Kittatinny Mountain.

The Pocono Plateau somewhat abruptly meets the lower surrounding land mass with a drop in elevation of about 1000 feet (see Figures 2.5 and 2.6). This juncture is the Pocono escarpment (or Pocono Front), and has sufficient visual impact on the eastern edge to be called the "Pocono Mountains". The escarpment is very pronounced along the southern and eastern sides of the plateau, but fades away gradually into the north. Much of the escarpment is part of a larger formation called the Allegheny Front. In those places where streams drop rapidly from the plateaus, the result is a landmark of the Poconos: waterfalls.

An Abundance of Waterfalls

Pennsylvania has seventy-five named waterfalls, thirty in the Pocono area. The drop from the Pocono Plateau is about 1000 feet to the Low Plateau Section, which, in turn, drops some hundreds of feet to the Delaware River. These two general bands, called "fall lines," are where the many streams drop rapidly off their respective plateaus and continue to wear down the edges of these plateaus. The Pocono Escarpment group includes Buck Hill, Swiftwater, and Paradise Falls, while the Delaware group includes Silverthread, Dingmans and Bushkill Falls. Fourteen of the more notable falls are included in Figure 2.7. Their locations, along with some commentary, are shown in Table 2.1. Typically, the falls have cut into the plateaus and formed deep, dark scenic gorges, often densely shaded by hemlock, white pine, and great rhododendron. It is in these low-light, high-humidity microclimates that many of the nonflowering plants, such as mosses, liverworts, and ferns, thrive in enormous variety.

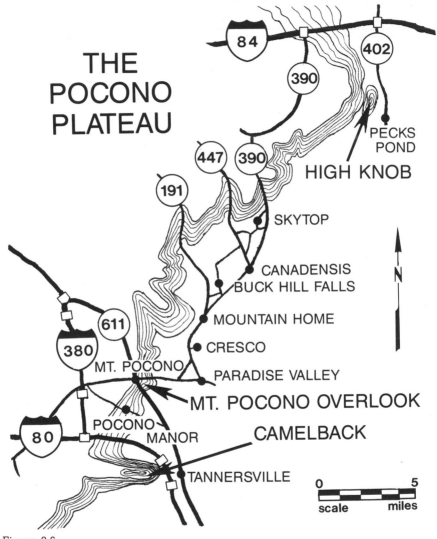

Figure 2.6
Eastern Escarpment (Pocono Front) of the Pocono Plateau. The contour line intervals at the escarpment are generalized and omitted from the rest of map for emphasis.

BOX 2.2 29

Where to See the Pocono Plateau

Flagstaff Park, near Jim Thorpe, offers an excellent view of the southern edge of the plateau, the Lehigh River, and part of the Appalachians.

Camelback Mountain (Pocono Knob, within Big Pocono State Park) is a very high (el. 2131 feet) and eastward prong (see Figure 2.6) of the Pocono Plateau, with an excellent view of the plateau to the north, the Blue Mountain and its gaps to the Southeast, and—on a very clear day—the Catskills to the northeast.

Mount Pocono Overlook is located on Knob Road, a short distance east of Mount Pocono Borough (Figure 2.6).

High Knob (el. 1941 feet), located about 2 miles northwest of the town of Pecks Pond (Figure 2.6), offers a magnificent view from this well-defined, most northeastern point of the Pocono escarpment.

The Moosic Mountains (Figure 2.5), at an elevation of about 2000 feet, are transversed by a number of roads from which one can see the Pocono Plateau to the east and the Wyoming Valley to the west.

From the monument at High Point State Park (el. 1803 feet), New Jersey, one can get an excellent view of the Poconos.

While the previous sites offer spectacular views at the rim of the plateau, a place to experience the climb up onto the Pocono Plateau, for many travelers, is the gradual rise along the northeastern extension of the Pennsylvania Turnpike. About six miles north of the Lehigh Tunnel, the traveler starts a long gradual climb up the southern escarpment of the Pocono Plateau; just beyond the top of the climb, the plateau is marked with a turnpike service plaza.

More dramatic ascents up onto the plateau occur along most of the eastern escarpment (Figure 2.6).

The Fossil Record

Northeastern Pennsylvania was once (five hundred to two hundred and eighty million years ago) part of a warm shallow sea. Some of the primitive forms of life became incorporated in the bottom sediments and, under favorable conditions, left their record as fossils in the rocks that formed in the future. One may find fossilized parts of a variety of brachiopods (scalloplike animals), crinoids (cousins of our

Table 2.1.
Waterfalls of the Poconos

Name	Location	Comments
1 Tobyhanna Falls	About 0.5 mi. W. of PA 115, just south of Blakeslee	Tobyhanna Creek drains several Pocono lakes. Check locally
2 Swiftwater Falls	On the estate of Pocono Manor	On Swiftwater Creek. Fine rhododendron stand
3 Paradise Falls	On the grounds of the Paradise Lutheran Association, Paradise Valley	On Paradise Creek. Private property
4 Buck Hill Falls	Near Canadensis; 0.5 mi. N. of Buck Hill Falls Boro	Falls drops over sandstones and siltstones. Admission charge
5 Indian Ladder Falls	4.2 mi. N. of Canadensis. Skytop Lodges property	Permission required. Sandstone, siltstone, and claystone rocks
6 Shohola Falls	Near Shohola Falls Village, on State Game Land 180	Shale and siltstone rocks
7 Pinchot Falls, or Saw Kill Falls	Milford, Rt. 209; on Pinchot Estate (open 8–4)	100-foot narrow gorge, cut through Devonian rock
8 Raymondskill Falls	Midway between Milford and Dingmans Ferry	Falls drop about 175 feet. In the DWGNRA
9 Silver Thread Falls	Dingmans Ferry, Rte. 209	Water flows over shales, siltstones and sandstones. DWGNRA
10 Dingmans Falls	Dingmans Ferry, Rte. 209	DWGNRA
11 Fulmer Falls	3 mi. W. of Dingmans Ferry; in Childs State Park	Very scenic falls and trails
12 Bushkill Falls	1.5 mi. N. of Bushkill, Rte. 209	The "Niagara of Pennsylvania" 100-foot drop over siltstone and shale. Admission charge
13 Winona Falls	2.4 mi. N. of Shoemakersville, Rte. 209	Very scenic. Admission charge
14 Resica Falls	5 mi. E. of Bushkill, Rte. 209	Creek descends over sandstones and shales

BOX 2.3

Places to See the Waterfalls

Figure 2.7 and Table 2.1 direct the reader to a number of the more notable falls of the Poconos. As they are a natural magnet for the Poconos, directions to the falls are widely advertised along roadways. Eight waterfalls are adjacent to Route 209 between Stroudsburg and Milford.

starfishes), bryozoans (mosslike animals), corals, clamlike pelecypods, and trilobites. Trilobites, as the name implies, had three longitudinal body divisions. Since these animals had an exoskeleton, and hence grew through molting, frequently only parts of the exoskeleton are found—most commonly, the abdominal portion, illustrated in Figure 2.8.

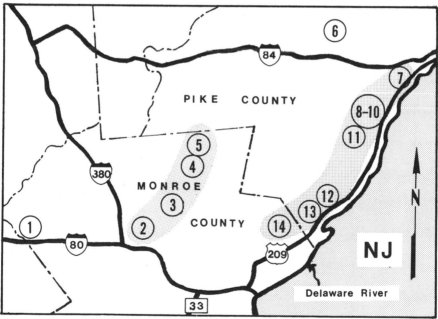

Figure 2.7
Major waterfalls in the Poconos. The numbers refer to Table 2.1. The major ski slopes largely coincide with these two bands. Roadside signs to the falls are numerous.

B R A C H I O P O D

B R Y O Z O A

C R I N O I D (stalk & xs)

H O R N   C O R A L

T R I L O B I T E

F E R N   (Fragment)

S O M E   P E L E C Y P O D S

Figure 2.8
Common fossils of the Pocono area. The drawings include the
shell of a brachiopod, an animal similar to the present-day
scallop but with unequal shell halves; a colony of very
small bryozoan (moss-like) animals; a stalk of a crinoid; a horn
coral; a fern fragment from coal; the abdomen of a trilobite;
and several bivalve pelecypods, which have equal-sized shell
halves.

BOX 2.4

Places to See Fossils

Beltzville State Park has a designated fossil-collecting site open to the public.

Route 209, between Raymondskill Creek and Milford, has a number of rubble pits along the west side of the road. Parking is ample and a variety of Devonian fossils can be observed.

Saylorsburg. About 0.5 mile northwest of Saylorsburg, on the right side of L.R. 930, there is an excellent outcropping of the "center field fossil zone" of the Devonian Age. Parking is available on the left side of the road.

Weissport. A good place to collect invertebrate fossils is along the old Lehigh Canal about 0.8 mile north of Weissport, in Carbon County. Fossils can be found in a broad rubble area just east of the canal.

Exhibits relating to the fossil record can be seen at the Anthracite Museum in McDade Park and the Everhart Museum in Nay Aug Park, both in Scranton, and the Wyoming Historical and Geological Society Museum in Wilkes-Barre.

In addition to these animal fossils, plant fossils may commonly be found in the nearby anthracite fields (Figure 2.9), as coal itself consists of accumulated fossil plant material. Among the more common plant fossils are those of ancient fern fragments and other simple vascular plants. Peat bogs contain fossilized pollen grains of the postglacial period, and occasionally a bog will turn up a mastodon skeleton (as was the case several years ago in John Leap's peat bog, near Marshalls Creek in Monroe County).

The Ice Age Cometh

A short geological time ago (in excess of one million years), a different series of natural forces started to reshape the surface of the Poconos. As Earth's climate cooled, great snow and ice masses accumulated and spread southward from Canada—these were the continental glaciers. As they slowly moved into the Poconos, the last two glaciers, like giant road scrapers, scoured the area and carried with them great loads of rock debris. The earlier glacier, called the

Illinoian, stopped at the Lehigh Valley, but the most recent one, called the Wisconsin, halted in the Poconos about fifteen thousand years ago.

The terminus of the Wisconsin Glacier (called an end, or terminal, moraine) is a band about a mile wide stretching from Belvidere, New Jersey, to Hickory Run and west. This end moraine can be observed from a number of roads transecting the Poconos. Typically, the topography is in hill and swale form, with a variety of rock types and debris scattered in the band. The moraine, shown in Figure 2.10, is not easily detected from afar because of the tree cover, but a little hiking about will reveal its knobby nature and heterogeneous surface deposits.

To the north of this terminal moraine, the glacier deposited considerable debris in ground moraine, or till, covering much of the Poco-

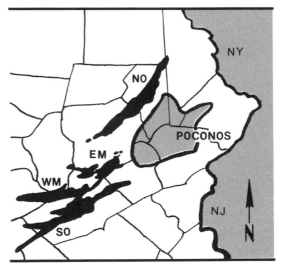

Figure 2.9
Northeastern Pennsylvania coal beds.
NO = northern field; EM = eastern middle;
WM = western middle; SO = southern.
They are south and west of the Pocono Plateau.

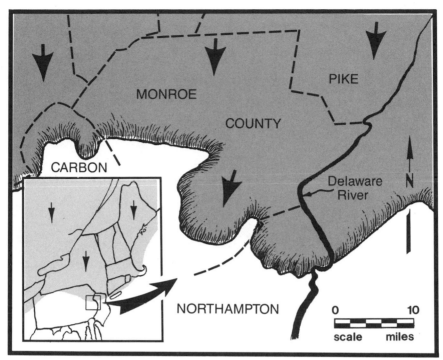

Figure 2.10
Extent of the last glacier (Wisconsin) in the Poconos. The terminal (end) moraine is
at the junction of the dark and light areas and is typically about a mile wide. It
passes through Brodheadsville and McMichaels near Route 215, around Camelback,
and then along Route 80 to the Hickory Run area. North of this band, the surface
is covered with ground moraine and lakes are abundant.

nos to a depth ranging from a few feet to nearly a hundred feet.
These were surface deposits, and the glacier did not modify the basic
structural landforms of the Poconos. It did, however, pile up enough
till in places to dot the plateau with poorly drained areas.

As the glaciers melted, outwash—water mixed with rock debris
—poured into the drainage channels of the Susquehanna and Delaware Rivers and their tributaries, and accumulated to great thick-
nesses. It is upon such deposits in the Wyoming Valley that Wilkes-
Barre, Kingston, and Forty Fort are built and in the Delaware Valley,
Philadelphia! Smaller outwash deltas that built up in the Delaware
River include those on which Milford and Port Jervis are built.

Figure 2.11
Hickory Run Boulder Field, Hickory Run State Park. A registered national landmark, the boulder field is approximately 400 by 1800 feet. The inset shows the end of the glacier and its meltwater. Extreme temperature fluctuations broke up the neighboring sandstone rock, and the pieces slowly moved to the present boulder field. This field is the largest of its kind in the Appalachian Mountains.

Glacial Signatures

When one walks across a beach, a series of "signatures" is left behind in the form of footprints. A 1000-foot sheet of slowly moving ice could not pass without leaving signatures. Perhaps the most characteristic signature of continental glaciation is the presence of numerous lakes. South of the glaciated area lakes are few, usually manmade and called impoundments. The Poconos abound in glacial lakes including Lake Harmony, Deep Lake, Saylors Lake, and Bruce Lake. Some of the lakes, clogged with vegetation, are now treated as swamps and/or bogs (see Chapter 5). The lake country is also characterized by the previously-mentioned ground moraine—a generally thin soil mixed with a debris varying from clay to boulders.

In some cases near the terminus of the glacier, the diurnal oscillation of freezing and thawing repeatedly broke large boulders loose. As a result of later movement caused by gravity, these accumulations made striking "fields" of rocks, such as Hickory Run Boulder Field.

Other glacial evidence includes the occasional deep scratches (or

BOX 2.5

Places to See ———————
Glacial Signatures

The Terminal Moraine location is illustrated in Figure 2.10. Conspicuous places to see it are at the base of Camelback, the drive along Route 715 between Brodheadsville and McMichaels, the base of Blue Mountain near Bangor, and much of the western aspect of Route 80 to Hickory Run State Park.

Outwash deposits occur along much of Route 209 between Bushkill and Metamoras.

Boulder fields are found at Hickory Run State Park (Figure 2.11) and the "Devil's Potato Patch" at Little Gap. The "Patch" is near the top of Little Gap on the east side of the road north of Danielsville.

A drumlin can be observed one-half mile east of the U. S. 209 intersection at Middle Smithville.

The famous Archbald Pothole is illustrated in Figure 2.12. Located about six miles northeast of Scranton along Route 6, this is one of the world's largest potholes.

Glacial scratches (striations) can be seen on rock surfaces along the Appalachian Trail just south of Lake Lenape in the Delaware Water Gap.

Glacial lakes abound in the Poconos. A few examples are Lake Sciota, Lake Harmony, Deep Lake, Saylors Lake, and Bruce Lake. Sunfish Pond, just northeast of the Delaware Water Gap and along the blue-blazed trail, is a good example in New Jersey.

striations, striae) on exposed bedrock, where the rocks imbedded in the ice sheets scarred the bedrock surface. Sometimes the bedrock was polished, and when fragments were torn loose, they were carried south by the ice. All telltale markings indicate a generally north-to-south ice movement. This directional pattern is also suggested by occasional drumlins, elongated hills composed mostly of till. As the last glacier finally melted, much of the suspended load was deposited as outwash in the major valleys.

One of the most impressive, though uncommon, glacial signatures is the large pothole. Swirling glacial meltwater, laden with rock fragments, occasionally wore large holes into the bedrock. One of the world's largest natural potholes is located on the fringe of the Poconos. This Archbald Pothole is roughly forty by forty feet in size.

Figure 2.12
Archbald Pothole, Archbald Pothole State Park. It was formed during the
last glacier by abrasive action of the meltwater.

After the Glaciers

When the last glacier began its slow melting, the Pocono climate was
cold—perhaps like the northern climes of present-day Canada. Under those cold conditions, the invading plant community consisted
largely of northern tree types, such as fir, spruce, and larch. With the

BOX 2.6

Places to See
Some Miscellaneous Geologic Features

The Devil's Wall is illustrated in Figure 2.13. It is a conspicuous rock formation visible from the Northeast Extension of the Pennsylvania Turnpike just above the Lehigh Valley Tunnel.

Bluestone is the construction stone of the Grey Towers (Pinchot Institute), Milford and the Sherman Underwear Mills in Hawley.

Private slate quarries (Figure 2.14) are located along the southern margin of Blue Mountain. Inquire locally. Piles of waste slate are seen along some of the roads in that area as, for example, along Route 33 at the town of Wind Gap.

Split Rock, located at the western end of Lake Harmony, is illustrated in Figure 2.15.

continued glacial disappearance the climate gradually warmed, bringing a change in the dominant plant community to such trees as beech, maple, and oak.

But how do we know this history of thousands of years ago? Interestingly enough, the plants left their signatures in the form of pollen grains, which rained onto the bog and lake surfaces. As the pollen sank, it remained preserved in the oxygen-free (anaerobic) sediments, and naturally the oldest pollen and sediments accumulated on the bottom while the present pollen is still being deposited on the top sediment layer. A palynologist (pollen expert) can remove sequential cores from these "buried history books" and reconstruct the vegetational sequence.

Would the Pocono landscape of William Penn's time 300 years ago, look much like that of today? Yes and no. Yes, because the major landform features of ridges, plateaus, and escarpments created by long-term geological events are little changed; and, yes, because glacial activity only modified surface features such as ponds and bogs, which have changed little in a few hundred years. No, because in a very short time a new agent, the human species, has rapidly modified the Poconos.

Some Miscellaneous Geologic Features

The Devil has had a long association, in name, with geological features that are scraggly, ugly, or somehow less than harmonious with the surrounding area. An excellent example is the "Devil's Wall" or

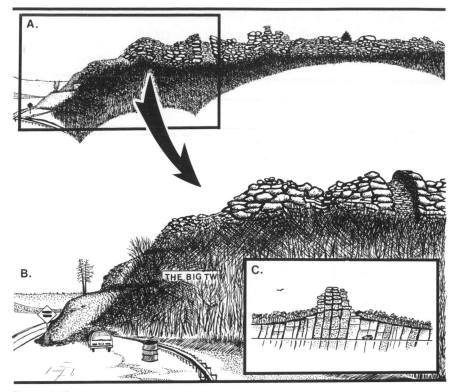

Figure 2.13
"Devil's Wall" or Stony Ridge, just above the Lehigh Valley Tunnel. A view to
the right (east) by the northbound traveler on the northeast extension of the
Pennsylvania Turnpike. A. distant view. B. at the pull-off. C. sectional view.

Stony Ridge (Figure 2.13), a narrow ten-mile-long fractured ridge of
resistant sandstone in the Appalachians. The originally horizontal
layers were folded here into a nearly vertical position (called a mono-
cline); subsequent erosion left the resistant sandstone silhouetted
against the sky.

Two construction stones that have a Pocono identity are bluestone
and slate. Bluestone is a type of flagging siltstone of the Milford area
used for building construction and sidewalks. While bluestone extrac-
tion is no longer active, the slate industry is still at work along a narrow belt just south of the Blue Mountain. Appropriately called the
Slate Belt (with towns of Slatington, Slatedale, Slateford, etc.), it is

WASTE SLATE

Figure 2.14

Slate Operations in the 1960s. The Slate Belt, paralleling the southern edge of the Blue Mountain, annually produces about four million dollars' worth of slate products. The drawing is after a photograph in Subitzky, S. (ed.): *Geology of Selected Areas in New Jersey and Eastern Pennsylvania: And Guidebook of Excursions*. Copyright © 1969 by Rutgers University, the State University of New Jersey.

the only area in the United States that now produces billiard-quality slate. Slate is a type of very fine-grained rock which is metamorphosed (recrystallized by pressure and heat) from sedimentary siltstones and other clayey sediments. In many of the southern approaches to the Poconos, the visitor will see huge piles of waste slate. More recently, the waste is being dumped into the many abandoned quarries of the area. Products from the Slate Belt exist throughout the Poconos and the world as chalkboards, billiard-table tops, curbing, and burial vault walls.

To conclude this topic of miscellaneous features, we note the Split Rock. Pocono visitors have all heard of the town of Split Rock, or of

Figure 2.15
Split Rock, Carbon County. The split (by joint separation) rock is much less known than its more famous town and lodge, located due east of this geologic anomaly. The six-foot-wide split occurs in sandstone.

the lodge, both located at the western end of glacial Lake Harmony. The actual split rock is a curious geological joint separation of rock (see Figure 2.15) located a short distance due west of the town and lodge.

For a relatively small area, the Poconos offer a diverse and interesting variety of geological features.

CHAPTER 3

Vegetation of Pocono Forests

> "Every region and, often, even every small
> locality has its peculiar kind of forest. The
> composition of the forests along streams, on
> slopes, and upon mountain tops usually
> shows great differences. The more varied
> the factors of the habitat are, the more var-
> ied the composition of the forest usually is."
> —JOSEPH ILLICK, *Pennsylvania Trees*, 1923

The Pocono forests are richly varied because of the variety of envi-
ronments atop and around the Pocono plateau—ridges and ravines,
lakes and streams, bogs and barrens. As classified by foresters, the
Poconos are in a transition zone between two major subdivisions of
the eastern deciduous forest: mixed oak and northern hardwood (or
beech-birch-maple). Three other major forest types—scrub-oak barren, chestnut oak ridge, and white pine-hemlock ravine—are well
represented in the Poconos. Indeed, detailed forest classification
maps for the region resemble jigsaw puzzles (see Figure 3.1). Even
so, such maps are over-simplified, since much of the Poconos is covered by mixed forest, with the various types blending into each other
(see Table 3.1). There are also three kinds of unforested areas: bare
rock, bogs, and marshes.

The Scrub-Oak Barrens

The neophyte barrens visitor is initially impressed by their monotony
and strangeness. A tough tangle of scrubby oaks and woody heaths
forms a lower layer from one to six feet high; a few emergent scrag-

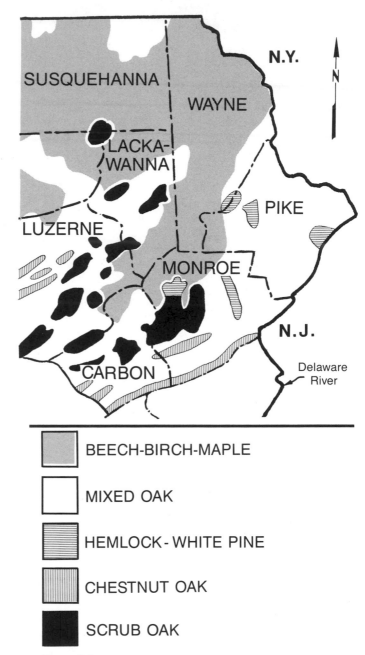

Figure 3.1
The five major forest types of the Poconos. (Modified after Grimm and Whitebread, *Mammal Survey of Northeastern Pennsylvania*. Pennsylvania Game Commission, Harrisburg, 1952.)

gly pitch pines, sassafras trees, or taller scrub oaks help to relieve the monotony. The pines, especially on the exposed higher places, are often lopsided and windshapen; such asymmetrical tree shapes are called "flag-forms." The soil is very shallow and the surface rock is mostly exposed and of resistant sandstone.

The barrens appear to be the result of unfavorable climatic conditions, poor soil, and repeated burnings. They are not new: diaries of the troops from General Sullivan's 1779 expedition unmistakably refer to the barrens. The native Americans of the upper Delaware Valley apparently used fire to clear the underbrush of the forests as well as to drive game; early European settlers often cleared land by the slash-and-burn method; lightning causes many forest fires. The mix of reasons for the repeated burnings of the present scrub-oak barrens is uncertain. One thing is certain: occasional fire does encourage the growth of the heaths such as blueberry and huckleberry. But frequent burnings will exhaust the root reserves.

The scrub-oak barrens of the Poconos are similar in a number of ways to the Pine Barrens of southern New Jersey. In both sites the soil is poor; the parent material is sand or sandstone; fire has been a contributing influence; and scrubby pines, oaks, and heaths dominate the landscape. Pitch pine, one of the most fire-resistant trees of the forest, can readily re-sprout after fires. Scrub (bear) oak, which also re-sprouts vigorously soon after a fire, has another fire-defying characteristic—it can produce acorns just three years after germination. Most oaks need a decade or more. Other typical plants of the Pocono barrens, such as sweet fern (an aromatic fernlike low shrub) and the colorful sheep laurel, are shown in Figure 3.2. Other plants common to the barrens are listed in Table 3.2.

To the immediate southwest and west of the Poconos there are areas that superficially resemble the barrens. These are the "strippin's," the strip-mined areas of the anthracite fields (see Figure 2.9). Sometimes called barrens, they differ in several ways. The surface is a loose mixture of broken rock called "culm," which is removed to get at the coal. The typical invading plants are gray birch, aspen, and a variety of weed species.

Invaders of Bare Rock

In a number of places throughout the Poconos, such as the ridge tops, the glacial ice sheets stripped the surfaces of their soil mantle and vegetation. Since the last glacier a number of small but very hardy plants have been invading the exposed rock surfaces. This invasion is the process of primary xeric (dry) succession.

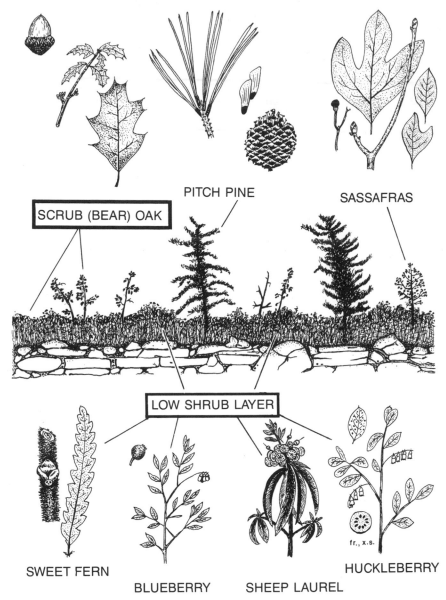

PITCH PINE

SASSAFRAS

SCRUB (BEAR) OAK

LOW SHRUB LAYER

SWEET FERN

BLUEBERRY

SHEEP LAUREL

HUCKLEBERRY

fr., x.s.

Figure 3.2
Typical plants of the Pocono scrub-oak barrens. Sectional view.

BOX 3.1

Places to See the Barrens

Camelback and State Game Lands No. 38. Much of the top of Camelback is of the barrens type of vegetation. Parts of State Game Lands No. 38, immediately to the west of Camelback, is similar and easily accessible for hiking.

Route 115 North of Effort. A few miles north of Effort, on the slow climb up the Pocono escarpment, there is a sign for Sierra View. Barrens are on the right.

Mount Pocono Overlook. The location is described in Chapter 2. It, like some of the southeastern edge of the Pocono escarpment, is a scrub-oak barrens area. A number of secondary roads cross the barrens area.

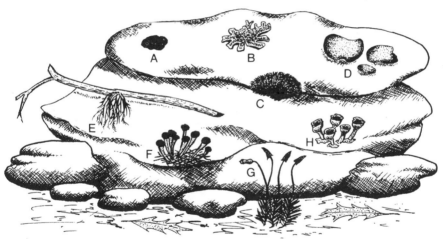

Figure 3.3
Some common pioneer nonflowering plants. On exposed rock surfaces one might expect to see one or more of the following: A. crustose lichen. B. foliose lichen. C. cushion moss. D. Rock Tripe, a foliose lichen. E. Beard Lichen, a foliose lichen on a twig. F. British Soldiers, a fructicose lichen. G. Haircap Moss. H. Pixie Cup (or Goblet) Lichen, a fruticose lichen. Each plant is about one-half-inch to two inches in diameter.

The earliest invaders are the crustose lichens, a group of flat (crustlike) simple plants that look like mere stains on the rock. They aid in the corrosive breakdown of the rock and also provide some organic material for later invaders such as the foliose (foliagelike) and fructicose (shrublike) lichens and the simple mosses. Figure 3.3 illustrates some of these common pioneer types in their harsh environment. Small herbaceous plants will follow if the rock has accumulated sufficient debris and organic material to provide for anchorage and adequate moisture. These, in turn, pave the way for pioneering shrubs such as blueberry, sheep laurel, and sumac; and, later, trees such as the chestnut oak, scrub oak, and pitch pine.

Chestnut Oak Ridges

As any hiker along the Appalachian Trail from the Delaware Water Gap to the Lehigh Gap knows, the trail is rocky and the trees are

Table 3.1.
The Major Forest Types of the Poconos and Their Characteristics

Characteristics	Scrub oak barrens	Chestnut oak ridges
Dominant vegetation	Scrub oak and pitch pine Heaths	Chestnut oak
Climatic conditions	Exposed to wind, storms, and ice. Fire important	Exposed to wind, storms, and ice
Soil	Sterile and very shallow	Sterile and shallow
Pocono location	Exposed and scattered areas on some of the drier parts of the Pocono Plateau	Narrow, dry ridge tops, as the Kittatinny
Layering (or stratification)	Dense and tangled lower layer; emergents	Somewhat layered; few herbs
Floor aspect	Dense, nearly inpenetrable tangle of branching oaks and heaths; rocky	Variable to approaching the scrub oak environment; rocky

BOX 3.2

Places to See
Rock Invasion

Exposed ridge tops, rocks of the barrens, boulder fields, and glacially deposited erratic rocks are all good places to see primary succession.

small. The soil that is formed on the ridges tends to wash down the slopes, and the resulting soil shortage limits the growth of the trees.

In addition, the ridge tops are maximally exposed to the extremes of the area's climate. In short, a combination of factors limits both the

Mixed oak forests	Northern hardwood forests	Cool ravines and some slopes
White oak Red oak Black oak Hickory	Beech, maple, yellow birch, hemlock, ash, white pine	White pine, hemlock
Moderate for the area	Similar to the mixed oak forest, but cooler	Protected in ravines; cool, humid
Somewhat infertile	Somewhat infertile	Strongly acid Mixed with needles
Mostly in the southern area of the Poconos and extending up the Delaware and Wyoming Valleys	Mostly on the Pocono Plateau and northward into N.Y. State	Occasional cool ravines in scattered places
Trees, shrubs, and herbs	Trees, shrubs, and herbs	Heavy canopy Shrub and ground cover sparse
Many spring wild flowers; summer aspect of ferns	Many spring wild flowers; summer aspect of ferns	Sparse growth Needle-covered Dark

tree composition and tree size. The species most common to this harsh environment is the chestnut oak. Its other name, ecologically more descriptive, is rock oak. It is easily recognized by its oblong leaves margined with coarse rounded teeth (the American chestnut, shown in Figure 3.29, is similar but the teeth are sharp, not rounded) and a roughly fissured bark. On the downslopes, where the chestnut oak grows a straighter trunk, it is used commercially much like white oak; but, unlike white oak, it sprouts readily from cut stumps and hence multiple stems are common.

A sectional view through a ridge, such as the Blue Mountain, is illustrated in Figure 3.5, along with some of the common woody plants. Table 3.3 lists other plants common to the ridge tops. The understory on the ridges varies considerably. In some places heaths,

Table 3.2.
Typical Plants of the Scrub-Oak Barrens

Trees	Big-toothed aspen	Quaking aspen
	Chestnut (sprouts)	Red maple
	Choke cherry	Sassafras
	Gray birch	Scrub (Bear) oak
	Pitch pine	
Shrubs	Blueberry	Mountain azalea
	Brambles	Mountain laurel
	Chokeberry	Sheep laurel
	Huckleberry	Sweet fern
	Meadowsweet	Witch hazel
Herbs and ferns	Aster spp.	Fly poison
	Bracken fern	Grasses and sedges
	Checkerberry	Spreading dogbane
	Cow-wheat	Whorled loosestrife
	Fireweed	Wild indigo

Table 3.3.
Typical Plants of the Chestnut Oak Ridge Tops

Trees	Big-toothed aspen	Pitch pine
	Black gum	Red maple
	Chestnut oak	Oaks (several spp.)
	Chestnut (sprouts)	Sassafras
	Gray birch	Sweet black birch
	Hickorys (several spp.)	
Shrubs	Blueberry	Sheep laurel
	Catbrier	Sweet fern
	Huckleberry	Witch hazel
	Mountain laurel	
Herbs	Narrow-leaved milkweed	Wintergreen
	Sarsaparilla	Grasses
	Whorled loosestrife	Few other herbs

Figure 3.4
A multiple-stem chestnut oak.

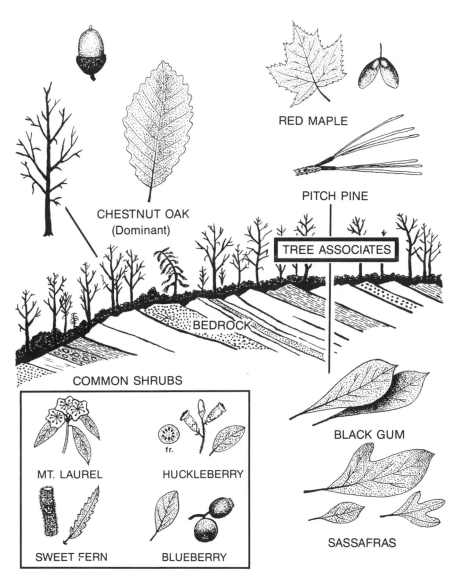

Figure 3.5
Sectional view of a chestnut oak ridge top and its woody plants. The bedrock of the ridge tops is typically resistant sandstone or conglomerate.

such as blueberry, mountain laurel, and huckleberry, dominate, while in other places the cover is sparse, with a scattering of sprout saplings and a mixed assortment of smaller plants.

The Mixed Oak Forest

If you descend from the higher Appalachian ridge tops, you will encounter another major forest type in the drained uplands: the mixed oak forest. It roughly follows the Appalachian Mountains from southern New England to Tennessee and forms much of the forest land of the southern section of the Poconos (Figures 3.1 and 3.6). Before the devastating chestnut blight, it was called the oak-chestnut forest. Through much of the region you can still frequently find young American chestnut trees sprouting from old roots, but they are short-lived as they become inevitable victims of the blight. With the loss of the once magnificent chestnut the common element of this Pocono forest type is the blend of three oak species: black, red, and white. Frequently, white pine trees mingle among these three dominant oaks, as do scarlet and chestnut oaks. The mixed oak forest grades into surrounding forest types as illustrated in Figure 3.7.

The three dominant oaks are not evenly distributed through this forest type. White oak prefers rich and moist soil and is common on the moist bottomlands and the better upland soils. Red oak does better on sandy-gravelly soil and will not tolerate wet soil conditions. Black oak is more characteristic of the dry uplands and, like red oak, is not a bottomland species. The common trees of the mixed oak forest are illustrated in Figure 3.8. Other large trees that occur with some regularity include sugar maple, black cherry, black gum, pitch pine, and hemlock. In places where the forest has been clear-cut or farmed recently, some of the sunloving trees, such as gray birch, the aspens, and red cedar, persist.

There are relatively few sub-canopy tree species. Growing among the replacement saplings, one might find hornbeam, hop hornbeam, sassafras, dogwood, and shadbush (juneberry). The latter two are quite conspicuous, as they both produce showy white flowers in the early Spring before the general forest leaves emerge (see Figure 3.9). Shadbush precedes dogwood by about one week.

The variety of shrubs is much greater than that of the sub-canopy trees. Common shrubs include deerberry, hobblebush, witch hazel, spicebush, mapleleaf viburnum, great rhododendron, and arrow-

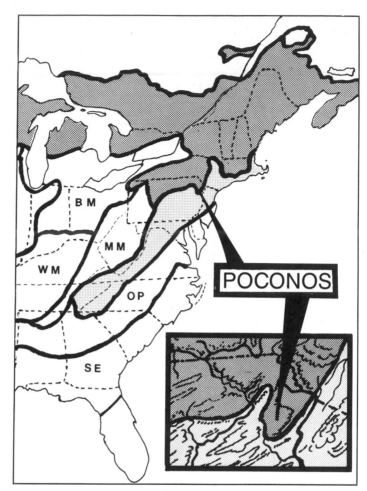

Figure 3.6
The subdivisions of the eastern deciduous forest. The Poconos are
in a transitional zone between the hemlock-white pine-northern
hardwood forest (dark shading) and the oak-chestnut forest
(light shading, and now treated as the mixed oak forest). Other
subdivisions include: BM, Beech-Maple; WM, western Mesophytic;
MM, Mixed Mesophytic; OP, Oak-Pine; and, SE, southeastern
evergreen forest. (Modified from E. L. Braun, *Deciduous
Forests of Eastern North America*. 1950. Macmillan Publishing
Co., Inc. Permission to use map from the Cincinnati
Museum of Natural History).

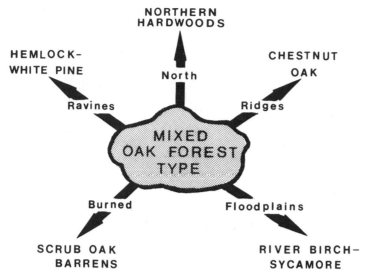

Figure 3.7
The mixed oak forest relative to surrounding forest types. Depending on environmental factors such as slope, repeated burning, and moisture, the mixed oak forest grades into surrounding habitats.

wood. Some of these are illustrated in Figure 3.10. In addition, many of the shrubs discussed and illustrated for other forest types appear in the mixed oak forest. Although the white laurel, or great rhododendron, is by far the most common woodland member of the genus *Rhododendron*, others in much lesser numbers include pink azalea, mountain azalea, and rhodora.

Four woody vines appear throughout the Poconos: Virginia creeper, poison ivy, fox grape, and catbrier. Each can be distinguished by its leaves, as illustrated in Figure 3.11. They are most commonly found in openings or at the edges of the woodlands. Poison ivy has quite varied growth patterns—it may grow erect as a small shrub in open fields, or as a clambering vine on fencelines, or it may grow high into the treetops with a lower stem diameter in excess of two inches! Always look for the three shiny leaflets and *avoid* any contact with poison ivy, as it can cause inflammation of the skin in susceptible persons.

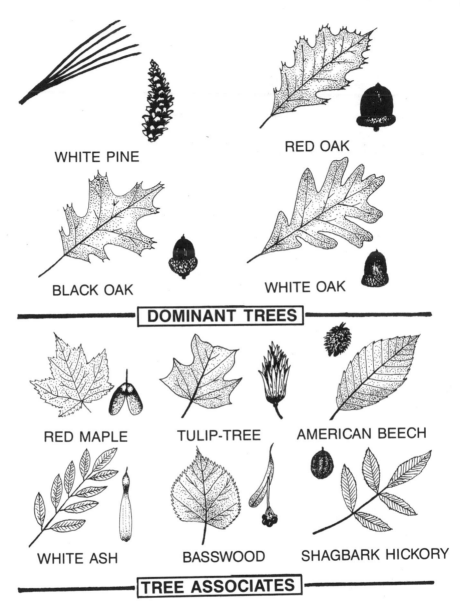

WHITE PINE

RED OAK

BLACK OAK

WHITE OAK

DOMINANT TREES

RED MAPLE

TULIP-TREE

AMERICAN BEECH

WHITE ASH

BASSWOOD

SHAGBARK HICKORY

TREE ASSOCIATES

Figure 3.8
Dominant trees and tree associates of the mixed oak forest.

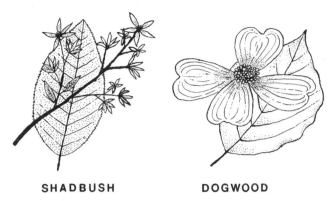

SHADBUSH **DOGWOOD**

Figure 3.9
Two conspicuous flowering sub-canopy trees. Shadbush has
small white petals, and dogwood has four large white
petal-like bracts. Both flower before most of the forest trees
have fully leafed out. Both have leaves about two to five
inches long.

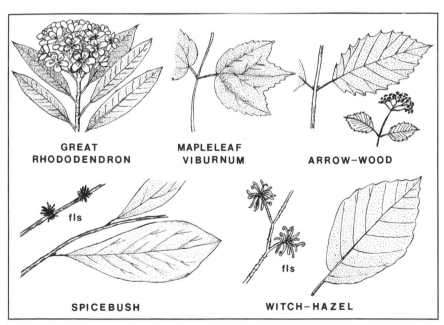

GREAT RHODODENDRON **MAPLELEAF VIBURNUM** **ARROW–WOOD**

SPICEBUSH **WITCH–HAZEL**

Figure 3.10
Common woodland shrubs of the Poconos. Native great rhododendron occurs
mostly in dense colonies and adds sporadic splashes of color to the understory of
the Poconos in July. Witch hazel, with its strap-like yellow petals, atypically
flowers in the fall, while spicebush, with its small clustered yellow flowers, blooms
in April and May.

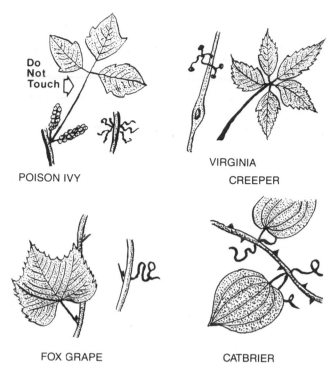

POISON IVY

VIRGINIA
CREEPER

FOX GRAPE

CATBRIER

Figure 3.11
Woody vines. Most common in open woodlands, on fence
rows, and at the edges of the forest.

The herbaceous plants vary according to the time of their flowering as well as their location within the forest. Unsurprisingly, the
variety of spring wildflowers is much greater than that of the summer
and fall. The months prior to the big surge of June vacationers are excellent times to observe the spring wildflowers. Many of the early
season flowering herbs are illustrated in Figure 3.12, and some of
the summer and early fall ones in Figure 3.13. As many of the spring
flowers die back, ferns become a conspicuous part of the forest floor.
Among the more common ones are the grape, hayscented, bracken,
sensitive, beech, shield, and Christmas ferns (Figure 3.22).

The Northern Hardwoods

As you move to the higher elevations and north of the mixed oak
forest, you will find the oaks gradually decreasing in importance as
the forest type grades into northern hardwood. The northern hard-

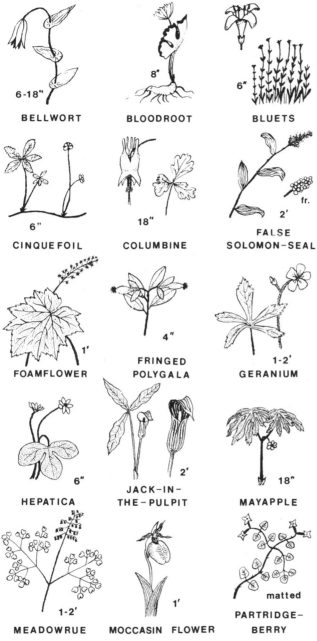

BELLWORT 6-18"

BLOODROOT 8"

BLUETS 6"

CINQUEFOIL 6"

COLUMBINE 18"

FALSE SOLOMON-SEAL 2' fr.

FOAMFLOWER 1'

FRINGED POLYGALA 4"

GERANIUM 1-2'

HEPATICA 6"

JACK-IN-THE-PULPIT 2'

MAYAPPLE 18"

MEADOWRUE 1-2'

MOCCASIN FLOWER 1'

PARTRIDGE-BERRY matted

Figure 3.12
Common spring and early summer woodland flowers.

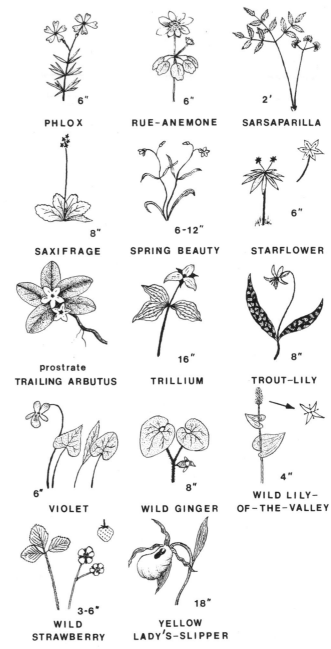

PHLOX 6"

RUE-ANEMONE 6"

SARSAPARILLA 2'

SAXIFRAGE 8"

SPRING BEAUTY 6-12"

STARFLOWER 6"

prostrate
TRAILING ARBUTUS

TRILLIUM 16"

TROUT–LILY 8"

VIOLET 6"

WILD GINGER 8"

WILD LILY–
OF–THE–VALLEY 4"

WILD
STRAWBERRY 3-6"

YELLOW
LADY'S–SLIPPER 18"

Figure 3.12 (continued)
Common spring and early summer woodland flowers.

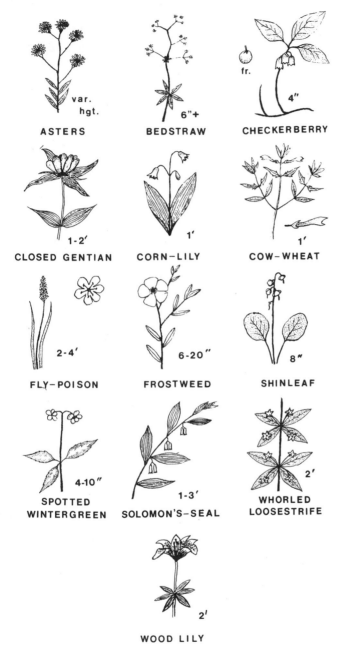

ASTERS   BEDSTRAW   CHECKERBERRY

CLOSED GENTIAN   CORN–LILY   COW–WHEAT

FLY–POISON   FROSTWEED   SHINLEAF

SPOTTED WINTERGREEN   SOLOMON'S–SEAL   WHORLED LOOSESTRIFE

WOOD LILY

Figure 3.13
Common summer and early fall woodland flowers.

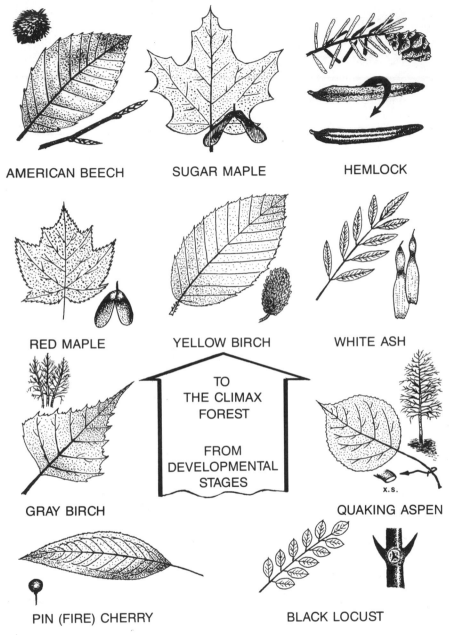

AMERICAN BEECH   SUGAR MAPLE   HEMLOCK

RED MAPLE   YELLOW BIRCH   WHITE ASH

TO
THE CLIMAX
FOREST

FROM
DEVELOPMENTAL
STAGES

GRAY BIRCH   QUAKING ASPEN

x.s.

PIN (FIRE) CHERRY   BLACK LOCUST

Figure 3.14
Dominant trees of the northern hardwood forest at developmental
and climax stages.

BOX 3.3

Places to See
Chestnut Oak Ridges and
Mixed Oak Forest

Chestnut oak dominates the narrow, dry ridge tops of the Appalachians, such as along the Appalachian Trail; and it is common on the drier, soil-starved hilltops throughout the Pocono Plateau.

The Mixed Oak Forest occurs along the trails of the Bruce Lake Natural Area, the State Forest Lands along route 402 near Ludleyville, and at the Shuman Point Natural Area at the northern end of Lake Wallenpaupack.

woods occupy much of the Pocono Plateau and extend further northward into New York state (Figures 3.1 and 3.6). The dominant forest trees include American beech, sugar maple, hemlock, red maple, yellow birch, and white ash. White pine, once a major tree of this forest type, is found in scattered places throughout the forest. Other trees include black walnut, black cherry, and some of the previously described oaks. While the dominant trees (Figure 3.14) together comprise the region's climax forest (generally a forest in which young individuals can develop under mature individuals of the same species), some sections have not reached this climax status. Seeds from mature trees may take root in the ground or on the surface of old dead trees (Figure 3.15). In recently lumbered areas or those having had

Figure 3.15
A prop-rooted tree. If a seedling starts on top of a fallen dead
tree, it sends roots around the log; as the seedling grows to
a mature tree, the dead log slowly disintegrates, leaving the new
tree "propped up." (Drawing of a mature yellow birch at
Buck Hill Falls.)

repeated burns, the developmental stage is evident, characterized by aspens, fire cherry, and gray birch. Several large tracts of this type are intersected by the Pennsylvania Turnpike just north of the Lehigh River.

In general, the canopy of the northern hardwood forest is a bit more closed than that of the mixed oak type; and, as increasing numbers of both white pine and hemlock enter the canopy, heavy shading becomes a factor in reducing the understory plants. The sub-canopy trees are much like those of the adjacent mixed oak forest, but with a decreasing number of flowering dogwoods and much more striped maple. Likewise, the shrub assemblage (Figure 3.10) is similar as are the common woody vines (Figure 3.11). In some locations, there are large tracts without any of the heaths (mountain laurel, rhododendron, etc.); in others, these shrubs are abundant.

The flowering herbaceous plants are similar to those previously illustrated for the mixed oak forest (Figures 3.12 and 3.13). However, the overall number of plants is somewhat lower, while there are larger numbers of partridge berry, wild lily-of-the-valley, starflower, and beechdrops. The ferns are also similar to those elsewhere in the Poconos (Figure 3.22), but with increasing numbers of Christmas fern, which prefers a cooler environment.

Hemlock-White Pine Ravines

Where the Pocono brooks and streams cut sharply into the less resistant bedrock, ravines develop. They typically slope steeply on either side of the rushing water. In the cool, moist ravines, another Pocono forest type prevails—the hemlock-white pine community. The hemlock stands may be pure or mixed with white pine. Because of the ravines' inaccessibility, many were not lumbered out. As a result, one often can see magnificent trees forming a high dense canopy. In fact, the canopy often becomes so dense that the forest floor receives little sunlight; reduced solar energy, coupled with acidic soil caused by the needle drop, results in a specialized understory growth.

Compared with the other four Pocono forest types, ravines contain a larger variety of ferns, mosses, and liverworts. In ravines, such as those at Dingmans Falls, much of the exposed rock surface is clothed almost entirely with ferns (Figure 3.22) and liverworts (Figure 3.16). Other plants include occasional shrubs such as the Canada yew, striped maple, hobblebush, and the largeleaved holly. Close to the water, luxurious stands of rhododendron frequently thrive.

If the ravine has north- and south-facing slopes (as many do), the

BOX 3.4

Places to See the Northern Hardwood Forest

Both Tobyhanna and Gouldsboro State Parks have good examples of this forest type. Other locations include the Ledgedale Natural Area, near the southern end of Lake Wallenpaupack and owned by P.P. & L., and along the access road off Route 940 to Brady's Lake on State Game Lands 127. All of these have marked trails. Long Pond, off route 170 near Seelyville, is a good example near the northern limits of the Poconos. One of the most mature stands is Jenkins Woods on the private grounds of Buck Hill Falls. Visitors are welcome, but should check at the entrance to the falls.

flora may vary according to slope. Obviously the south-facing slopes are warmer and drier than the north-facing slopes. Hemlock favors the cooler and wetter north-facing slopes, while white pine favors the south-facing slopes (Figure 3.17). Tree associates may include yellow birch, red maple, and other species from the surrounding upland communities.

The Wetter Sections

In all five major types of forest found in the Poconos—as well as the many mixed forest sections—the mix of trees and other plants depends partly on the wetness of the soil. For instance, white oak likes moister soil than red or black oak; ferns, mosses, and liverworts thrive on dampness; and hemlocks want wetter ground than white pines.

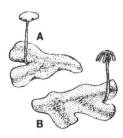

Figure 3.16
Liverworts. A male (A) and female (B) plant with their characteristic reproductive structures. Each plant is flat and about an inch long.

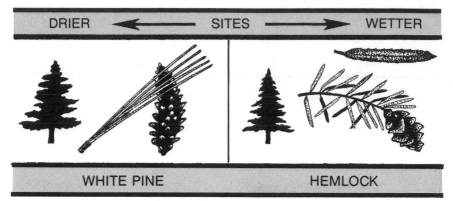

Figure 3.17
White pine and hemlock.

Besides these forest floors of varying degrees of wetness, the Poconos contain much wetter sections known as bogs, swamps, and marshes. In the nearby Delaware River there are areas sometimes totally under water: the floodplains. And, of course, rich plant life exists within the water itself—in streams, ponds, and lakes. The amount of aquatic and semi-aquatic life in the Poconos is so great that it requires a separate chapter (Chapter 5, Watercourse and Wetland Communities).

The Delaware Cliffs

Some of the cliffs at the Delaware Water Gap and further north at Milford and Matamoras deserve a special comment, even though they are not forests. The cliffs are dry, exposed to the sun and wind, and thus have a specialized desertlike flora. Red cedar is found here, but the most interesting plant is the prickly pear cactus—a plant usually associated with the desert of the Southwest—highlighting the varied flora of the Poconos. Indeed, in a day's outing, one can experience a touch of the desert, the coolness of a hemlock ravine, the sogginess of a boreal bog, and a host of other natural communities.

The Tree Plantations

Throughout the Poconos one sees tracts of evergreen trees with a strikingly different character from those in the five types of forest. The trees are usually the same species in each tract; they are close to-

BOX 3.5

Places to See ——————
Hemlock-White Pine
Ravines

The ravine communities are associated with the many Pocono Waterfalls (Figure 2.7 and Table 2.1). Dingmans Falls, in the Delaware Water Gap National Recreation Area, is an excellent example. Another fine example is at the G. W. Childs Park, where towering evergreens preside over a meager subcanopy and nearly barren ground cover, creating an almost cathedral-like setting.

gether and evenly spaced; and they are all the same age. These are the plantations.

As in the hemlock-white pine ravines, understory light is much diminished in the plantations; but, unlike the natural forest, the plantation trees have been systematically planted at predetermined close distances. The effect is twofold: first, the floor is almost barren of vegetation and carpeted with fallen needles; second, the lower, light-starved branches die and eventually self-prune. At the later stages, this creates an open parklike atmosphere beneath the canopy. If the trees are being grown for lumber, the owner may prune the lower branches before they die. The obvious effect of growing a tall straight tree without branches is that it eliminates knots. The price difference between knotty wood (sheathing grade) and clear wood (select grade) is about threefold.

Although some plantations are grown for lumber, some are planted as soil conservation measures, and others, such as Douglas-fir tracts, for Christmas trees. Figure 3.18 shows the self-pruning effect and illustrates some common Pocono plantation trees.

Farms, Pastures, and Roads

Tree plantations are an obvious result of human activity. Roads are another. Indeed, roads have had so large an impact on Pocono flora and fauna that this book devotes Chapter 6 to roadside natural history.

Some effects of human activity are not so obvious. Where virgin trees were removed for lumber, new forests often grow; where stone and clay have been quarried, the wounded land often heals. Man-

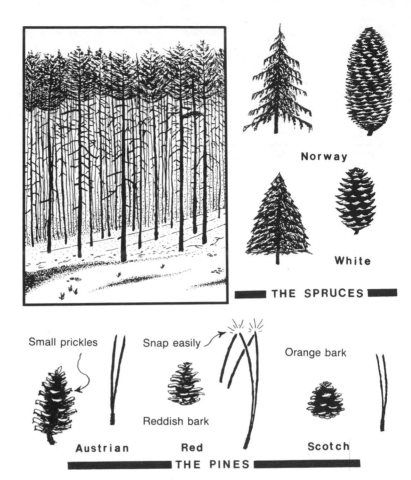

Norway

White

THE SPRUCES

Small prickles

Snap easily

Orange bark

Reddish bark

Austrian   Red   Scotch

THE PINES

Figure 3.18
Pocono conifer plantation trees. Norway spruce has very large
cones and pendulent branchlets. Austrian pine has small prickles on
the cone scales; red pine does not. Red pine has long needles which
snap easily. The orange upper bark on Scotch pine is distinctive.
Hemlock and white pine (Figure 3.17) are also commonly cultivated,
as are several varieties of the deciduous larch.

INSET: a typical pine plantation.

made bodies of water often look quite "natural," as Chapter 5 makes
clear. The effects of fires set by humans are noted in the description
of the scrub-oak barrens at the beginning of this chapter. A history of
human activity in the Poconos is the subject of Chapter 7, but the decline of the region's agriculture deserves mention here because of its
impact on forests. As flatter and more fertile farmlands opened to set-

Figure 3.19
An old stone row fence in the winter. Scene from along the trail to
the Tannersville bog. Large oak trees are at the fence line, while the
abandoned fields to either side have shorter-lived invading trees
like those in Figure 3.20.

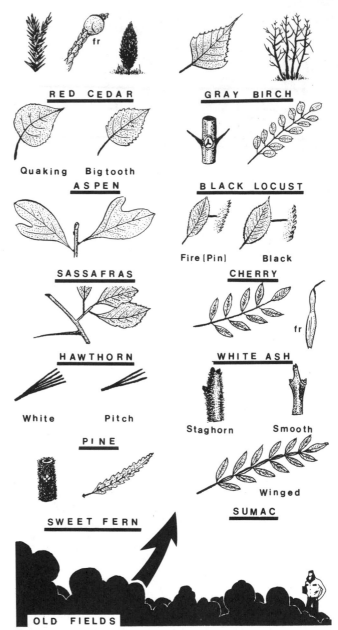

RED CEDAR

GRAY BIRCH

Quaking   Bigtooth
ASPEN

BLACK LOCUST

SASSAFRAS

Fire (Pin)   Black
CHERRY

HAWTHORN

WHITE ASH

White   Pitch
PINE

Staghorn   Smooth

SWEET FERN

Winged
SUMAC

OLD FIELDS

Figure 3.20
Common woody plants of abandoned pastures and croplands.
Each such old field has its own flora, depending on prior
land use, proximity to seed trees (or their roots from which
sprouts may grow), soil conditions, and slope.

tlement in the West, Pocono pasture and cropland gradually converted to recreational use.

The numerous abandoned farm and pasture lands of the Poconos are recognizable by the stone row fences that traverse many of the woodlands. Among the stones of these fences one often can observe large old trees, remnants of an earlier forest, while on either side the former fields are in varying stages of transition (Figure 3.19). Both the rate of change and the mix of plants in the changing fields depend on the time of abandonment, the soils, and arrival of invading plants. Some common woody invaders of old fields are illustrated in Figure 3.20. Former turnip patches are now transitional woods viewed from busy tennis courts.

Woodland Ferns

Most of the plants discussed in this chapter have been the "higher plants" or those that produce seeds. A group of nonflowering plants that form a conspicuous part of the woodlands, swamps, and roadsides is the ferns. There are at least thirty species of ferns throughout the Poconos. They vary greatly from the rare climbing fern (Figure 3.21) to the lacy common hayscented fern, which often grows in circular patches to the exclusion of other plants. Throughout spring and early summer the many wildflowers and flowering shrubs dominate the forest floor. In the summer and fall, however, ferns are often the most striking of the smaller flora. A few, such as the Christmas and shield ferns, are evergreen and add a delightful contrast of green through the drab winter months.

A few of the most common ferns of the Poconos are illustrated in Figure 3.22. Most of these are identifiable by their shape or spore-bearing structures, but it is necessary to have a hand lens to distinguish among a number of the similar species. Individual species also vary considerably in their structure, size, and shape. Many hybridize, or cross, quite readily—adding some difficulty to the identification process. Nonetheless, their study is worth the effort—with the assistance of one of the good fern guides on the market. Also included in the illustration are four representatives of the fern-allies —club mosses and horsetails. The club mosses, such as ground pine and ground cedar, are evergreen, and add a small touch of fresh-

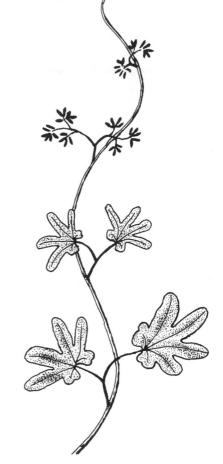

Figure 3.21
The climbing fern, *Lygodium palmatum*. This most unfernlike fern is rarely seen in roadside thickets in the moist, acid, and poor soils of the Poconos. The lower palmshaped fronds are vegetative and the upper few, of smaller size, produce spores. Unfortunately, the climbing fern has been picked for ornamentation, and was the subject of the first conservation law for a fern (Hartford, Connecticut, 1869). Its alternate name is the Hartford fern.

ness to a midwinter day. Unfortunately, excessive numbers of club mosses are still picked for holiday decorations.

Pocono Phenology

Phenology is the study of natural phenomena that recur periodically, such as yearly blossoming and foliage coloration, in relation to climate and changing seasons. The coronation ceremony of the Laurel Blossom Queen at Split Rock Lodge occurs within a few calendar days in early June of each year. The chosen date falls well within the laurel-flowering time zone of the Poconos. Choosing initial flower-

SOME FERNS OF...

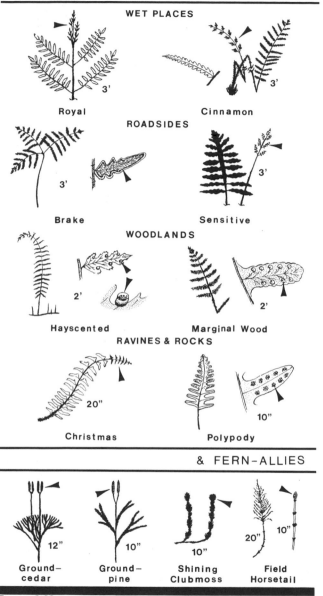

Figure 3.22
Common fern and fern-allies. The small arrowheads indicate
the reproductive spore-bearing structures. If the spores are
borne on the regular leaves, as in the brake and polypody
ferns, they are found on the underside of the leaf blades.

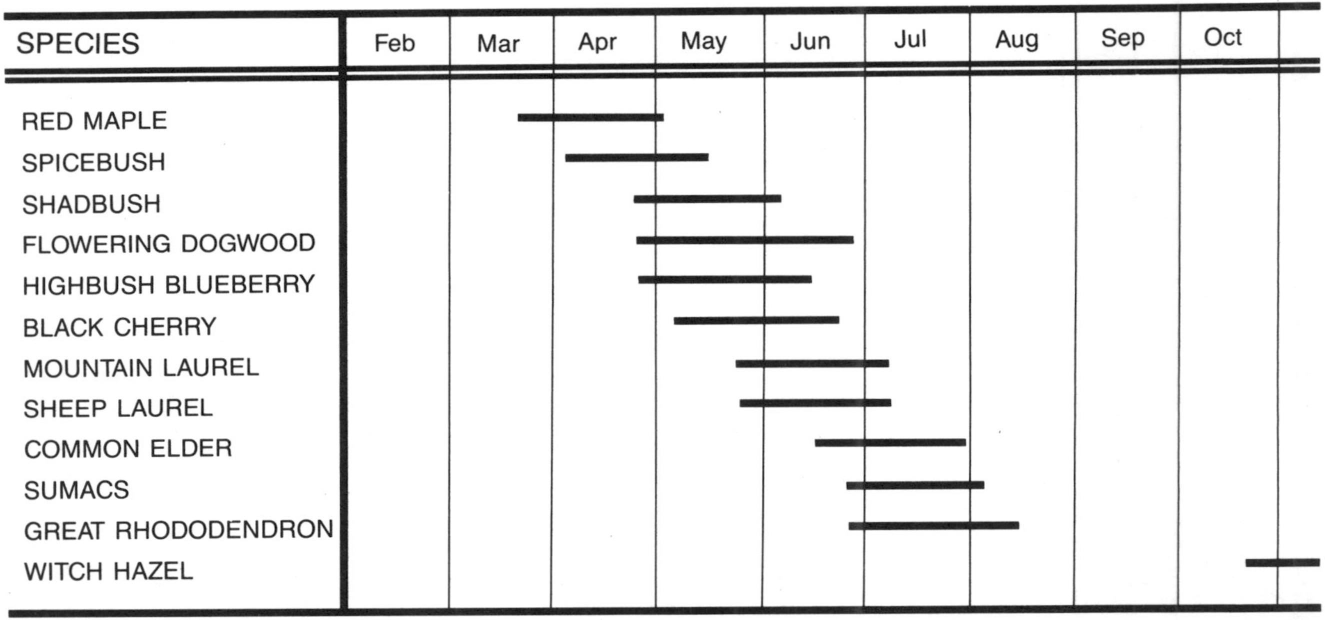

VEGETATION OF POCONO FORESTS

SPECIES	Feb	Mar	Apr	May	Jun	Jul	Aug	Sep	Oct
RED MAPLE									
SPICEBUSH									
SHADBUSH									
FLOWERING DOGWOOD									
HIGHBUSH BLUEBERRY									
BLACK CHERRY									
MOUNTAIN LAUREL									
SHEEP LAUREL									
COMMON ELDER									
SUMACS									
GREAT RHODODENDRON									
WITCH HAZEL									

Figure 3.23
Approximate flowering times for some conspicuous trees and shrubs of the Poconos.

ing dates or the flowering dates of plants in diverse habitats is less simple.

Two primary factors govern blossoming dates: the genetic program of a species and its physiological response to increasing warmth and the photoperiod. The dates also vary according to environmental factors: elevation, latitude, slope, aspect (direction of slope), and the progression of the macroclimate. In general, blossoming is delayed by about one day per 100 feet of elevation; by about one day per twenty miles of latitude at the same elevation; by as much as a week by slope and aspect; and, by an indefinite period because of the late "arrival" of spring. From Allentown (el. 400 ft.), for example, to the top of Camelback (el. 2100 ft., and thirty-five miles to the north), one normally expects a blossoming-time delay of two to three weeks. Within the Poconos, since the region has a north-south extent of about sixty miles, one normally expects a latitude-governed difference of up to three days. If we also consider elevation, slope, and aspect—as well as macroclimatic factors—we see that predicted flowering dates cannot be exact.

At the risk of oversimplification (in light of the previous discussion), a generalized blossoming chart for the Poconos is presented in Figure 3.23. If nothing else, it suggests that for more than three months there are some interesting and colorful trees and shrubs in flower throughout the Poconos, but the favorite is still mountain laurel.

Mountain Laurel

From "the laurel highlands" of western Pennsylvania to the Laurel Festival of the Poconos, mountain laurel has a special meaning for Pennsylvanians; indeed, in 1933 it became the official state flower.

Figure 3.24
Mountain laurel, the state flower of Pennsylvania. It blooms from late May into early July.

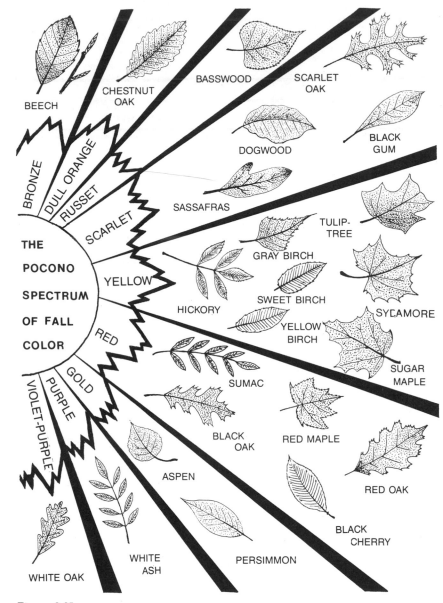

Figure 3.25
Pocono autumn leaf colors.

Mountain laurel reaches its flowering climax in June in much of northeastern Pennsylvania, including the Poconos. Mountain laurel is an interesting and colorful shrub common in both the moist and dry woods of the Poconos. Technically it is a heath, a member of the

Where to See Mountain Laurel

Although mountain laurel can be seen throughout the Poconos, some areas give better views than others. A list of about twenty roads, informally called the "Laurel Blossom Trail," appears seasonally in *This Week in the Poconos* or can be obtained from the Pocono Mountains Vacation Bureau. The plant flowers from late May into early July.

acid-loving plants of the family Ericaceae, exhibiting colorful white to pinkish flowers in loose floral blooms on a shrub three to six feet high. The leaves are evergreen and alternately arranged on crooked and branched stems. Mountain laurel also goes by the name of "spoonwood" and "calicobush." Cultivated varieties are available from nurserys.

Pocono Fall Color

While spring brings flowering shrubs and herbs to the Poconos, autumn brings the "flaming foliage." Warm days coupled with cool nights are ideal for setting off the series of leaf pigment changes re-

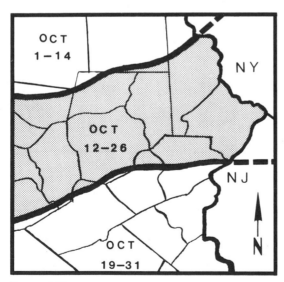

Figure 3.26
Peak fall coloration zones for the Poconos and adjacent areas.

sulting in the wide spectrum of fall color (Figure 3.25). The color parade starts in the northern counties and moves southward—as well as from higher to lower elevations—in a reverse of the blossoming progression. The periods of best leaf coloration are shown in Figure 3.26.

Finally, of course, the leaves die and drop. Many of the oaks and beech trees hold their brown leaves until late into the winter. All eventually decay and become the raw material of future recycling.

Nature's Recycling

When one thinks of the process of decay, two groups come to mind: bacteria and fungi. The microscopic bacteria act primarily on animal tissue, while the fungi are the primary decomposers of plant material. The fungi are void of chlorophyll, and are either saprophytic (living on decaying organic matter) or parasitic (living on other living organisms)—or between these two extremes. Being both nongreen and often fairly large, fungi are frequently encountered in the Poco-

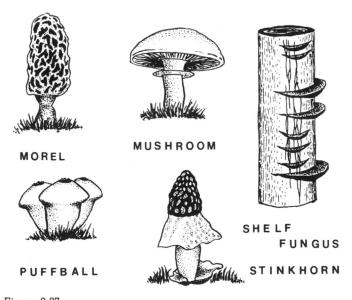

Figure 3.27
Some common fungal types of the Poconos. Morels are edible, as are puffballs when they are young. Some mushrooms are edible, and some are deadly poison—a distinction reserved for the experts only!

Where to See Fall Coloration

Figure 3.25 can be used as a color and leaf-shape guide. Figure 3.26 suggests peak coloration zones. The best period is mid-October. Many bus companies schedule Pocono fall color day tours. Check locally or with the Pocono Mountain Vacation Bureau.

nos. Since the group is so large and diverse, Figure 3.27 merely suggests some of the common fungal types to look for. Were it not for the continued activities of fungi, the Pocono landscape would be hopelessly buried under a dead "plant junkyard." Unfortunately, a number of fungi are destructive. Among the more notorious culprits are those responsible for the chestnut blight (since 1904), the Dutch elm disease (since 1930), and the catastrophic potato blight of Europe in the mid-1800s. Less familiar but nonetheless important are the "Rogue's Gallery" of fungi, such as the various rusts, smuts, and molds which attack our foods and crops and sometimes our bodies. Like bacteria, fungi are a mixed blessing!

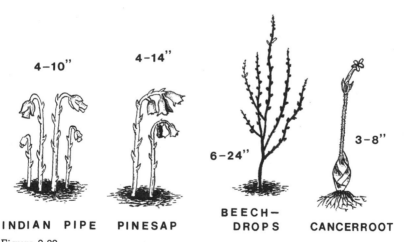

Figure 3.28
Four non-photosynthetic flowering plants. Indian pipe and beechdrops are common. Indian pipe and pinesap are in the same genus (*Monotropa*), but the latter always has several flowers per stalk. Beechdrops are parasitic on beech roots.

In addition to the fungi, several flowering plants lacking chlorophyll are likely to be seen in the Poconos. They are an apparent offshoot from the main line of higher plant evolution. The principal varieties include pinesap, cancerroot, beechdrops, and Indian pipe (Figure 3.28). The careful observer will note that they produce flowers; the fungi do not.

Forest Disturbances

The idealized model of a pristine Pocono forest with sparkling clear waters, an absence of diseases and pests, and an endless euphoria-like balance of nature are but visions in the eyes of poets and promoters. Any area has a history and the Pocono forests, being no exception, are checkered with a series of perturbations. Most, no doubt, are lost in the thousands of years of postglacial time, but for the last several centuries we can look at the record to help understand the present.

The loss of the American chestnut (Figure 3.29), due to a fungus, is but one of the many perturbations in the Pocono forests; other agents which have caused changes include fire, hurricanes, the gypsy moth, and the Dutch elm disease.

Of all the forest changes, the most extensive and wholesale one was caused by the lumbering industry. Only areas confined to steep slopes, on private preserves, and inaccessible ravines escaped; hence, most of the Pocono forests are now in second growth. Considering the excessive lumbering of the last century, the Pocono visitor is sometimes startled to see lumbering in the Delaware and Lackawanna State Forests (combined 71,579 acres) of the Poconos. There is no need for alarm, as the activities in the state forests are all part of the Forest Management Plan, summarized in one of the Bureau of Forestry publications:

> Multiple-use forest management is the *key* to providing a continuous supply of quality timber products, protection of watersheds for maximum yields of potable water, wise development of mineral resources, and providing recreation opportunities for millions of urban and suburban residents who are only hours away from the Poconos. Timber management is an important activity on all State Forests. Most State Forest land is under an even-aged forest management system which is designed to regenerate valuable light demanding tree species and provide food for wildlife.

fr.

lvs.

fls.

Figure 3.29
American chestnut. Leaves, lacy
flowers, and spiny ball-like fruits
(called burs) are depicted about
one-half size.

A multiple-use approach, or "compromise approach" as it is some-times called, implies use of a given environment for several purposes simultaneously. Each compartment (approximately two square miles) is managed for recreation, environmental protection, forest yield and/or education. Thus we observe such diverse activities as hiking, picnicking, snowmobiling, hunting and fishing, but also find natural areas, experimental tracts, wild areas, demonstration zones, and tim-ber management activities. For this last activity, the state policy as-sures diversity through the continuation of openings and tracts of evergreen cover, the encouragement of young woody growth areas, the preservation of large seed trees and cavity trees, and a laissez-faire policy on wet areas. In brief, the exploitation of the past has graduated to the managed policies of today. History has taught its lessons.

CHAPTER 4

Animals of Pocono Forests

Before population was greatly advanced in this part of Pennsylvania, game of all description found within that range was extremely abundant. The Elk itself did not disdain to browse on the shoulders of the mountains near the Lehigh."
—JOHN JAMES AUDUBON, *Episodes,* 1829

The forest vegetation types of the Poconos have reasonably discernible patterns of distribution, although gradations and transitions occur. Plant populations spread; environmental conditions change over time; and thus patterns change. Animal populations also spread and do so much more rapidly. Some species have special requirements and thus a restricted distribution, but many animals are able to adapt to varied environmental conditions.

In addition, animals do not stay put for easy viewing by visitors. Many times indirect signs can lead to possible direct sightings, if patience is employed. The presence of nests, gnawed bark, shed skins, patches of hair, feathers, tracks in mud or snow, fecal droppings, or distinctive calls are the clues which the visitor must use to gain knowledge about forest dwellers that are often secretive, alert to danger, or nocturnal. Sadly, animals have little defense against motor vehicles, and dead animals beside roads are unpleasant indications of which animal species occur in a particular region.

Forest Invertebrates

The most numerous animals in forests are invertebrates—that is, those that lack a vertebral column. In the soil, the crossroads of terrestrial communities, a great diversity and abundance of animals dwell.

Many soil organisms reside in the thin film of water that exists between soil particles. Here microscopic protozoans, rotifers, and round worms may reach population levels of tens of thousands of individuals per cubic foot of soil. Somewhat larger animals, such as white or pot worms, mites, ticks, springtails (primitive wingless insects), and the larvae of many insect species live in the soil and the litter which accumulates on the soil surface. Still larger forms, such as earthworms, roaches, sowbugs, beetles, termites, ants, millipedes, centipedes, spiders, slugs, and snails are more easily discovered in soil litter. Many soil animals are detritus feeders, playing an important role in converting dead plant and animal organic matter into inorganic substances for later absorption by roots of trees and other forest vegetation.

Other forest invertebrates are foliage dwellers. Ants, spiders, leafhoppers, aphids, beetles, and many insect larvae, particularly caterpillars, are good examples of this group. Flying insects—sawflies, deerflies, horseflies, "no-see'ems," bees, wasps, moths, and butterflies—range widely through the forest vegetation. Figure 4.1 shows a profile of a mature oak forest with some representative invertebrate creatures.

Sometimes foliage dwellers are so numerous—for example, spruce budworms or gypsy moth caterpillars—that the sound of their excrement dropping to the ground sounds like the patter of rain drops. These forest insects may reach such population levels that they are termed "pests". Many battles have been waged to control these pests, which can do considerable damage to forest growth and yield. Bark beetles, hardwood borers, aphids, sawflies, spruce budworms, hemlock loopers, tent caterpillars, and gypsy moth caterpillars are major forest pests. In Pocono forests, the gypsy moth caterpillar is of greatest concern. A discussion appears in the next section.

A daytime visit to forested tracts enables one to see some of the invertebrates. A nighttime visit, especially in summer, is more revealing since many soil and foliage dwellers show themselves as air

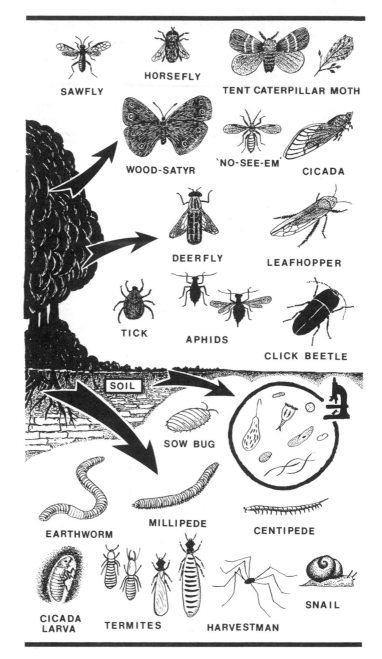

Figure 4.1
Representative invertebrates of the Pocono woodlands and upper soil.

temperatures moderate and relative humidity rises. Under these conditions, many creatures can be seen with the aid of a flashlight or lantern. The light will attract other forms, particularly flying insects. The calls of still other insects such as crickets and katydids will be heard on warm summer evenings.

Gypsy Moth

The most serious insect pest in Pennsylvania's forests is the gypsy moth. This native of Europe, Asia, and North Africa was accidentally introduced into Massachusetts in 1869, when an American naturalist imported some gypsy moth egg clusters. He hoped to develop a hardier variety of silk-producing insects by crossing the gypsy moth with the silkworm. A hardier variety might withstand the disease causing severe problems in some silkworm industries at the time. Some caterpillars escaped, found favorable conditions plus a lack of natural enemies, and thus gained a foothold in North America.

Gypsy moths were widespread by 1902 in all of the New England states, eastern New York, and New Jersey. The species disperses by an unusual method. Adult female moths are so laden with eggs that they do not fly. Male moths detect, from some distance, a sex attractant emitted by the females and thus locate the female. It is in the earliest caterpillar stages that dispersal occurs. The hairy caterpillars float downwind, and these larvae help by spinning a silkthread sail to catch the wind. Figure 4.2 illustrates the mature caterpillar and other life stages of the gypsy moth.

By 1932, gypsy moth infestation covered 400 square miles of Luzerne and Lackawanna counties. Since that time, gypsy moths have extended their range so that by the early 1980s the species had spread throughout 46 counties in the commonwealth. Over two-and-a-half million acres of forests felt serious effects during 1981, a peak gypsy moth population year.

Most of the damage is done by the caterpillars, which are general feeders on many types of trees as well as shrubs. Food plants favored at all larval stages include aspen, birch, sumac, willow, larch, blue spruce, and all species of oak, especially white oak and chestnut oak. Chestnut oak is the dominant tree on nearby mountain ridges and in many places on the Pocono plateau. In fact, gypsy moths have spread southwestward across Pennsylvania, mainly along the ridges where chestnut oaks predominate. In recent decades, dispersal of gypsy moths has had the unwitting aid of campers and other travelers who transport egg masses, larvae, and other stages of the moth

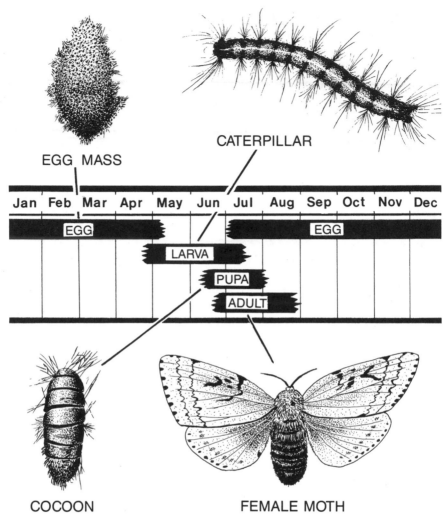

EGG MASS

CATERPILLAR

| Jan | Feb | Mar | Apr | May | Jun | Jul | Aug | Sep | Oct | Nov | Dec |

EGG

EGG

LARVA

PUPA

ADULT

COCOON   FEMALE MOTH

Figure 4.2
Gypsy Moth life cycle. Beginning in late June, the female moth deposits egg clusters on tree trunks and other protected sites. Embryonic development is completed within four to six weeks. Larvae stay within their egg cases for seven to eight months. Hatching begins in late April and early May. Larvae undergo a series of molts in the next month or so. Mature larvae pupate in a sparse silk cocoon by late June. The pupal stage lasts about two weeks after which the adult moth emerges.

attached to trailers and other vehicles. As a result, the species has tures. Other vertebrates also parcel out the habitat, but the inter-relationships have not been as well studied.

Birds

Of all types of vertebrate animals, birds are the most familiar and most likely to be encountered when people venture outdoors. Approximately 260 species of birds have been recorded for the Poconos. The more common species are listed in Table 4.1 according to those habitats where the species is most likely to be observed. Uncommon species, designated by an asterisk, are also listed. Since birds are highly mobile animals, visitors may expect to discover a species outside its principal habitat. As Roger Tory Peterson stressed in his renowned field guide to birds, certain key features such as bill shape, length and position of the tail, eye bars, wing bars, etc., are quick, useful aids to identification. As mentioned earlier, birds will generally be seen whenever one ventures outdoors. However, there are numerous places in the Poconos especially well-suited for birding. Some of these sites are listed in Box 4.1.

Figure 4.3
Black-capped chickadee.

Table 4.1.
Pocono Birds and Their Principal Habitats

Species	Deciduous Forest	Mixed Forest	Hemlock Ravines	Fields, Woodlots	Flood Plains	Lakes	Ponds, Marshes	Bogs
Common loon					●	●		
Pied-billed grebe					●	●	●	
Horned grebe*					●	●	●	
Great blue heron					●	●	●	
Great egret*					●	●	●	
Snowy egret*					●	●	●	
Green-backed heron					●	●	●	
Mute swan*					●	●		
Snow goose*					●	●		
Canada goose					●	●	●	
Wood duck*					●	●	●	
Green-winged teal*						●	●	
Blue-winged teal*						●	●	
American black duck					●	●	●	
Mallard					●	●	●	
Northern pintail*						●	●	
American widgeon*					●	●	●	
Canvasback*					●	●	●	
Ring-necked duck					●	●	●	
Lesser scaup*					●	●	●	
Common goldeneye					●	●	●	
Bufflehead					●	●	●	
Hooded merganser*					●	●	●	
Common merganser					●	●	●	
Turkey vulture	●	●		●				

ANIMALS OF POCONO FORESTS

Species	Deciduous Forest	Mixed Forest	Hemlock Ravines	Fields, Woodlots	Flood Plains	Lakes	Ponds, Marshes	Bogs
Osprey					•	•	•	
Bald eagle*					•	•		
Golden eagle*	•							
Northern harrier				•	•	•	•	
Sharp-shinned hawk	•	•	•		•			
Cooper's hawk*	•	•	•		•			
Northern goshawk*	•	•	•		•		•	•
Red-shouldered hawk	•	•	•		•		•	•
Broad-winged hawk	•	•	•		•		•	•
Red-tailed hawk	•	•	•	•	•		•	•
Rough-legged hawk	•							
American kestrel				•	•		•	
Ruffed grouse	•	•	•					•
Ring-necked pheasant				•				
Wild turkey	•	•	•					
Common moorhen*						•	•	
American coot*						•	•	
Killdeer				•		•	•	
Greater yellowlegs*						•	•	
Lesser yellowlegs*						•	•	
Solitary sandpiper*						•	•	
Spotted sandpiper						•	•	
Least sandpiper*						•	•	
Pectoral sandpiper*						•	•	
Common snipe							•	•
American woodcock							•	•

Table 4.1. (*continued*) 91

Species	Deciduous Forest	Mixed Forest	Hemlock Ravines	Fields, Woodlots	Flood Plains	Lakes	Ponds, Marshes	Bogs
Ring-billed gull				•		•		
Herring gull					•	•		
Rock dove				•				
Mourning dove				•				
Black-billed cuckoo	•	•						
Yellow-billed cuckoo	•	•						
Barn owl*				•	•			
Eastern Screech owl	•	•			•			
Great Horned owl	•	•	•		•			
Barred owl*	•	•	•		•			
Long-eared owl*		•	•					
Short-eared owl*							•	
Northern saw-whet owl*	•							
Common nighthawk				•				
Chimney swift				•				
Ruby-throated hummingbird				•				
Belted kingfisher					•	•	•	
Red-bellied woodpecker*	•							
Yellow-bellied sapsucker*	•	•		•				
Downy woodpecker	•	•		•				
Hairy woodpecker	•	•		•				
Northern flicker	•			•	•			
Pileated woodpecker*		•	•		•			
Eastern wood pewee	•	•			•			
Alder flycatcher*					•		•	•
Least flycatcher	•			•				

Table 4.1.   (*continued*)

ANIMALS OF POCONO FORESTS

Species	Deciduous Forest	Mixed Forest	Hemlock Ravines	Fields, Woodlots	Flood Plains	Lakes	Ponds, Marshes	Bogs
Eastern phoebe	●	●		●	●			
Great crested flycatcher		●			●			
Eastern kingbird				●				
Horned lark				●				
Purple martin				●				
Tree swallow				●	●	●	●	●
Rough-winged swallow				●		●		
Bank swallow				●	●	●		
Cliff swallow*				●				
Barn swallow				●		●		
Blue jay	●	●	●	●	●			
American crow	●	●	●	●	●			
Fish crow*					●			
Black-capped chickadee	●	●	●	●	●			●
Tufted titmouse	●	●	●		●			
Red-breasted nuthatch*	●	●	●					
White-breasted nuthatch	●	●	●		●			
Brown creeper	●	●	●					
Carolina wren*	●			●	●			
House wren	●	●		●	●			
Winter wren*		●	●					
Marsh wren*							●	
Golden-crowned kinglet	●	●	●		●			●
Ruby-crowned kinglet	●	●	●		●			●
Blue-gray gnatcatcher	●	●			●			
Eastern bluebird				●				

Table 4.1. (continued)   93

Species	Deciduous Forest	Mixed Forest	Hemlock Ravines	Fields, Woodlots	Flood Plains	Lakes	Ponds, Marshes	Bogs
Veery	•	•	•		•			
Gray-cheeked thrush*		•	•		•			
Swainson's thrush*		•	•		•			
Hermit thrush	•	•	•					
Wood thrush	•	•			•			
American robin	•	•		•	•			
Gray catbird				•	•			
Northern mockingbird				•				
Brown thrasher				•				
Water pipit*							•	
Cedar waxwing	•	•			•			
European starling				•	•			
Solitary vireo*		•	•					
Yellow-throated vireo*	•							
Warbling vireo	•			•	•			
Red-eyed vireo	•				•			
Blue-winged warbler	•				•			
Golden-winged warbler*	•							
Tennessee warbler	•	•			•			
Nashville warbler	•	•			•			•
Northern parula	•	•	•		•			
Yellow warbler	•				•		•	
Chestnut-sided warbler	•	•			•			
Magnolia warbler	•	•	•					•
Cape May warbler	•	•	•					
Black-throated blue warbler	•	•	•		•			

Table 4.1. *(continued)*

Species	Deciduous Forest	Mixed Forest	Hemlock Ravines	Fields, Woodlots	Flood Plains	Lakes	Ponds, Marshes	Bogs
Yellow-rumped warbler	●	●	●		●			
Black-throated green warbler	●	●	●		●			
Blackburnian warbler	●	●						
Prairie warbler	●	●	●					
Palm warbler	●	●			●			
Blackpoll warbler		●	●		●			
Cerulean warbler*	●							
Black-and-white warbler	●	●			●			
American redstart	●	●	●		●			
Worm-eating warbler*	●							
Ovenbird	●	●			●			
Northern waterthrush*	●		●					
Louisiana waterthrush*	●				●			
Common yellowthroat	●	●	●		●		●	●
Hooded warbler*	●	●	●		●			
Wilson's warbler*		●						
Canada warbler*	●	●	●		●			●
Scarlet tanager	●				●			
Northern cardinal	●			●	●			
Rose-breasted grosbeak	●	●			●			
Indigo bunting				●				
Rufous-sided towhee	●	●			●			
American tree sparrow				●				
Chipping sparrow				●				
Field sparrow				●				
Vesper sparrow*				●				

Table 4.1. (continued)   95

Species	Deciduous Forest	Mixed Forest	Hemlock Ravines	Fields, Woodlots	Flood Plains	Lakes	Ponds, Marshes	Bogs
Savannah sparrow*				•				
Fox sparrow				•				
Song sparrow				•	•		•	
Swamp sparrow					•		•	•
White-throated sparrow				•				
White-crowned sparrow*				•				
Dark-eyed junco	•	•	•					
Snow bunting*				•				
Bobolink*				•				
Red-winged blackbird					•		•	
Eastern meadowlark				•				
Rusty blackbird*					•		•	
Common grackle				•	•		•	
Brown-headed cowbird				•				
Orchard oriole*	•							
Northern oriole	•	•			•			
Purple finch	•	•			•			•
House finch				•				
Common redpoll*				•				
Pine siskin		•						
American goldfinch				•				
Evening grosbeak		•		•				
House sparrow				•				

NOTE: Certain species may be common but only at specific seasons; occasional, rare, and very uncommon species are not included in this list. Detailed checklists with common, uncommon, and rare species are available. "A Checklist of the Birds of the Pocono Plateau of Pennsylvania," by T. Master and L. Rymon, may be obtained from the Biology Department, East Stroudsburg University, Pennsylvania. "Birds of the Delaware Water Gap National Recreation Area, New Jersey and Pennsylvania," by J. Padalino, is available at DWGNRA Visitor Centers.

* indicates uncommon species

On any woodland hike, visitors should encounter one of the most tame and inquisitive Pocono birds, the black-capped chickadee. Easily identified by its prominent black "cap" and throat markings, this bird even announces its name with a buzzy *chick-a-dee-dee-dee*. See Figure 4.3.

Because of popular interest in eagles and hawks, the next section of this guide focuses on these striking birds, together with their less handsome but beneficial cousin, the turkey vulture.

Rare Raptors of the Poconos

The rivers and lakes of the Poconos, especially the Delaware River, were once the haunts of two magnificent birds of prey, the osprey and the bald eagle. The steady decline of these and other birds of prey coincided with the introduction and steady increase of DDT as an agricultural pesticide. High levels of DDT and its breakdown products DDD and DDE accumulated in the fat of these predators at the top of the ecological pyramid as they consumed prey that had picked up substantial quantities of DDT from their own diet or from their immediate surroundings. This process of biological magnification proved devastating to many bird species. The accumulated DDT and its derivatives interfered with calcium metabolism in the female's reproductive system, resulting in the production of eggs with thinner, weaker shells. These eggs cracked as adult birds attempted to incubate them.

Since the banning of DDT in 1972, the situation has improved for some species, but for ospreys, bald eagles, and several other raptors, the status is still critical. The Poconos in recent years have become a site for reintroduction programs for the bald eagle and the osprey. In 1983, the first year of the Bald Eagle Recovery Program conducted by the Pennsylvania Game Commission, twelve eagles obtained in Canada were brought to two sites along the Susquehanna and Delaware Rivers. The Delaware River site is near Shohola Falls in Pike County. Plans call for the subsequent release of forty eagles.

The method used by the game commission to encourage eagles to breed in the state is termed "hacking." Thirty-feet-tall towers supporting nesting compartments were built at sites where natural nest sites exist. Young birds were reared in the compartments for two months. During their confinement, trained handlers fed the young birds on fish and venison salvaged from road-killed deer. Release of the eaglets came in late August. If all goes well, in four or five years the immature birds will become sexually mature, with the white head and tail feathers that mark the transformation. The birds after wan-

BOX 4.1

Some Pocono Birding Sites

Delaware Water Gap National Recreation Area
> Hidden Lake. Nature trail around lake, also grassy areas adjacent to lake, near DWGNRA headquarters on River Road off of U. S. 209.

> Dingmans Falls. Trail to the falls, hemlock ravine, and rhododendron thickets, off of U. S. 209 north of Dingmans Ferry.

> Thunder Mt. Trail encircles a beaver pond, woody swamp nearby, on Thunder Mt., about three miles south of Peters Valley, New Jersey.

Promised Land State Park
> Conservation Island. Nature trail on island in Promised Land Lake, off of PA 390 onto Park Ave. In village of Promised Land.

> Little Falls. Trail along lake and stream edges, off of PA 390 onto Lower Lake Road at Park Office.

Bruce Lake Natural Area
> Bruce Lake Road. Well-marked two-and-a-half mile-trail through hardwood forest to isolated glacial lake, manmade lake (Egypt Meadows) at about halfway point, off of PA 390 just north of Promised Land State Park.

Hickory Run State Park
> Sawmill Trail. Two-mile nature trail through grassy areas, swampy sections and along stream, just north of Park Office on PA 534.

> Hawk Falls. Steep trail through hardwood forest to natural 25-foot waterfall, off of PA 534 about five miles east of Park Office.

> Deer Trail. Woodland path which crosses stream, also hemlock thicket, off of PA 534 about one mile east of Park Office.

Tobyhanna State Park
> Lakeside Trail. Five-mile woodland trail encircles lake, north of Tobyhanna on PA 423.

Shohola Waterfowl Management Area
> In State Game Lands 180. Open water birding sites plus swamps, meadows, along U. S. 6 at Shohola Falls.

BOX 4.1 (CONTINUED)

Brady's Lake
Fish Commission managed lake. Open water birding sites with meadows, swamps, extensive woodlots adjacent, off of PA 940 near Pocono Pines.

Decker Marsh
No trails but good vantage point for surveying shallow water habitats, grassy meadows, along U. S. 6 about one mile east of junction with PA 507.

Lake Wallenpaupack
Ledgedale Natural Area. Several trails through mature woods, at west end of the lake off of PA 507 near Greentown.

Shuman Point Natural Area. Three miles of trails along lake edge and woods, east end of lake off of PA 590 near Hawley.

Beech House Creek Wildlife Refuge. No trails but good roadside views of meadow and swampy areas, PA 590 west of Hawley.

dering over much of the eastern United States may return to the hacking tower area as breeding adults.

Another encouraging sign is the recent use of the upper Delaware River sites as wintering places for bald eagles, which nest further north and had, in past years, wintered in more southern locales. A slow drive along the Delaware, especially in the Delaware Water Gap National Recreation Area, during mid-morning or mid-afternoon could reward the visitor with a glimpse of our national emblem. (See Box 4.2.)

The bald eagle, as it appears in flight, appears in Figure 4.4 with two other birds that the novice often misidentifies as "eagles," the osprey (a fish-eating hawk) and the turkey vulture (a carrion-eating relative of the condor).

The osprey, or "fish eagle," suffered a fate similar to that of the bald eagle. It, too, accumulated DDT with the same disastrous consequences on population levels. An osprey reintroduction program began in 1980 with the release of birds in the lake regions of the Poconos. This appears to be a success story, as transplants have re-

BOX 4.2

Places to Observe Wintering Eagles

A route suggested by the National Park Service starts at Shawnee, Pennsylvania. Head north from Shawnee on River Road, stop at Smithfield Beach for observation, continue north to Dingman's Ferry Bridge. Cross the bridge into New Jersey and follow signs to Peter's Valley. Turn right at Peter's Valley and follow the road along the river. Several vantage points are located along this road (caution is advised on this poorly maintained road). Continue south, following signs to Millbrook Village. At Millbrook, bear right and continue south to the Pocono boat launch and through Worthington State Forest. From there, it's only a short drive back to I-80.

mained in the area. In 1986, six osprey nests were detected. Four chicks were hatched, the first in Pennsylvania in forty years.

Hawk Watching along the Kittatinny

In many towns and cities, activities of bird watchers are noteworthy. Christmas counts of birds conducted by local Audubon Society members generally serve as the basis of a column or two in the local newspaper. In northeastern Pennsylvania, another bird watchers' pursuit is frequently a news feature: counting hawks during their autumn migration.

In large measure the interest in this particular natural history adventure is due to the influence of Hawk Mountain Sanctuary, located along the Kittatinny Ridge (Blue Mountain), about thirty miles southwest of the southern border of the Poconos. Established in 1934, Hawk Mountain Sanctuary served first to prevent shooters from slaughtering hawks at promontories within the sanctuary. A short time later, visitors from near and far experienced the joy of scanning the skies at the sanctuary lookouts, spotting, identifying, and counting raptors.

The many ridges of the Appalachian Mountains, including the Kittatinny Ridge, are excellent sites to observe migrating hawks. Many of these birds of prey nest in forests to the north of the Appalachians, then head south along the ridges to wintering areas in southern coastal states and even into South America.

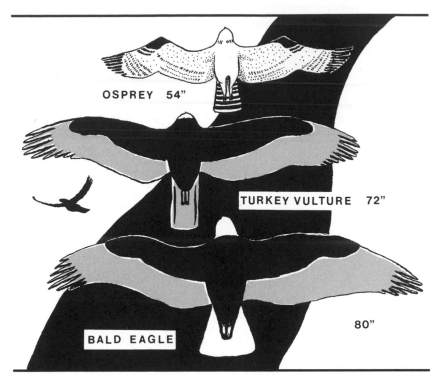

Figure 4.4
Three birds of prey. The bald eagle has a steady flight with the wings held
flat. The turkey vulture, almost as large as an eagle, glides with uplifted wings
and has a distinctive tipping from side to side as it soars. The osprey, a
large hawk with long gull-like wings, usually flies with a characteristic bow or
crook in the elbow of the wing.

One reason migrating hawks follow the ridges is that convection
currents, which frequently develop amidst the ridges, permit the mi-
grants to conserve energy. The most favorable wind currents for
hawks heading south are updrafts produced as northwest winds
blow against the ridges. Aided by these updrafts, hawks may travel
as much as 240 miles in the six hours typical of a day's flight. On
clear warm days, especially when the winds are light, the air close to
the ground becomes heated and then rises as a bubble. A number of
hawks, but particularly the broadwings, circle upward by the lift of
these thermal air currents. Such a flock of thermaling hawks is called
a "kettle." At the top of the thermal, the birds then glide south, slowly
losing altitude, until they pick up another thermal to repeat the process. Another reason that birds tend to stay along the Kittatinny is
that extensive lowlands, the Great Valley, to the east generally have
turbulent air currents over them rather than the updrafts of the ridges
so useful in gliding flight patterns. In addition, there is a considerable

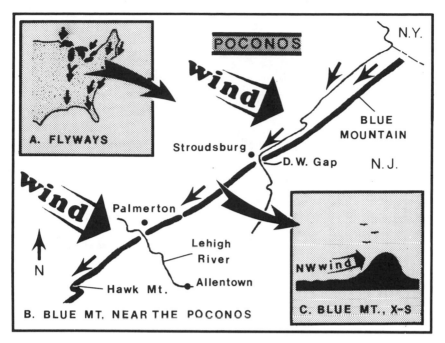

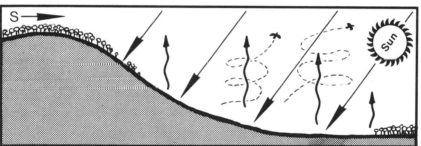

Figure 4.5
Fall hawk migration. Upper panel: A. eastern U. S. flyways. B. Blue Mountain
near the Poconos. C. updrafts. Lower panel: thermal air currents rising from
the heated surface.

narrowing of the Appalachians in northeastern Pennsylvania causing a "funneling effect" on the migratory patterns of birds of prey.
Figure 4.5 indicates the major hawk flyways of Eastern United States
as well as the relationships of wind direction to migration.

Other wind and weather systems produce different flight patterns
and levels of hawk activity. For instance, during inclement weather
hawks rarely move any distance at all. Such variables make interest-

ANIMALS OF POCONO FORESTS

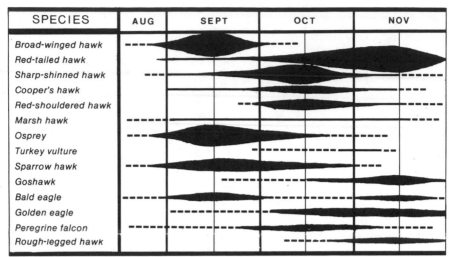

Figure 4.6
Autumn raptor migration patterns along the Kittatinny Ridge. (Redrawn, with
permission, from *The Mountain and The Migration* by James J. Brett.)

ing times for birders as they record the numbers and kinds of hawks
observed throughout the spring or autumn season. Figure 4.6 indicates the peak fall migration periods for the principal birds of prey
heading south along the Kittatinny Ridge in Pennsylvania.

Although Hawk Mountain Sanctuary remains the primary location
for hawk watchers and counters, Pocono sites along the Kittatinny
Ridge are finding favor with birders (see Box 4.3). Further information
is available at Hawk Mountain.

Mammals

Some mammals dwell exclusively in forests. Many other species
spend some time in forests to feed, hibernate, or bear young. Where
a forest abuts a field, meadow, or other habitat, mammals and other
forms of life generally occur with increased diversity and abundance.

Like birds, mammals tend to partition the forest in a vertical manner. Some species—squirrels, for example—use mainly the upper
and middle heights for shelter and food, with some ventures onto
the forest floor. Others, such as chipmunks and deer mice, tend to
stay on or near the forest floor, with occasional forays to the lower
heights. Voles, shrews, and especially moles, spend almost all of
their time within the forest litter or below the soil surface. In direct
contrast, one group of highly specialized mammals—bats—feed at

BOX 4.3

Places to Observe Hawks and Eagles

Tott's Gap. In the village of Delaware Water Gap, Pennsylvania, follow Cherry Valley Road to the edge of a golf course, turn left onto Poplar Valley Road, continue several miles to the Tott's Gap Road to the top of the mountain. At the top, follow an unpaved road to a radio tower and pipeline right-of-way.

Raccoon Ridge. From Blairstown, New Jersey, drive west on Route 94 to a sign for the Yards Creek Pump Storage Station. Secure permission from gatekeeper, continue to parking area. Walk uphill to powerline, proceed along powerline to top of ridge, walk along Appalachian Trail eastward to lookout.

Sunrise Mountain. From Newton, New Jersey, drive north on Route 206 to Stokes State Forest. Follow directional signs to lookout.

night above the forest canopy and spend the day in a hollow tree or some other sheltered spot.

Like birds, mammals also partition the forest horizontally according to the habitats they prefer. The large number of microhabitats suitable as dwelling places, the varied food supplies, the mobility of mammals, their ability to survive cold weather by hibernating, and the transitional nature of the Pocono forests result in a substantial mammal species list for the Poconos. Table 4.2 lists these Pocono mammals and their usual habitats.

White-Tailed Deer

North American Indians and, later, European settlers prized the white-tailed deer for food and as a source for clothing and even weapons. The dense forests that once covered much of the eastern part of the continent could not have supported a large population of deer, which are primarily browsers and feed on the tips of woody vegetation. The clearing of forested lands for farms and settlements created habitats that favored increases in deer population. At the same time, the increased harvest of deer for food and sport almost eliminated the species from the state by the end of the nineteenth century.

A Board of Game Commissioners was established in 1895 to regulate recreational hunting. This control, combined with reforestation of timbered tracts and the extirpation of predators such as mountain lions, enabled deer populations to build. By 1930, there were estimates of more than one million white-tailed deer present in the state. To avoid the problems of excessive populations and destruction of habitat, the state permits harvesting of adult does as well as bucks. This is, indeed, necessary since a deer population has the potential for doubling every two years. Each adult doe, two-and-a-half years

Table 4.2.
Pocono Mammals

Species	Usual habitat(s)
Opossum	Lowland forests, wooded swamps
Eastern mole	Fields, meadows
Hairy-tailed mole	Open, dry woodlands
Star-nosed mole	Wet bottomland forests, swamps
Masked shrew	Moist woods, bogs, meadows
Long-tailed shrew	Moist yellow birch-hemlock forests
Smoky shrew	Moist yellow birch-hemlock forests
Least shrew	Fields, marshes
Short-tailed shrew	Widespread; forests, marshes, fields
Northern water shrew	Along streambanks in conifer forests
Little brown bat	Retire to hollow trees, caves, tunnels, etc., during day, feed at night over fields, lakes, open spaces
Silver-haired bat	
Eastern pipistrelle	
Big brown bat	
Red bat	
Hoary bat	
Black bear	Forests, swamps
Raccoon	Widespread along streams and lake borders
Long-tailed weasel	Open woods, fence rows
Short-tailed weasel	Open woods usually near water
Mink	Along streams, marshes, swamps
Otter	Lakes, streams in dense woods
Striped skunk	Woods, swamps, fields
Coyote	Woodlands

Table 4.2.   (*continued*)   **105**

Species	Usual habitat(s)
Red fox	Farmlands, open woods
Gray fox	Rocky upland forests
Bobcat	Rocky upland forests
Woodchuck	Fields, meadows, road banks
Eastern chipmunk	Widespread; deciduous forests, parks
Eastern gray squirrel	Deciduous forests, parks
Red squirrel	Conifer forests, wooded swamps
Southern flying squirrel	Deciduous forests
Northern flying squirrel	Deciduous forests
Beaver	Streams, lakes, ponds
White-footed mouse	Wooded and brushy areas, near cabins
Deer mouse	Forests, forest edges
Eastern woodrat	Rocky ridges
Southern red-backed vole	Conifer forests, stream banks
Meadow vole	Grasslands, marshes, swamps, orchards
Rock vole	Moist, rocky woods
Woodland vole	Deciduous forests
Southern bog lemming	Bogs, wet meadows
Muskrat	Wet meadows, marshes, along watercourses
House mouse	Fields near buildings
Norway rat	Fields, farm buildings, rubbish heaps
Meadow jumping mouse	Moist meadows, forest edges
Woodland jumping mouse	Forest edges, stream borders
Porcupine	Mature woods, rocky areas
Snowshoe hare	Shrub swamps, rhododendron thickets
Eastern cottontail	Forest edge, abandoned fields, near homes
White-tailed deer	Open woods, forest edges, farmlands, orchards

or older, typically has two fawns each spring. In 1988, the reported statewide harvest of white-tails was 163,106 bucks and 218,293 does. Approximately 5 percent of the total kill occurred in the Poconos. Other deer are killed by dogs, poachers, and natural or accidental causes. With over 25,000 reported highway kills, the total annual kill of white-tailed deer may be as high as 400,000. As a result, the number of white-tailed deer in Pennsylvania remains at about a million.

A white-tail's home range has an area of about one-and-a-half square miles, although most of the time the animal stays within a more restricted area of about forty acres. Although primarily browsers, deer will eat herbaceous vegetation in spring and summer and apples and acorns in fall. Winter is the most stressful period, when deer move to protected areas such as conifer groves. To help it through the lean times of winter, a deer can lower its metabolic rate as much as one-third, and thus conserve food reserves. Also, the winter pelt is twice as dense as the summer coat, and the hollow hairs are effective insulators.

The white-tailed deer, Pennsylvania's state animal, is a fascinating, remarkably adaptable creature. Since natural predators are now lacking, hunters perform that role, maintaining deer populations at levels which avoid destruction to habitat, important for the long-term well-being not only of deer but also of other plants and animals. With wise management, the white-tails' beautiful form and graceful movements will continue to be a regular sight when visitors come to the Poconos.

Black Bear

The largest animals hunted in Pennsylvania, black bears are found in about forty of the state's sixty-seven counties. Almost 70 percent of the Pennsylvania black bear population is in the more remote mountainous regions of the north-central and northeastern portions of the state. The species ranges through much of North America and exhibits considerable variation in size, color, and behavior patterns throughout this range. Black bears may be brown, bluish-gray, or cinnamon-color, but most are glossy black with a tan muzzle. Adults are 50–85 inches in length, stand about 30 inches at the shoulder, and weigh from 140 to 400 pounds, with a few individuals weighing over 600 pounds.

Bears are mainly nocturnal but can occasionally be spotted during the daytime as they move to feeding areas. Bears feed on a wide variety of items including shadbush fruits, blueberries, acorns, beechnuts, grubs, honey, honeybee larvae, small vertebrates, carrion, and garbage.

Figure 4.7
The black bear. Primarily a woodland inhabitant, bears are not infrequently seen crossing Pocono roads—as in this sighting by the authors along route 447 south of Canadensis. The bear, oblivious to traffic, crossed the road, leisurely scratched its rump on the utility pole, and meandered into the woods. Inset A, bear tracks. Inset B, scratch marks on a tree.

The Poconos are the site of extensive investigations by Pennsylvania Game Commission researchers of the Bear Research Project. Bears, trapped in culvert traps, are tranquillized, weighed, measured, and released. The largest bear trapped weighed 650 pounds. Female bears averaged 250–300 pounds, whereas males averaged 400–450 pounds. Some bears have been equipped with radio collars. The signal emitted by the radio collar is located by receivers carried on trucks or, more frequently by aircraft. In this fashion, studies of home range and movement patterns continue. The average home range for adult males studied has an area of sixty-three square miles and fifteen square miles for females.

Another aspect of the Bear Research Project involves black bear denning activities, especially of females. In autumn, bears feed heavily to gain weight to sustain themselves over winter. Females den in more protected sites than do males—for example, a hollow tree, a crevice in a rock ledge, or a drainage culvert. Males generally use a mound of twigs, which they build. Pregnant females and males den alone, but females den along with their first-year cubs. Bears are not true hibernators. Their body temperature is not drastically reduced, as is the case of hibernators such as jumping mice, although their breathing and heart beat rates do slow considerably.

Throughout most of its range, the black bear begins breeding at three-and-a-half to four-and-a-half years of age. The Game Commission's study of tagged bears revealed that in Pennsylvania almost all females had bred by three-and-a-half years of age. The abundant, dependable foods of the region probably promote this early reproductive maturity. Once they reach maturity, females breed only every other year. Intervening years are spent caring for the cubs. In a study of 120 bear litters, researchers found that most cubs are born in January in winter dens. The litter size average of 2.9 cubs was higher than that found in any other state. The largest litter observed was a litter of five cubs.

When cubs are born, they are almost hairless, their eyes are closed, and their weight ranges from ten to sixteen ounces. Emerging with the mother from the den in late March or early April, the cubs weigh about three to eight pounds and are capable of walking short distances. Cubs remain with the female throughout the first year and den with her in winter. The yearlings travel with the female after emergence from the den until May or June, then go off on their own.

Black bears are not only fascinating animals for the researcher to study or the visitor to see, but are also important game animals. In recent years, hunters in Pennsylvania annually killed over 1000 bears, approximately 200 of these in the Poconos. With proper management and protection of habitat, the black bear will remain a symbol of the Pocono wilds for years to come.

Poconos' Wild Cat and Wild Dog

The bobcat and the coyote are symbols of the wild with a special mystique. Perhaps they remind us of childhood tales of native Americans, pioneers, and the wild frontier.

Based on trapping and bounty records (from 1810 to 1938, a bounty of fifteen dollars prevailed), bobcats were fairly common in most counties of the Keystone State. Now bobcats are rare, found only in more remote areas, including wilderness pockets in the Poconos.

Bobcats, although fierce carnivores, are not large. A mature animal averages thirty-six inches in length and generally weighs about fifteen to twenty pounds. The stubby, six-inch tail accounts for the common name. Bobcats hunt mainly at night, utilizing a variety of prey including small rodents, rabbits, hares, grouse, and other small birds. Occasionally, they will consume insects, fish, frogs, and winter-starved deer.

As the Pocono forests matured, a decline in small rodent populations probably contributed to the decline in bobcat numbers. In 1970, when the state's bobcat population was estimated to be about 500, it was granted full protection, so the population may be on the rise. A 1985 survey conducted by the Pennsylvania Game Commission provided estimates based on confirmed and unconfirmed sightings gathered by District Game Protectors. Statewide, about 2300 bobcats may be present in forty-seven of Pennsylvania's sixty seven counties. In the northeastern area of the state, a population density of one animal per twenty square miles was estimated. But it is unlikely that bobcats will ever become common; thus the sighting of the Pocono "wild cat" will continue to be a highlight of any naturalist's experience.

The Poconos' wild dog, the coyote, moved into the region recently. Originally, coyotes were an open plains animal of the western United States and Canada. These doglike carnivores extended their range into the New England states during the past fifty years and into the Poconos about two decades or so ago. The eastern coyote is typically bigger than its western relative, weighing as much as eighty pounds, according to one authority. Weights ranging from thirty-five to fifty pounds are more common. The coyote resembles a small collie dog but is more slender, with straighter, more erect ears and distinctive eyes with a round pupil and yellow iris. The bottle-shaped tail, tipped with black at its base and tip, is also characteristic.

In the East, coyotes dwell in brushy areas bordering second-growth hardwood forests. They are chiefly nocturnal but may be seen at dawn or dusk. A bark and, especially, the distinctive flat howl might also be heard by an alert visitor. Coyotes eat a variety of prey, with rabbits, squirrels, mice, grouse, and other ground-nesting birds the prime dietary items. One New England study found white-tailed deer carrion to be a major portion of the coyote diet.

Coyotes are unprotected in Pennsylvania, so only time will tell whether this hardy, opportunistic canid will become a dominant member of Pocono habitats. Nevertheless, the sighting of a coyote, once a novelty, is now a distinct possibility for the Pocono visitor.

Shrews and Moles

The short-tailed shrew (Figure 4.8), about the size of a mouse, eats insects and a variety of small invertebrates and vertebrates. With sharp front teeth and poisonous saliva, shrews are well-equipped to kill

Figure 4.8
The Short-tailed shrew. Shown eating a cucumber beetle, this small mammal
eats its own weight in insects, millipedes, earthworms, etc., each day. Length
may be four to five inches.

mice and other small vertebrates. Other species of shrews probably
possess poison, as does one of the oddest of all mammals, the duck-
billed platypus of Australia. The use of venom, however, is rare
among mammals.

The short-tailed shrew is probably the commonest mammal in
Pennsylvania, but it is nocturnal, usually burrowing under leaf mold,
and generally goes about its activities undetected. Dead shrews are
regularly seen on roadways, where the gray velvet fur, tiny eyes,
long snout, and short, hairy tail are easily noted. Five other Pocono
species of shrews and three species of their relatives, moles, are
listed in Table 4.2. Moles are larger and darker than shrews, and
their heads appear to rest between their shoulders. Mole burrows
can often be seen under the surface of soft ground (including lawns).

Bats

Bats are unique among mammals, and their appearance and behavior do little to suggest that their closest living relatives are shrews and
moles. There is a great deal of myth and folklore about bats, but the
truth is just as fascinating. Probably no aspect of bat biology is more
intriguing than the bat's ability to use an echo-location technique for
navigational and feeding purposes. During flight, bats emit bursts of
supersonic sound ranging in frequency from 40,000 to 100,000 cycles

per second and with durations of only 2/100th of a second. These bursts are emitted at rates of about twenty to thirty per second. The reflected sound waves, detected by the bat's sensitive ears, provide it with all the information needed to navigate at night and catch flying insects.

The commonest bat of the Poconos is the little brown bat, which has a body only two inches long and a wing span of ten inches. They may be seen before dusk flying over open fields, ponds, and lakes near forested tracts. Bats spend the day hanging head downward, in a lethargic state, in a hollow tree, an attic, behind a cabin shutter, or, yes, even in a belfry.

Weasels, Otters, Skunks

Another major group of mammals, the mustelids (weasels and their allies) are represented in the Poconos by a diverse array of species including long-tailed and short-tailed weasels, mink, otter, and striped skunk. Most members of the group have paired anal scent glands capable of producing a musky odor, but it is the skunk which has specialized in this trait. Skunks are found in abundance in the region and use "chemical warfare" only as a last resort. Sadly, this defense is not effective against cars, and many dead skunks are seen on the region's highways.

Foxes

Mystique rather than musk surrounds two other Pocono mammals. Foxes, gray and red, are a rare and thrilling sight. Both belong to the canidae, the family to which dogs, wolves, and coyotes also belong.

The red fox is only about the size of a small beagle and weighs eight to twelve pounds. The thick, full reddish-brown coat gives the red fox the appearance of being larger and heavier than it actually is. The gray fox is slightly longer than the red but, with a shorter muzzle and legs, appears smaller than the red fox. A grizzled gray and black coat, and a tail with a black tip instead of a white tip as in the red fox, also serve to differentiate the gray from the red.

Red foxes tolerate the presence of humans and are found in farm areas, open woods, swamps, and marshes. Grays are more secretive, and their primary habitats are dense woods and swamps, as well as rugged mountain ridges. Where the ranges of the two species overlap, the more aggressive gray is the dominant species. The gray fox, originally a southern species, has extended its range into southern Canada. Both foxes are primarily nocturnal but may occasionally be seen abroad near dusk or dawn.

Although both species are classified as carnivores, they actually are omnivores, consuming among other items berries, fruits, grains, grasses, insects, birds, birds' eggs, rodents, rabbits, and even young deer. Only when natural foods are scarce does Reynard raid the henhouse.

Squirrels and Chipmunks

Squirrels and their close relative, the chipmunk, are probably the most conspicuous forest dwellers of a major group of mammals, the rodents. Red, gray, and flying squirrels are present in the Poconos.

The nocturnal behavior and almost exclusively arboreal existence of flying squirrels makes them the least well-known of the group. Gliding, rather than flying, describes the locomotion of these seldom-seen squirrels. Loose flaps of skin along the animal's sides are stretched taut when the limbs are extended. Flying squirrels nest in hollow trees and abandoned woodpecker holes, so that their habitat along with their nocturnal behavior makes them hard to discover. One sign suggesting that flying squirrels are in the area is the presence of empty walnut or hickory shells with small oval openings. Other squirrels typically produce more irregularly shaped holes as they open shells. Actually two species, a northern and a southern flying squirrel, have overlapping ranges in the transition zone of the Poconos.

Gray squirrels are found in mixed deciduous woods as well as every community park and campground in the region. In the woods they are alert, wary, and readily sound a warning to their group. These familiar animals live both in hollow trees and in conspicuous outside nests constructed of leaves and twigs. These nests are generally eighteen inches or more in diameter and located thirty or more feet above the ground.

The red squirrel, about half the size of the gray, is also called the pine squirrel, reflecting the preference of this species for conifer forests. This alert, active squirrel quickly spots intruders into its domain and then proceeds to chatter, chirp, whistle, scold, and, in general, announce the intruder's presence to one and all. Red squirrels use old nest cavities of flickers and other woodpeckers, as well as building outside nests. These nests usually are composed of more twigs and shredded bark than are seen in gray squirrel nests.

Red squirrels cut loose pine and spruce cones, which they gather and store in conspicuous food caches. A mound of cone scales covering up to several square yards, called a midden, is a sure sign of red squirrel presence. Smaller piles of cone scales on a log or stump are another good sign that red squirrels reside there. A variety of nuts, berries, buds, fungi, and occasionally a clutch of eggs are dietary items.

The eastern chipmunk is well-known to all Pocono visitors, and its sharp single alarm note is familiar to all who hike in the woods. A chipmunk digs an extensive burrow system within its small home range of less than one acre. Even here, it spends most of its time in an area not much more than about 100 feet in diameter.

This small rodent consumes a wide variety of plant and animal foods. Chipmunks, in turn, serve as food for many predators such as hawks, owls, foxes, cats, snakes, and, especially, weasels. A weasel will enter a chipmunk burrow and kill an entire family of chipmunks in a few minutes. Chipmunks use two large internal cheek pouches to transport seeds, nuts, and other items to its burrow or other cache. Although chipmunks do not hibernate, they become lethargic in winter. Periodically, they awaken to feed on stored food items. During the hot weather of midsummer, chipmunks retreat to their burrows for a shorter period of lethargy.

Other Rodents, including Porcupines

Several other species of rodents live in Pocono forests. Pine voles, red-backed voles, woodland jumping mice, wood rats, and other small rodents are present, often in relatively large populations, but generally go undetected. Voles are stouter than mice and rats, and have blunter noses and shorter ears and tails. One species, the white-footed mouse, is well-known to Pocono visitors, particularly those who own cottages and cabins in the area. White-footed mice frequently become "guests" in these dwellings, especially during colder months. The brown dorsal color, underparts of white, four white paws, and big ears and eyes make the white-footed mouse a most distinctive rodent. A closely related species, the deer mouse, may also utilize cabins and outbuildings but is normally an inhabitant of moist, mature mixed hardwood and conifer forests.

A large rodent, the porcupine, has made a comeback in the Poconos during recent decades (Figure 4.9). An adult porcupine weighs ten to twenty pounds, and is readily identified by its highly modified hairs, called quills. With as many as 30,000 spines, this compact, slow-moving animal is appropriately nicknamed "quill pig." The spines can be as long as three inches on the back and tail. A porcupine cannot throw its quills but, when provoked, raises the quills on its back and thrashes its tail. The quills may pull out, being loosely attached to the skin, and being barbed may embed themselves in the

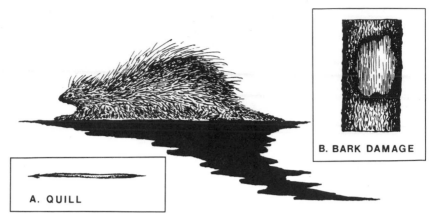

A. QUILL

B. BARK DAMAGE

Figure 4.9
The porcupine. This large rodent (twenty-five to thirty-six inches long) is becoming more common in Pocono forests. A. Detail of quill to show barbs. B. Bark damage, resulting from distinctive feeding habits of the "quill pig."

attacker's flesh. Backward-pointing barbs cause the quills to work their way deeper into the flesh as the attacker's muscles move. Few predators manage to get around the porcupine's clever defenses. The fisher, a large weasel relative, is a known attacker, as are the bob-cat, mountain lion, and coyote. The porcupine's defense is inade-quate against motor vehicles, and dead animals may be seen along Pocono highways.

Live porcupines are most likely to be discovered in winter when they spend most of their time in a restricted territory, about six acres, and may spend several days in one large hemlock or white pine tree. Since they consume the inner bark of trees, distinctive patches of ex-posed wood a foot square on the upper trunks of conifers attest to the presence of porcupines. Dens can sometimes be located in rock crev-ices, caves, and hollow trees. The presence of broken quills and fecal scats, ovals about one inch long containing mostly wood fibers, help identify the den's owner. In spring, porcupines add leaves, flowers, and aspen catkins to their diet. Their craving for salt is legendary, and they gnaw even camping equipment such as axe handles bear-ing traces of sweat.

Hares and Rabbits
One last group of mammals is seen in Pocono forests: hares and rab-bits. The snowshoe hare, sometimes called the snowshoe rabbit, is not a true rabbit. In addition to structural differences, a more impor-

tant difference is that hares are *precocial*. The young are born with
fur and with open eyes. Rabbits are *altricial*; that is, the young are
born hairless and blind. Snowshoe hares, abundant in the Poconos
when dense forests covered the region, are now uncommon and restricted to dense spruce woods, shrub swamps, and bogs. Another
common name, "varying hare," comes from its pelage color changes,
which occur seasonally. From spring until fall, the coat color is
brown. In late autumn, a molt occurs, in patches, and the brown
coat is replaced by a white winter coat. The process takes about ten
weeks to complete, so that, for a time, the hare is a mixture of brown
and white.

The eastern cottontail, a forest edge dweller, is a close relative of
the snowshoe hare. It is smaller than its cousin and has a year-round
sandy brown coat contrasting with its distinctive white tail. The
number one game animal as well as a major food source of many
predators, the cottontail has managed to withstand these hunting
pressures. Although populations fluctuate markedly in any given lo-
cale, throughout the region the cottontail is likely to remain the number one game animal since the female can produce about five litters
of from three to eight (usually five) young a year.

If Pocono visitors cooperate with the region's wildlife managers,
the large and varied mammal population of Pocono forests will be a
lasting delight.

Amphibians

Amphibians, creatures that live both on land and in water, are discussed fully in the chapter on watercourse and wetland communities.
Some amphibians, however, are seen (or heard) in Pocono forests,
especially in moist hemlock ravines and lowland groves and near
woodland streams and ponds. The clear note of the tiny tree frog, or
spring peeper, and the trill of the American toad are common forest
sounds. Lizardlike amphibians, the salamanders, may be found in
the forest litter and under fallen logs or rocks. Among these are the
red-backed, slimy, and two-lined salamander, and the red eft, the terrestrial immature stage of the red-spotted newt.

Perhaps the most secretive of all forest vertebrates, the mole salamanders, occurs in the Poconos in three species: the marbled, Jefferson, and spotted salamanders. As the family name suggests, mole
salamanders spend most of their life underground, emerging mainly
to breed in woodland ponds. Here one has the best opportunity to observe these large (four to seven inches) salamanders. More often seen
than the animal itself are its gelatinous clumps of eggs attached to

twigs and debris or floating at the pond surface. Spotted and Jefferson salamanders breed in early spring, whereas the marbled salamander is one of the less common autumn breeders among amphibians. Most amphibians are dependent upon water as a medium for mating and providing a suitable environment for development of the young.

Reptiles

Reptiles are better suited for terrestrial life than their amphibian relatives. Their bodies are covered with dry, cornified skin usually in the form of scales or plates that prevent dehydration. They are able to reproduce on land. The eggs are large, with much yolk, and protected with a leathery shell. The eggs are usually laid, but some lizard and snake females retain the eggs within their bodies until hatching. Forests and forest edges are a major habitat for about half of the reptilian species common to the Poconos. However, many reptiles are secretive, patterned to blend in with their surroundings, quick to hide if a person approaches, and thus frequently undetected by visitors. The main kinds of reptiles found in the Poconos are turtles, snakes, and lizards.

Turtles

Moist woodlands are the home of two of the most terrestrial species of Pocono turtles: wood turtles and box turtles (see Figure 4.10). The more aquatic turtles are discussed in Chapter 5.

Wood turtles are easy to recognize by the rough sculptured shell and orange markings on the neck and limbs. The common name is appropriate, since this species is found in a wide variety of forest areas. Wood turtles do wander, especially in summer. In addition to forests, they occur in fields, meadows, along roads, and on roads, often with tragic consequences for the animals.

The box turtle derives its name from its ability to close up tight by means of a hinged lower shell, which fits snug against the high-domed upper shell. This species has been the focus of several studies. One investigator spent three years trailing turtles around 29 acres of rich bottomland forest in Maryland. Box turtles establish definite territories. As evidence, this scientist determined a home range of approximately 350 feet in diameter. In addition, we now know that a box turtle spends each night in a hideout that the turtle makes by pushing aside litter and soil. In autumn, turtles locate a pond and push into the muck on the bottom or tunnel into a soil bank to a depth

BOX TURTLE   **WOOD TURTLE**

Figure 4.10
Two common woodland turtles. The box turtle has a high, domelike back with
yellow-to-orange blotches; its underside (plastron) is hinged. The wood turtle, the
less common species, is marked with orange on both the head and legs and
has a deeply sculptured carapace (upper shell).

below the frost line. Here, in a lethargic state, these ancient reptiles
may survive the cold weather. In aquatic settings, cutaneous gas exchange replaces the more usual lung gas exchange employed on
land.

After mating, the female digs a hole in loose soil, deposits four or
five leathery eggs, covers the clutch, and moves away. The young
hatch in about three months if the eggs are not eaten by raccoons or
skunks. Young turtles emit a vile odor which may repel certain predators. They are also secretive. Box turtles that survive the early days
may live to a ripe old age, probably forty to fifty years.

Snakes

Snakes are the best representatives of forest reptiles but tend to be secretive, well-camouflaged, and thus often go unnoticed. Snakes are
most likely to be discovered in spring, shortly after they emerge from
hibernation, as they go about searching for mates, or in autumn,
when they tend to sun themselves on exposed rock slabs before en-
tering hibernating dens. At least half of the fourteen species of snakes
listed in Table 6.1 utilize forested tracts to some extent.

Of the smaller nonpoisonous species, garter, the ringneck, red-
bellied, and milk snakes are the species likely to be detected. The
garter snake (twenty-four to thirty inches) is variable in color but normally has three yellow lengthwise stripes. The ringneck snake is a
small (ten to fifteen inches) brown snake with an orange collar. The
red-bellied snake is equally well-named since a distinctive bright red
belly is a feature of this small (eight to ten inches) reptile. The dorsal
coloration is normally brown, but gray and black individuals exist.
The milk snake is larger (twenty-four to thirty-six inches) than the
previous two species and much more highly patterned. Large dorsal

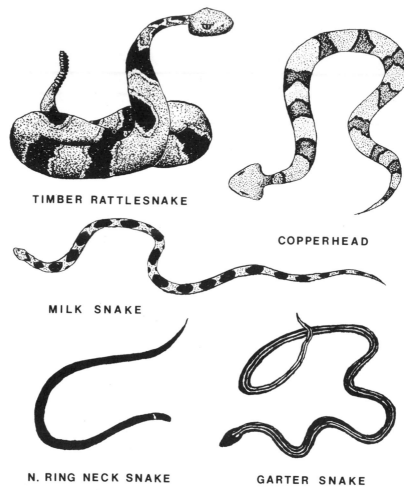

TIMBER RATTLESNAKE

COPPERHEAD

MILK SNAKE

N. RING NECK SNAKE

GARTER SNAKE

Figure 4.11
Representative snakes of the Poconos. The two venomous snakes of the
region, the timber rattlesnake and the copperhead, are infrequently
encountered. The three species of non-venomous snakes are more common.
The milk snake is often misidentified as a copperhead. The distinctive
orange band of the ring neck and the equally distinctive stripes of the garter
snake facilitate easy identification of these common reptiles.

blotches of brown or reddish-brown alternate with smaller, lateral
blotches. Ground color ranges from gray to tan. Milk snakes are
frequently mistaken for the poisonous copperhead and often killed on
that basis—a fate which should not befall a copperhead, let alone a
harmless milk snake (see Figure 4.11).

Larger nonpoisonous species—black rat snakes, black snakes (racers), and hognose snakes—may sometimes be seen sunning themselves along a hiking trail. Black rat snakes, also called "pilot" or "mountain black snakes," are large (forty-two to seventy-two inches), heavy-bodied, and uniformly black. They are good climbers. Also a good climber, the black snake (racer) is thinner-bodied than the rat snake and somewhat smaller (thirty-six to sixty inches); usually a white chin can be seen. The hognose snake, named for its distinctive upturned snout, is variably colored. Blotches of yellow, brown, gray, or orange usually predominate, but jet black or plain gray specimens may occur. Another common name, "puff adder," stems from the hognose snake's habit of flattening the head and neck and hissing loudly when provoked. If this technique is unsuccessful in deterring the attacker, the snake will roll on its back, shiver a bit, and then lie still as though dead.

Old lumber mill sites, with piles of bark and scrap lumber, are favorite hiding places and egg-laying sites for many of these snakes. The same sites may also serve as a home for the Poconos' two poisonous snakes, the copperhead and timber rattlesnake. Both species are pit vipers, a family of snakes characterized by a triangular head with a small opening or "pit" located between the eye and the nostril. The pit contains a heat-sensing organ enabling these snakes to locate their warm-blooded prey, which they search for in dimlight conditions. The vertical-slit pupil is also characteristic of these nocturnal hunters. Figure 4.12 illustrates features useful in distinguishing between venomous and non-venomous snakes.

The copperhead has a copper or russet-colored head, as well as a dorsal row of distinctive chestnut brown hourglass patterns on a tan background. The belly is a uniform dusky color which contrasts sharply with the checkered belly of the milksnake. The copperhead is not aggressive and seeks to avoid confrontations. Copperheads are gregarious, especially in autumn, as they cluster around hibernating dens.

The timber rattlesnake at one time was found throughout the state but exists today only in sparsely settled mountainous areas, including some sections of the Poconos. Some experts believe that the timber rattler could be the next wild creature to disappear from Penn's Woods.

With two distinct color phases, yellow and black, the timber rattler is highly variable in appearance. Usually brown or black cross-stripes are evident except in the darkest, generally oldest, individuals. The rattle, hallmark of this group of about thirty species, is composed of horny remnants of shed skin. Two to four new segments are

ANIMALS OF POCONO FORESTS

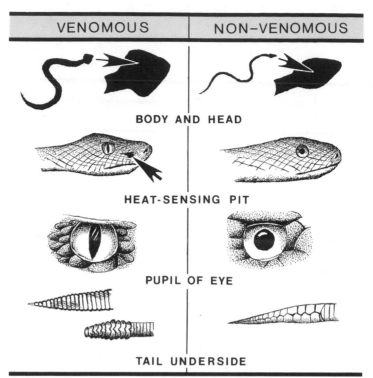

Figure 4.12
Distinguishing features of venomous and nonvenomous snakes.

added each year to the "button" present at the tail tip of the newborn rattler. The age of a rattlesnake cannot be told from the number of rattle segments. The vibration of the tail tip is common to many species of snakes when they assume a defensive posture. The sound produced by a rattlesnake rattle is variable but has been compared to sounds produced by escaping steam or that produced by seventeen-year locusts (cicadas).

Rattlers require safe hibernating places, such as rock fissures and underground crevices below the frost line. They tend to be gregarious during hibernation, and may coil together with copperheads—as well as nonpoisonous species—in a mass of several dozens of individuals. In spring, the snakes disperse and may move as much as a mile away from the dens.

The earlier practice of paying bounties on rattlesnakes and the more recent "sport" of organized rattlesnake hunts as the animals emerge from hibernation have contributed to the threatened status of the timber rattler. The slow reproductive rate of the species accentuates the threat. A female will not bear young until she reaches sexual maturity at about five years of age. Then she will give birth in late summer to a litter of seven to twelve young. This species and certain other types of snakes and lizards retain the developing young within their bodies. However, the young rely on their stores of yolk to provide nourishment for growth and development. Such organisms are called ovoviviparous—a sort of middle stage between egg layers and live bearers. Females reproduce only every two or three years; they need those years between to gain weight and to store yolk protein in the maturing eggs. A life span believed to be about fifteen years suggests that most females reproduce only three to five times in their lives.

Snakes, especially copperheads and timber rattlers, are more subject to indiscriminate slaughter than other kinds of wildlife. They do have their place in the scheme of things, and to an unprejudiced eye their bright colors and patterns and graceful movements make them as beautiful a work of nature as any bird or flower.

Lizards

Lizards are rare in northern temperate climates. One representative of this group, the five-lined skink, is sparsely represented in cutover woodlots containing rotting stumps and logs. With their shiny, smooth, flattened scales, skinks resemble large salamanders more than they do the rough-skinned, heavy-scaled desert lizards. Skinks do possess the clawed toes characteristic of lizards but lacking in salamanders, so that identification, at least close up, is possible. In the five-lined skink, dorsal stripes of yellow against a brown background are typical of young animals and adult females. Males tend to become more uniformly brown or olive in coloration. Skinks are active during the day as they search the forest litter for small invertebrates, but quickly dash for cover when approached.

Stop, Look, and Listen

A diverse assemblage of animals lives in the Poconos. It usually takes some effort on our part to observe and study animals but this effort is amply rewarded when we do see Pocono wildlife in a natural setting. Your efforts will be enhanced if you search during the earlier morning or late afternoon periods when many animals are most active.

CHAPTER 5 Watercourse and Wetland Communities

"All the rivers run into the sea; yet the sea is not full; unto the place from whence the rivers come, thither they return again."
—Ecclesiastes 1:7

Water is the essence of life; life began in water and the association endures. Most plant and animal cells have as much as 70–80 percent water in their composition, and even uptake of nutrients and gases by terrestrial organisms occurs only as these vital substances are dissolved in water.

The various habitats collectively called watercourse and wetland communities are determined largely by their water component. Thus, changes in these communities chiefly result from the influence of the quality and quantity of water.

The Paradox of Water

Water is both common and uncommon. Almost three-fourths of the earth's surface is water but at the same time water is a substance with many unusual, and, in some cases, rare characteristics. As figure 5.1 indicates, water is a polar molecule because the two hydrogen atoms, covalently bonded to one oxygen atom, are displaced to one side producing a slight positive charge to that side.

Water molecules readily interact with each other, forming weak hydrogen bonds. The state of water—liquid, gas, or solid depends upon the speed at which bonds form and break.

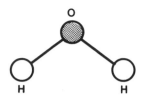

Figure 5.1
Water molecule. The many unusual
physical and chemical properties
derive in part from the asymmetrical
arrangement of two hydrogen atoms
with one oxygen atom.

When water freezes, the molecular arrangement is a lattice with open space between the crystals resulting in a decrease in density. Upon melting, water contracts as the lattice arrangement breaks down and density increases until the water temperature reaches 39.2° F. Beyond this temperature, the loose arrangement of molecules again results in a reduction in density. This aspect of water is of fundamental importance to aquatic life. For instance, ice forms at the surface of a pond, not the bottom.

Water has the highest heat of fusion and heat of evaporation of all known subtances that are liquid at ordinary temperatures. Water absorbs and releases heat much more slowly than does air, a fact that has a profound effect upon climate. It also means that aquatic life is not subjected to sudden and wide temperature fluctuations.

Additional water characteristics significant to life are the viscosity and high surface tension of water, which draw it through pore spaces within soils and move it through conducting networks in plants. Finally, water will dissolve more substances than almost any other liquid. Oxygen, carbon dioxide, nitrogen absorbed from the atmosphere, mineral salts dissolved from bed rock and soils—all are now available for use by aquatic plants and animals.

The Hydrologic Cycle

Distributed in land, sea, and atmosphere, water is moved in a global cycle driven by solar energy. Oceans cover 71 percent of the planet. Fresh water makes up only 3 percent of the earth's supply and three-quarters of that is locked up in glaciers and ice sheets. The atmosphere contains only 0.035 percent fresh water.

Precipitation originates as water vapor in the atmosphere. When air rises, it cools. Water vapor then condenses and coalesces into raindrops. When rain falls, it is intercepted by vegetation before it reaches the soil. Water that does reach the soil moves into the ground water.

Evaporation from the planet's surface into the atmosphere is at a

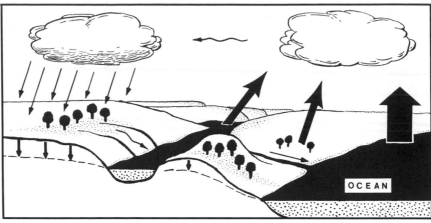

Figure 5.2
The hydrologic cycle. Oceans provide 84 percent of the total evaporation, more than they receive from precipitation. Land areas constitute 16 percent of the total via evaporation directly from land and freshwater surfaces and indirectly from plant transpiration. Rivers return surface runoff to the seas to balance the evaporation deficit of the oceans. Some water percolates into the subsurface and provides a zone of saturation whose upper boundary is known as the water table (the dashed line in figure).

rate governed by how much moisture the air contains. Plants take in water and lose some of it through leaves in a process called transpiration. At any one time, the atmosphere holds no more than a ten to eleven day supply of rainfall. Figure 5.2 presents additional details about this important cycle.

Pocono Aquatic Communities

The varied habitats of the Poconos, as elsewhere, are in essence formed by the mixture of the two basic media, air and water, and by the intricate relationships of land masses and water. Water seeping out of a rock crevice on a steep wooded slope may become a cool, well-aerated, fast-flowing mountain brook. Water trapped in a glacial depression with no drainage and little wind stirring may evolve into a bog.

The problem of designating aquatic communities is complicated, since communities change over time and space. Most lowland forested areas, swamps, and marshes are later stages in succession from lakes and ponds. Streams and rivers also go through stages from youth to maturity. In addition, varying depths of water bodies, varied exposure of stream bank or lake edge to sunlight, uneven terrain, and human activities all work to produce a complicated ecological mosaic for the Poconos. However, biologists widely use two major categories to group these varied aquatic habitats. The categories, *lotic*, or running water communities, and *lentic*, or standing water bodies, will form the basis of consideration in this chapter of Pocono aquatic habitats.

Whatever the designation, it was aquatic communities that first drew humans to the Poconos. Those who became our native Americans settled along the Delaware River and its tributaries. Later, European colonists used many of the same sites. Waterfalls were among the first tourist attractions and most resort communities utilized lake and stream settings. Aquatic areas are still a prime focus for recreational and natural history interests and possess some of the most fascinating biotic assemblages of the entire Pocono region.

Not as readily appreciated is the value of wetlands in flood control. Because of the nature of their soils and dense vegetation, swamps, marshes, and bogs absorb and retain much of the precipitation they receive. During dry periods, this stored water is slowly released to adjacent areas. Wetlands also serve as traps for pollutants that may get into ground water. This may especially be true when excess nitrates from human wastes and farmland fertilizers enter ground water. All in all, aquatic communities deserve our utmost efforts to preserve and protect them.

Lotic Communities

The one-way flow of water is the single most important environmental feature of lotic communities. The rock type predominating in the drainage basin and the nature of contributions from terrestrial life along the watercourse are also of great influence in determining the nature of life in lotic habitats.

Mountain Brooks

Brooks, originating from seeps, and springs, issuing forth where ground water reaches the surface, are numerous on the steepest slopes in the Poconos. Small, fast-flowing brooks unite to become the headwaters of the creeks and streams, which in some cases form spectacular gorges and waterfalls. (You may wish to refer to the section on waterfalls in Chapter 2.)

Brooks flowing three feet per second can carry stones three inches in diameter. Even flows of this magnitude are slowed by friction to produce a motionless boundary layer a fraction of an inch thick in the stream bed. Highly specialized plants, especially green desmids and yellow-brown diatoms, attach to rock surfaces at this boundary. Perhaps you can attest to the slippery rock surfaces produced by these microscopic plants from your own, possibly embarrassing, encounter in attempting to cross a small brook. These tiny plants and the more conspicuous, less numerous, filamentous green algae and aquatic mosses, the *periphyton*, provide food and dwelling sites for specialized animals.

Animals must overcome the major problem of life in flowing waters, staying put. They do so by clinging with sharp claws, by wedging into crevices, by producing adhesives to glue themselves to rocks, by wrapping stone anchors around themselves, and other ingenious devices.

Insects, especially larvae, are the group of animals best represented in Pocono brooks. These and other aquatic animals are not readily observed unless submerged rocks are removed from the brook for closer examination. Please return the rocks after your study. Remember it's "home" for many seen and unseen creatures!

Net-spinning caddisfly larvae wedge themselves into crevices and surround themselves in a case of silken threads produced by oral glands. Small stones added to the case provide additional anchoring. The larva sends out a fine-mesh net, which traps organic debris and drifting, dying creatures. Periodically, the larva collects the catch and repairs the net.

Also specialized for life in swift currents is the oval, segmented carapace of the riffle beetle larva. It can easily be overlooked. Carefully pry it from its attachment site on a rock and discover the insect's curved claws at the leg tips, which enable it to cling tenaciously. When undisturbed by inquiring naturalists, it browses slowly over the algal carpet.

Easier to detect are slow moving flatworms, tiny, wiggling, worm-

Figure 5.3
Net of net-spinning caddisfly larva. The small net is produced by the larva, which periodically collects the trapped detritus and repairs rips and tears in the net.

like midge larvae and active, darting larvae of stoneflies and may-flies, usually referred to as nymphs. These nymphs are even more abundant in other habitats and will be discussed in the section devoted to streams.

The current has a profound effect on the number of animal species in a stream, with numbers of species decreasing as the gradient of the stream increases. Similarly, few large animals are found in the steep headwaters of flowing water communities. It is a challenge for an animal with a large surface area to maintain a position in the swift current. Thus, brook fishes are tiny and species diversity is low. Small darters, two to three inches in length, with distinctive speckled scales reside in protected pockets in the bed. Highly modified pectoral fins enable these fish to skip over rocks in pursuit of prey. Longnose dace, a three-inch relative of minnows, and young brook trout may be seen occasionally.

If one spies a salamander wriggling out from under an overturned rock in the brook or at its edge, it is likely to be either a northern dusky or a two lined salamander. The northern dusky is tan or brown, stout-bodied with the hind legs noticeably larger than the forelimbs. Maximum length is five inches. The thinner, smaller (four inches) two-lined salamander could better be called "yellow salamander" since the belly is distinctly yellow and the dorsal regions have a yellow, sometimes bronze, coloration. A find, such as is shown in Figure 5.4, of a female salamander coiled against a small cluster of eggs as she lies beneath a rock or log at the brook's edge is rare.

Figure 5.4
Female two-lined salamander guarding egg mass. Length two to four inches.

The splash and seepage areas alongside a brook are not only favored sites of salamanders but also of mosses, liverworts and ferns.

Springs

Springs occur where ground water contained within a porous layer of soil or rock emerges at the surface. Water moves through the porous layer at rates varying from a few inches to several hundred yards per day. In many instances, the water rushes downhill as a brook, but where a basin exists a pool will form. Spring water is cold year-round, 48–54° F, and generally contains less oxygen and more carbon dioxide than surface water. In this setting, a distinctive biota will be found.

On stones in the basin are attached filamentous green algae, chains of diatoms and mosses. Watercress is one of the few vascular plants able to thrive in springs.

Dwelling among the plants is a gray-brown, shrimplike arthropod, a scud. These crustaceans are also called side-swimmers because of their distinctive swimming position. See Figure 5.5.

Scuds are nocturnal scavengers and may attain high population densities (10,000 individuals per square yard are reported in the scientific literature). Scuds, in turn, are the prey of the occasional diving beetle, frog, or salamander. A careful look in the clear spring water should reveal the movements of pinhead-sized, bright red or yellow orbs gliding beneath the surface—water mites. These relatives of spiders can afford to be conspicuous since few other animals eat them.

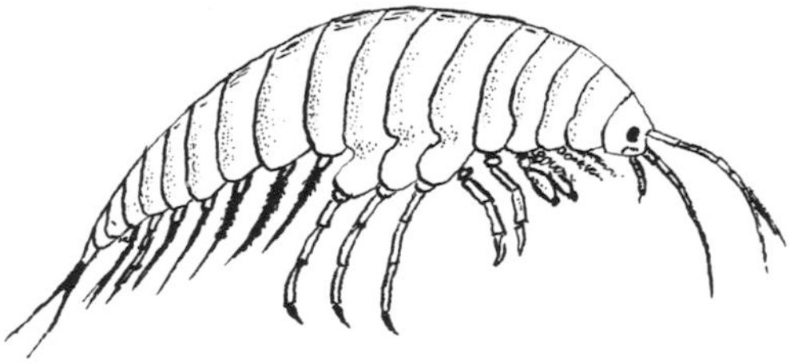

Figure 5.5
Scud. Magnified view of a quarter to three-quarter-inch crustacean widespread in unpolluted springs, brooks and ponds. As it swims, the scud usually rolls onto its side or back, hence another common name, "side-swimmer."

Salamanders discovered in or near springs probably are members of the following species. One is—appropriately—the spring salamander, the other—equally well-named—is the northern red salamander. Both are stout-bodied with flattened, keel-like tails. The spring salamander is salmon-pink to brownish pink dorsally, with a flesh-colored belly. The northern red is usually bright red, but reddish-orange individuals do occur. Irregular black spots, scattered over the dorsal and lateral regions, complete the pattern.

Springs and brooks are scattered throughout the Poconos and serve as sources for the most familiar flowing water community—streams.

Streams

The distinction between streams and rivers is vague but, generally, a stream is smaller, often with a steep gradient. Rivers are larger and usually have low gradients at lower elevations. Although it may appear otherwise, average river currents are faster flowing than most stream currents.

Brodhead, Pohopoco, Tobyhanna, Little Bushkill, Saw, Shohola—these and other familiar, outstanding trout streams are also great for nature study as well.

Streams have varied microhabitats determined largely by gradient and substratum. Fast, turbulent flow over shallow rocky beds, interspersed with quiet pools with mud and silt bottoms, typifies many Pocono streams. Horizontal meanders occur in flatter portions of some streams as water seeks the least energetic path. Meanders produce arcs with deeper, swifter flows near the eroding outer edge and, on the opposite bank, form shallow areas as gravel and sand are deposited by the currents.

Pennsylvania's worst water pollution problem, acid mine drainage, has contaminated an estimated 9000 miles of streams located mainly in the southwestern and northeastern sections of the state. Iron pyrites present in coal seams when exposed to water and oxygen are involved in a complex series of reactions yielding sulphuric acid (see Figure 2.9, which shows the location of coal seams in northeastern Pennsylvania). In addition, ferric hydroxide coats stream bottoms and colors the water red or yellow. Only a few specialized organisms can survive such harsh conditions. In the Poconos, some streams on the western edge, which drain into the Susquehanna River, and a few streams that drain into the Lehigh River have been severely degraded by acid mine drainage.

Fortunately, most Pocono streams are not contaminated and inhospitable. They are full of life and a delight to explore and study. To be sure, as streams increase in size, one must employ nets and other devices to gather most inhabitants for detailed study. However, the casual streamside visitor, perhaps with the aid of a hand lens, can engage in a satisfying study of stream life with just a bit of extra effort. Many of the stream organisms described below are those most likely to be detected by visitors without specialized collecting devices.

Stream Riffles

A major feature of streams, riffles are shallow, fast-flowing, well-aerated rapids over rocky beds. As in brooks, rocks provide anchoring and hiding places for many stream dwellers. Many of the dominant types are related to species found in the headwaters.

In sunny stretches of riffles, filamentous green algae may produce conspicuous waving strands on many rocks. Microscopic diatoms, protozoa, rotifers, and worms live among or attached to the algal filaments.

Algae and associates are the base of the stream food chain. Vascular plants are not a prime feature of flowing waters and contribute little to the producer base of the ecological pyramid. However, the base is significantly augmented by the contribution of living and dead organic matter that enters the stream from land. Leaf fall in autumn and other organic matter blown or washed into the stream at all seasons are major sources of nutrition for stream inhabitants. Much of this organic matter is partially decomposed by bacteria and fungi. The resulting detritus is consumed by many organisms.

As in most aquatic communities, insects, crustaceans, and fishes are dominant animals. Flatworms, roundworms, segmented worms, mollusks, and cold-blooded vertebrates—such as amphibians and reptiles—are present but rarely with the abundance or diversity of the dominant types.

Casual observation should reveal the presence of insects, especially larvae. Sometimes, an entire rock will be covered with small, cylindrical, wormlike creatures with the caudal end distinctly swollen. These are black fly larvae. The swollen end has many hooks that enable the larvae to maintain their position in swift currents. After two to six weeks as a larva, the animal spins a compact, cone-shaped cocoon in order to pupate. The animals emerge as small, two-winged (diptera), terrestrial adults well-known to hikers, campers, fishermen, and stream naturalists who've experienced the irritating bites of female black flies searching out a blood meal from warm-blooded vertebrates.

Caddisfly larvae also inhabit riffles and their distinctive cases of small stones anchored to rocks should be a common observation. If the case has the end sealed shut, the larva is undergoing pupation before emerging as a delicate, mothlike adult.

Dobsonfly larvae, also called hellgrammites, are well-known to fishermen as an excellent live bait. The stout, large (one to three inches long), brown larvae are active predators. The larvae, after an aquatic life of two to three years, transform into weak-flying adults. Adult males have conspicuous, elongate mandibles that make identification easy.

Perhaps the most frequently observed stream insects seen scurrying over rocks in riffles are stonefly and mayfly nymphs, which possess similar anatomical features as well as life cycle similarities. Both nymphs are depicted along with other insects in the stream profile shown in Figure 5.6.

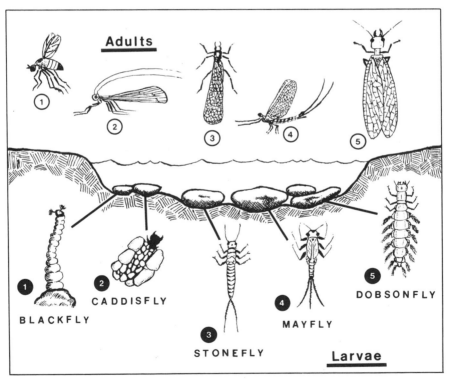

Figure 5.6
Stream riffle insects. Many stream insects have an aquatic larval life, sometimes lasting two or three years, followed by a terrestrial adult life, which is much shorter, generally a few months, but occasionally only a day or two.

Stonefly nymphs are a good indicator of stream quality since they are intolerant of pollution or low levels of dissolved oxygen. The best Pocono trout streams will have numerous stonefly larvae. Mayfly nymphs, which have a wider tolerance to stream conditions, occur in varied habitats. Both types are important dietary items of game fish.

Because of the similarities of stonefly and mayfly life cycles, and since the streamside visitor is likely to be more familiar with mayflies, only their life cycle will be considered in detail. Mayfly nymphs may exist in the aquatic stage for one to three years but the adult terrestrial existence is noteably short-lived. Some species last only a few hours, many species just days or a week. The scientific name for mayflies, Ephemeroptera, is certainly appropriate.

In some species, emergence of great numbers of adults from the water occurs in a brief period. In the Poconos, this "hatch" starts about the last week of April and continues throughout the summer. Mayfly nymphs require two molts to complete the transformation into adults. On an exposed rock or stream edge plant, a milky white subadult emerges from the exoskeleton. The "dun," as it's called by fishermen, soon flies upward and alights on vegetation. After a day or so, the fully formed adult, the "spinner," emerges from a final molt. Adults are easily recognized by the delicate, many-veined, transparent wings, long, slender legs, and two or three long filaments extending from the posterior of the abdomen. Swarms of adults, all males, can be seen hovering over the stream on a calm spring or summer day. Female mayflies enter the swarm and leave shortly thereafter accompanied by a male. Mating occurs during flight, and females lay the fertilized eggs as they alight on the water surface or even crawl beneath it briefly to deposit eggs on the bottom.

Crayfish, relatives of the larger oceanic crustacean, the lobster, are common, if infrequently observed, stream dwellers. These nocturnal scavengers will go undetected unless stones and debris are uncovered by the vistor. Even then, one will usually get only a quick glance as the crayfish dashes quickly backward, its usual escape maneuver. One may more readily discover the distinctive burrow openings surrounded by mud pellets, which some crayfish species produce along the stream bank. Occasionally a female crayfish might be discovered when she is carrying the developing young on specialized abdominal appendages. As is true with many stream dwellers, a way must be devised to keep the young from being carried downstream. This is the crayfish's way. Smaller crustacean relatives, copepods, sow bugs, and scuds are also riffle dwellers.

Other invertebrate groups are less well represented. Snails, freshwater limpets, flatworms, true worms— round and segmented, and even small, amorphous clumps of yellow and green sponges may be detected by careful searches.

Another major stream component, fishes, are easier to detect but more difficult to study. One can generally observe schools of minnows and an occasional sucker, bass, or trout moving through the water but many species will remain undiscovered.

Principal fish species found in riffles in Pocono streams are longnose and blacknose dace, darters, creek chubs, fallfish, common and spottail shiners, small catfish called "madtoms," and white suckers. Where streams are stocked, younger brook, brown, and rainbow trout also utilize riffle sections. (See Figure 5.7.)

Stream Pools

Interspersed with riffles, the quiet water stretches of streams, pools, have a less diverse biota. Fine sediments and decaying terrestrial debris that make up the bottom of pools do not provide as many suitable places for animals but do permit vascular plants to take hold. River weeds, milfoils, and pond weeds are present. Dwelling in the bottom sediments are worms, wormlike dipteran larvae, especially of midges and craneflies, some mayfly nymphs, snails, and fingernail-sized pill clams.

What is most easily detected by the visitor are the two specialists shown in Figure 5.8, water striders and whirligig beetles. These insects utilize the surface tension of water to skim over the pool surface in search of prey.

Larger individuals of such riffle species as brook trout, suckers, and shiners spend much of their time in pools. Sunfish, creek chubs, and smallmouth bass are other species found in Pocono streams.

Except for humans, the animal which does most to change the character of a stream is the beaver. Although brought close to extinction by fur trappers, this largest of all American rodents (two to three feet in length, thirty to sixty pounds) is now well established in most states. In fact, sometimes it seems that beavers are too well established, as beavers not only kill many trees directly by cutting and indirectly by flooding but, with their dams, force stream waters out of their bed with resulting damage to adjacent property.

Direct sightings of beavers are uncommon but the indirect evidence of beavers' presence is plentiful. Characteristically gnawed saplings, dams made of branches and mud, and dammed lodges also composed of branches are all a sure sign of beaver. The animals spend daylight hours in the lodge, which they leave by underwater

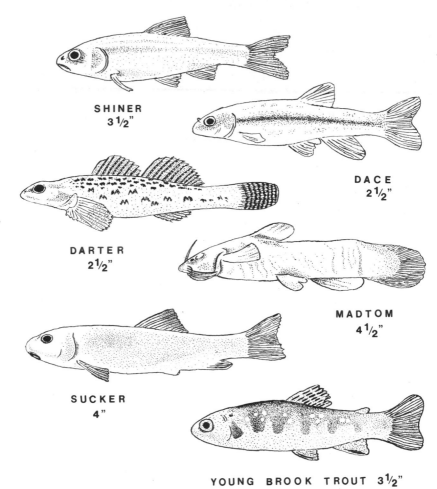

SHINER
3½"

DACE
2½"

DARTER
2½"

MADTOM
4½"

SUCKER
4"

YOUNG BROOK TROUT 3½"

Figure 5.7
Stream riffle fish species. Note the characteristic lateral blotches of skin pigments (parr marks) of young brook trout. Sketches based on photographs of actual specimens. (After E. L. Coopers' *Fishes of Pennsylvania*, The Pennsylvania State University Press, with permission.)

tunnels to feed on land at night. The tender bark of aspens and willows are favored foods. In ten minutes, a beaver can chip away sufficient wood with the use of sharp, chisel-like incisors to fell a sapling six inches in diameter.

Beavers mate in midwinter and have litters of three to four young called "kits." Parents, kits and offspring of the two preceding years

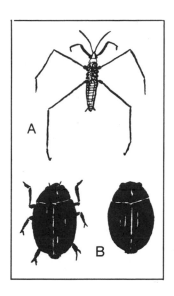

Figure 5.8
Two surface film dwellers of stream
pools and ponds. A. Water strider.
B. Whirligig beetle (at left with legs
extended, at right as it appears
while swimming).

stay together as a well-organized colony. The parents drive away the
two-year olds so that the colony size remains at about twelve members. The emigrants may move as much as thirty miles away to con-
struct a new dam.

After all suitable trees are felled and fed upon, the beavers move
away from the region and shortly thereafter the habitat will change.
The successional stages which follow when a beaver pond is abandoned are becoming a familiar sight throughout the Poconos, even
along the interstate highways that cross the region. Conspicuous,
mature, dead trees scattered across the marsh or meadow are generally a sign of past beaver activity.

Streams are a feature of many wetland communities and even of
forests. The plant and animal life one would see alongside a particular stream is therefore quite varied. Some stream-edge organisms in
conjunction with other communities are considered elsewhere in the
text.

Rivers

The Lackawaxen, Lehigh, and Delaware are the main rivers of the
Poconos. The Lackawanna River receives runoff from the far western
edge of the Pocono area. The drainage pattern of these rivers and
their major tributaries is presented in Figure 5.9.

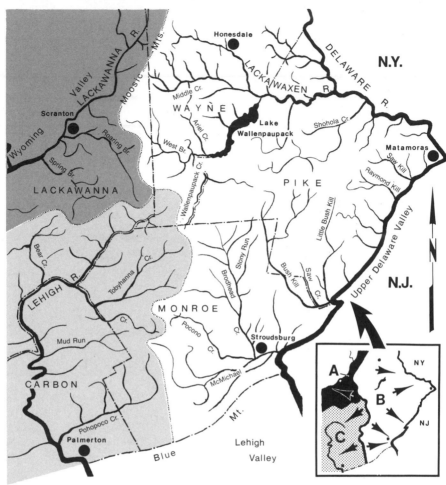

Figure 5.9
Major stream and river drainage patterns. Inset: the three drainage basins are
A. Lackawanna, B. Delaware, and C. Lehigh.

As with larger streams, much river life will go unnoticed by the visitor to the river's edge. Fishermen and boaters have the best opportunity to study river life.

Aquatic vegetation is sparse in swift water. In quiet stretches and shallow backwater eddies, attached filamentous algae and higher plants such as milfoils, pond weeds, and river weeds may be seen. The sediments and gravel beds, which favor the establishment of vascular plants, also harbor burrowing animals such as mayfly nymphs, worms, dipteran larvae, and leeches. More abundant here than in other lotic communities, mussels with dark blue or black shells dig into the sandy bottom. These efficient filter-feeding mollusks are, in turn, fed upon by fish, raccoons, and muskrats. Empty mussel shells along the river bank—a common observance—attest to nocturnal feasts, especially by raccoons.

Principal game fish in Pocono rivers are smallmouth bass, walleyed pike, muskellunge, white sucker, channel catfish, shad, and brown trout. Other species such as fallfish, rock bass, black crappie, pickerel, eel, yellow perch, and several kinds of shiners, sunfish (pumpkin seed, blue gill, green), madtoms, and minnows are common but known mostly to the avid fishermen and naturalist. Research biologists compiled a list, available at Delaware Water Gap National Recreation Area Visitor Centers, of fifty-five species of fish for the waters of Delaware Water Gap National Recreation Area alone.

The Delaware is the setting for many fish stories and what is more, the following two are true. Both the shad and eel have a fascinating life history.

American shad are slab-sided fish with a broad triangular head and a deeply forked tail. Shad are *anadromous*, that is, they come upriver to spawn in fresh water after spending most of their life in the ocean. Today, the only naturally spawning population in Pennsylvania is in the Delaware River, where the spring spawning run is estimated at half a million individuals.

Migration activity is stimulated by rising coastal and river water temperature. As a result, shad first appear in lower Delaware Bay in early March when surface temperature reaches about 41°F. At a rate of five to eight miles a day, the leading edge of the migration reaches

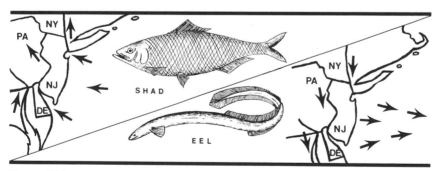

Figure 5.10
Delaware River migratory fishes. The arrows denote the migration of adults to spawning areas.

the Bushkill-Matamoras area by mid-April. Shad continue to move upstream into the east and west branches of the Delaware as spring advances. Incidentally, at the same time that shad are running up the Delaware, a small tree on the slopes above the river is in bloom with delicate white flowers. Called serviceberry in the southern Appalachians, here it is appropriately known as shad bush. (See Figure 3.9.)

Participants in the spawning run are males, mostly four and five years old and nineteen to twenty-two inches in length, and five- and six-year-old females averaging twenty-two to twenty-four inches. Spawning occurs from mid-April through June. Eggs are lodged in bottom rubble, and young fish hatch in 6–15 days when water temperatures are 52–63°F. As three- to five-inch fingerlings, the shad move to tidal waters and become ocean dwellers. Adults will return to the sea until the next spawning season.

The American eel is a long, slender, snakelike fish. (See Figure 5.10.) It is the only species of fish in North America which is *catadromous*, that is, it moves downstream to the sea to breed after living most of its life in fresh water.

Spawning occurs in subtropical Sargasso Sea waters southwest of Bermuda. Presumably the adults die after mating. The young develop into thin, transparent plankton dwellers and drift into the Gulf Stream, there to be carried northward along the North American continent. By the time the young eels reach coastal waters, they are three to four inches long, with darkened skin, and are then called elvers. Eels live as many as nine years in fresh water where they feed on a variety of invertebrates and other fish. Females may attain a length of 48 inches, whereas males seldom exceed half that length. When sexually mature, the fish stop feeding, change from olive to black, and move downstream in autumn. Females are joined by males in the estuary and together they travel to the Sargasso Sea.

Flood Plains

Flood plains are flat areas alongside rivers, which typically are inundated during spring runoff but for much of the year experience fairly dry conditions. The soil is mostly the sand and silt left behind when flood waters recede. It was the flood plains along the Upper Delaware River that were cleared first by native Americans, and later by European settlers, for use in agricultural activities. This region, the Minisink, is a good place to observe the flood plain community.

The annual fluctuation in the water table and the nature of the soil play important roles in determining the types of vegetation found on flood plains. Trees adapted to these sites are fast-growing species with extensive root systems. Usually, supple trunks and stems are

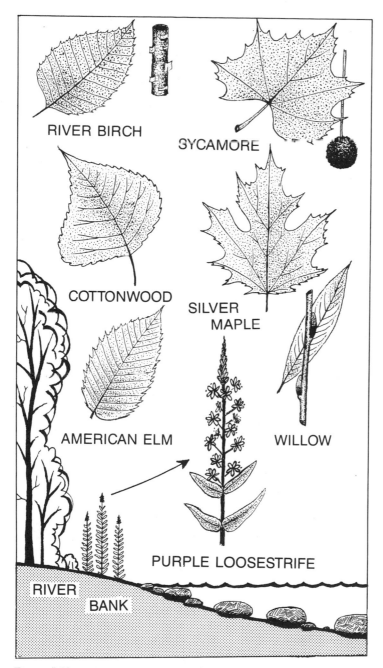

RIVER BIRCH

SYCAMORE

COTTONWOOD

SILVER MAPLE

AMERICAN ELM

WILLOW

PURPLE LOOSESTRIFE

RIVER BANK

Figure 5.11
Flood plain vegetation. Some trees have adapted to periodic flooding common to flat areas along rivers. Leaves of common flood plain trees are shown. Purple loosestrife, an imported herb from Europe, has become widespread and conspicuous along Pocono streams and rivers.

also a characteristic and help young trees, especially, to survive flood waters. Silver maples and sycamore are the most conspicuous trees on flood plains. River birch, willow, cottonwood, and American elm are also well represented. Figure 5.11 shows the leaves of these flood plain trees.

As Figure 5.11 indicates, a shrub layer is not typical of flood plains. An occasional elderberry, silky dogwood, or spicebush may be present. More often, vines such as Virginia creeper, poison ivy, and wild grape grow along the ground and high into the trees.

The most common annual plant, purple loosestrife, with its showy spike-like inflorescence of magenta flowers is familiar to summer visitors of river banks. Jewelweed, mints, and nettles are also abundant. One brush against the tiny, stinging hairs will positively, if painfully, identify the latter plant.

Animals are primarily transients in flood plains. Water snakes and snapping turtles are found here as they are in many semi-aquatic settings. A good population of an uncommon toad, Fowler's Toad, is found along the Delaware. Those mammals that come to these sites mainly to feed and drink include deer, muskrats, raccoons, skunks, and mink. A larger relative of skunks and mink, the river otter is one of the larger species of the weasel family. Sighting an otter would be a rare event. Today, otters live along secluded tributaries, many of which flow through restricted wild areas owned by private fishing clubs, rather than along the river itself. A recent study by a Pennsylvania Game Commission biologist indicates that the Poconos have the largest population of otters in the state, probably 260–450 individuals.

Waterways Wanderings

Flowing water communities are readily available for visits and nature study. Many Pocono roads run parallel to streams and rivers. Some of the most enjoyable hiking and nature trails in the state parks and in the Delaware Water Gap National Recreation Area follow the meanderings of streams. The modern traveler can trace the routes of the Poconos' first human inhabitants, native Americans, and, one hopes, develop an understanding and appreciation of waterways comparable to that of those earlier travelers.

Lentic Communities

Lentic, or standing water, communities lack the one constant common to lotic communities—the one-way flow of water. In lentic

BOX 5.1

Places to Observe Flowing Water Communities

DWGNRA. Nature trail to Dingmans Falls, starts at Dingmans Falls Visitor Center.

George W. Childs State Park. Steep trail into glen and gorge adjacent to three waterfalls.

Hickory Run State Park. Numerous trails of varying length and difficulty; Sawmill Trail, Hickory Run Trail, Sand Spring Trail, Hawk Falls Trail, Fishermen's path to fly fishing section of Mud Run Gorge.

Promised Land State Park. Also has several good trails along streams; Little Falls Trail, No. 1 and No. 2 Millbrook Trails, E. Branch Wallenpaupack Trail, Lower Lake Trail.

Selected Roadside Streams

Numerous Pocono roads are located, for at least a portion of their length, along streams. Pulloffs, often used by fishermen, are suitable stopping places for stream explorations. Of special note are:

Rte. 447 from Canadensis to Analomink which runs along the Brodhead Creek.

Rte. 590 from Kimble to Lackawaxen along the Lackawaxen River.

Rte. 615 along Flatbrook Creek and River Road (Old Mine Road) along the Delaware River, both in New Jersey section of Delaware Water Gap National Recreation Area (DWGNRA).

Canoeing and Rafting

Many opportunities from one-hour to overnight camping ventures; from white water to mild currents; for the novice to the advanced white water paddler. Inquire of the Pocono Mountains Vacation Bureau, or at the many rental facilities along the Delaware and elsewhere.

communities, there is considerable daily and seasonal variation in conditions, based in part on the size and shape of the basin holding the standing water. The distribution of factors such as light, heat, oxygen, and wind action is variable whenever a sizable basin exists. As a result of the interactions of these factors, zonation is characteristic of many lentic communities.

Zonation

In lakes and large ponds, a *littoral* zone extends from the shore to a depth where light is barely sufficient for rooted aquatic plants to grow. Beyond the littoral region, an *open water* zone exists in larger, deeper standing water bodies. A *euphotic* zone is found from the surface to a depth, the *light compensation level*, where the intensity of illumination is such that plants can just balance food production via photosynthesis with use of stored organic matter via respiration. Below, the *aphotic* zone, without light, extends to the lake bottom. Figure 5.12 illustrates the zonation of lakes and large ponds.

As might be expected, distinct biotic assemblages have adapted to these zones. In the littoral zone, there is a distinct pattern of plants which develops from the moist edges out to the open water zone. At the edge, emergent plants, such as cattails, grow with roots and

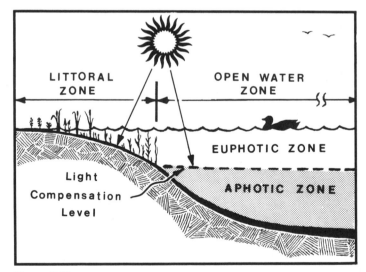

Figure 5.12
Lake zonation. Distinctive zones are present in lakes in large part determined by the extent to which light penetrates the water column. Many plants and animals have become adapted for life in a particular zone.

lower stem under water. Next, submerged plants grow in deeper water. Most submerged plants have thin, flexible stems and leaves and only tiny flowers poke above the water surface in some species. Floating leafed plants can grow in deeper water with the roots buried in the mud, but with the highly modified, waxy leaves resting on the surface. Floating plants, such as duckweed, can cover the entire littoral zone in some lakes.

The littoral zone, in addition to conspicuous aquatic plants, is the haven of many tiny to microscopic plants and animals attached to the rooted plants and on sticks and rocks. These are *periphyton*. Other organisms, the *benthos*, live in or on the bottom mud from the shoreline to the depths of the basin. Microscopic algae, *phytoplankton*, dwell throughout the euphotic zone from the littoral zone into the open water region. *Zooplankton*, mainly microscopic protozoans and rotifers, macroscopic crustaceans, and several other less abundant invertebrate types, are found in the same places as phytoplankton. Zooplankton can also live in the dark and many spend some time each day in the aphotic zone and move into the euphotic zone nightly. There are larger, active swimmers such as fishes, amphibians, and reptiles moving freely throughout the lake although, in general, younger individuals will be found in shallower waters whereas mature animals will spend most of their time in open, deeper waters.

Thermal Stratification

Larger lakes in temperate regions show another type of zonation because of seasonal changes in the solar radiation falling on the water. The main heat component of sunlight is in the infrared portion of the spectrum and these wavelengths are absorbed by water in the uppermost layer. As water temperature rises above 39.2°F, where maximum density occurs, density decreases and a lighter, warmer layer, the *epilimnion*, becomes established as summer advances. A cool, lower layer, the *hypolimnion*, may have a constant temperature of about 39°F for much of the summer. A narrow zone, the *thermocline*, where abrupt temperature change occurs, is found at about ten to fifteen feet below the surface in larger lakes by mid-summer.

In summer, the dissolved oxygen (D.O.) content in the water column is quite variable, due mainly to oxygen production by phytoplankton in the epilimnion. Dead plant and animal matter sinking to the bottom provide material for bacterial activity. However, these bacterial activities may deplete oxygen in the hypolimnion, presenting problems for fish dwelling at or near the bottom.

In autumn, epilimnion waters cool until maximum density is

reached and then sink as nutrient-laden bottom waters move up-ward. This thorough mixing, the so-called fall turnover, may permit a fall bloom of phytoplankton.

Temperate, deep-water lakes will experience an inverted tempera-ture gradient in winter when ice cover develops. Water temperature just below the ice remains slightly above freezing and somewhat warmer waters of maximum density occupy the middle and bottom regions. Dissolved oxygen values are variable. In many instances, the lowered water temperature and reduced activity of organisms re-sult in satisfactory oxygen levels. In some cases, sustained bacterial decomposition produces oxygen depletion in the hypolimnion and a winter "fish-kill" may ensue.

When the ice cover melts in spring, the lake experiences another turnover, the spring turnover, followed by a spring bloom of algae stimulated by longer periods of daylight, warming temperatures, and plentiful nutrients. Figure 5.13 shows the seasonal temperature and dissolved oxygen patterns which characterize larger Pocono lakes.

Succession

Lakes and ponds of varied size and age dot the Pocono landscape. Many of these bodies owe their origin to glacial events of the last ice age. Others, impoundments such as Lake Wallenpaupack and Beltz-ville Dam, were created when dams were built across stream val-leys. Standing water habitats are ephemeral, geologically speaking. Unless humans deliberately modify the sequence, standing water bodies typically fill with sediments. Lakes which originally may be deep, with limited plant and animal life, and low productivity, thus *oligotrophic*, will usually experience increased sedimentation, inva-sion of more plant life (especially rooted aquatic plants), and show increased productivity. The lake is then said to be *eutrophic*. A *meso-trophic* lake is sometimes designated for a middle stage in lake suc-cession. Over time, usually thousands of years, sediments accumulate to such an extent that rooted aquatic plants grow com-pletely across the area and a pond has formed. In turn, a pond may be succeeded by a bog, marsh, or swamp. Given enough time, a completely terrestrial habitat—a forest—ensues.

In actuality, ecological succession is not as clear-cut as presented in theory. Geologic events and local climatic conditions can greatly alter the nature and rate of succession in lakes and ponds. In the Poconos, sandstones only slowly release minerals, thus nutrient-poor waters prevail. High levels of humic acids seeping into the lake from adjacent vegetation and long, cold winters also combine to slow the

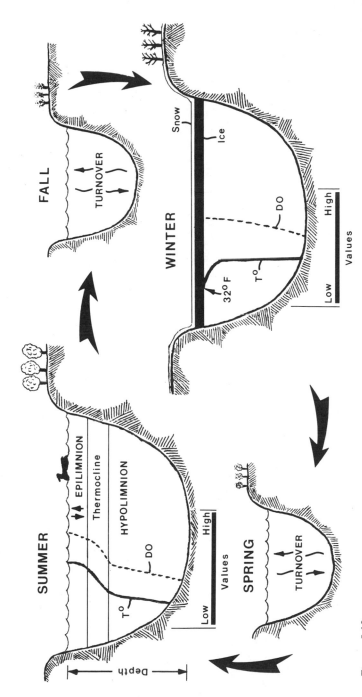

Figure 5.13
Seasonal lake dynamics. Temperature (T°) and dissolved oxygen (D.O.) profiles typical of many deep water lakes in temperate regions. Consult text for details.

eutrophication process. In man-made lakes and farm ponds, enrichment of water, mainly by nitrates and phosphates from animals and human wastes, will speed the process of increased productivity, thus the phenomenon *cultural eutrophication*. In such artificially enriched waters, only a few specialized organisms, especially blue-green algae, can thrive. Farm pond blooms, a "pea-green soup" readily seen by summer visitors to the Poconos, are a good example of this phenomenon.

Lakes

The focus of much resort and recreational activity, lakes of varied size, age, and origin exist in the Poconos. A consideration of three representative lakes will show the varied nature of these lentic communities.

Lake Wallenpaupack is the largest impoundment in the Poconos. The 13-mile long lake was created in 1926 by damming Wallenpaupak Creek on the Pike and Wayne Counties boundary. Originally a major hydroelectric project of Pennsylvania Power and Light Company, the lake today serves only as an auxiliary generating source. It's become a major recreational facility with a surface area of almost 5700 acres and 52 miles of shoreline. A visitor center at the eastern edge of the lake utilizes photographs and a slide show to inform visitors about the construction and operation of the power project. An excellent taxidermic exhibit of the lake's principal game fish is a valuable nature study aid. Figure 5.14 shows the location of the visitor center and other features discussed in this section.

Lake Wallenpaupack has a maximum depth of approximately 60 feet. The lake level fluctuates as much as five to ten feet in the course of a year as water is periodically released. With such shoreline changes, few rooted aquatic plants can get established. A few tufts of wild celery and milfoil may be noted. More frequently seen are the young shoots of willows and buttonbush, which germinate on the exposed shore when water level is low and survive the periods of partial submersion. A few floating leafed plants such as watershield and spatterdock are present in the shallowest, protected coves of the impoundment. Phytoplankton populations are sparse here also. As is true of most fresh water habitats, green algae and diatoms are dominant types along with blue-green algae, dinoflagellates, and chrysophytes—but microscopic examination is required to identify most species.

Zooplankton representatives are also principally microscopic protozoans and rotifers. However, one may detect slightly larger mem-

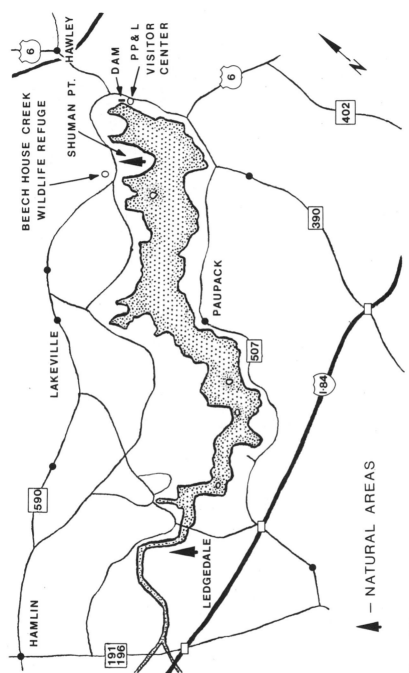

Figure 5.14
Lake Wallenpaupack.

bers of this community. If one holds a glass of lake water up to the light, one should see, dancing up and down in the water, crustaceans such as copepods and water fleas. Figure 5.15 shows a magnified view of these two common zooplankton.

A variety of larger animals—invertebrates and vertebrates—are present in this large lake but not in abundance. Many of these animals will be considered with other lentic communities where the likelihood of seeing such animals is greater.

The game-fish populations in Lake Wallenpaupack are sustained in large part because of stocking. Principal game-fish species are yellow perch, walleyed pike, smallmouth and largemouth bass, rock bass, pickerel, muskellunge, rainbow, and brown trout.

One last natural history feature of Lake Wallenpaupack should be noted. There are two well-marked and maintained nature trails, which one may hike to gain an appreciation of the surrounding countryside. The trail near Ledgedale follows old logging roads through a mixed hardwood forest on a slope above the lake. Rocky ledges and glacial boulders are conspicuous features along the one-and-one-half mile trail.

The Shuman Point trail parallels the lake shore for much of its three mile length. Along the lake edge, buttonbush, willow, swamp azalea, and blueberry bushes may be seen. Patches of royal, cinnamon, and chain ferns grow in moist areas. Numerous American chestnut sprouts are a prominent feature of the trail. Forest succession in abandoned farm fields, which are bordered by attractive stone walls, can easily be observed as one hikes this trail. An adjacent area, the Beech House Creek Wildlife Refuge, an open, grassy

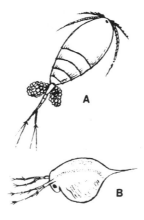

Figure 5.15
Two common freshwater
zooplankton. A. Copepod with
egg masses. B. Water flea.
(Both highly-magnified views.)

wet meadow lacks trails but observations of wildlife may be made by
stopping along Route 590, which passes by the refuge.

Near the Ledgedale region, Lacawac Sanctuary is located. This National Natural Landmark is a pristine glacial lake surrounded by a nature preserve used for education and research. Summer nature walks and progams plus a self-guided nature trail are available. Call the sanctuary for visiting times and progam details (717-689-9494).

Bruce Lake, a few miles south of Lake Wallenpaupack, is a fine example of an oligotrophic lake. It is located within the 2845-acre Bruce Lake Natural Area which is part of Delaware State Forest. The three-mile hike to Bruce Lake is a pleasant hour walk on a marked trail that traverses an oak-maple forest. Interesting variations in understory vegetation are seen along the trail, with early stretches going through parklike patches of grasses and ferns, while other trail sections go past an understory mainly of blueberry bushes interspersed with sheep laurel and mountain laurel.

About halfway to Bruce Lake, the trail crosses the causeway that divides Egypt Meadow Lake. This shallow lake, average depth about four feet, was constructed by the Civilian Conservation Corps in 1935. Before this time, meadow grass that grew along the stream was harvested for use as packing material for the glassware produced by the Dorflinger's glass works near Honesdale. The water of Egypt Meadow Lake is tinted brown and is acidic mainly because of humic acids from Balsam Swamp, which is adjacent to the lake. The shallow regions of this lake show increased numbers of rooted aquatic plants characteristic of a lake which is becoming eutrophic.

After another mile and a half, the trail ends at another grassy parklike setting on the northern edge of Bruce Lake. This glacial lake covers about forty-eight acres and has an average depth of seven feet and a maximum depth of about twenty feet. There is no inlet as springs provide water for the lake. The outlet at the southern end becomes the headwaters for Shohola Creek.

The blue water, typical of oligotrophic lakes, indicates sparse populations of phytoplankton. Larger plants are not abundant. Plants such as water shield, white water lily, spatterdock, mud plantain, and golden club are represented by a few individuals. Equally sparse populations of submerged plants such as wild celery and milfoils may be seen. (See Figure 5.17, which depicts some aquatic plants typical of a eutrophic lake—some of which are also present in oligotrophic lakes like Bruce Lake.)

Lakes with sparse floating vegetation, such as Bruce Lake, are promising locales for the discovery of a most interesting plant. The plant, when in bloom, has tiny yellow flowers poking just above the water surface to aid one's search. Just below the surface, the plant has fine-forked leaves with numerous tiny sacs. The entire plant may be several square feet in area. This plant is the carnivorous bladderwort whose bladders serve to trap water fleas, mosquito larvae, and even motile algae such as diatoms and desmids. Figure 5.16 shows a magnified view of several of these fascinating bladders. The bladder trap is set when special cells lining the sac take up water, in turn causing the sac to become slightly indented and form a partial vacuum. At the bladder mouth, several tiny bristles serve as triggers. When a bristle is touched by a passing organism, the door of the bladder opens for a quarter of a second and the prey is sucked in as water refills the sac.

Few fish—mainly sunfish, yellow perch, pickerel, smallmouth and largemouth bass—are found here. Those fish present in remote lakes got there by swimming upstream as young individuals or were conveyed there as eggs on the mud-laden feet of ducks and wading birds. Fishermen who empty bait-buckets make their contribution to fish distribution also.

Some of the amphibians and reptiles discussed in the section on pond life are also found in Bruce Lake, but only one ancient and durable reptile is highlighted here.

Snapping turtles, the most widely distributed turtle east of the Rockies, are found in diverse aquatic habitats from southern Canada to northern Florida. Easily recognized by its large head, small ventral

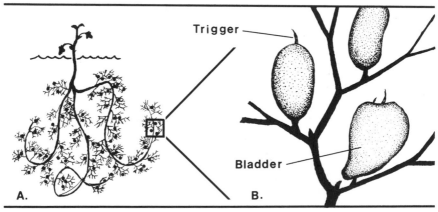

Figure 5.16
Bladderwort. A. Habitat sketch. B. Bladders and trigger bristles (highly magnified).

shell, and long, saw-toothed tail, the turtle is well-named. It lunges and snaps at its prey and at a potential attacker on land. Aquatic vegetation and stunted pan fish, dead or alive, are primary dietary items.

The female snapper moves onto land to lay her eggs. She selects a spot free of vegetation and open to the warmth from sunlight, which serves to incubate the eggs. Several test holes may be started by the turtle before the actual nest, a flask-shaped hole about eight inches deep is dug into the ground with the use of her hind limbs. Usually about thirty to forty eggs, each slightly smaller than a ping pong ball, are deposited in the nest which the female then covers with the excavated soil. Incubation takes about seventy to one hundred and twenty days.

Many nests do not go undisturbed since raccoons, skunks, and mink are experts in locating nests and digging out the eggs. As many as 60 to 70 percent of all nests may be discovered. One will be detecting the remains of such nest-robbing activity if one notices shriveled, leathery, split-open "ping pong balls" along a lake edge.

Those nests not disturbed will produce young that hatch by September and, if the soil has not been baked too hard from a dry summer, the young will dig upward until they break through the soil. The young quickly move into aquatic sites, perhaps guided by an open horizon and the sun's position. Diverse predators such as herons, crows, muskrats, mink, bullfrogs, large turtles, bass, and pike, all eat young snappers. If the young do get to about the four- or five-pound size, they are well able to defend themselves and may then attain a long life for wild animals, as much as twenty-five years.

At the southern end of Bruce Lake, a developing sphagnum bog and beaver meadow are also worth exploring. The plants and animals of these habitats are described elsewhere in the text.

Lake Lenape, located in Delaware Water Gap National Recreation Area near the village of Delaware Water Gap, is a good example of a eutrophic lake and may be readily visited. In the village, take the road that bears left off of Mountain House Road. This road then leads to a parking lot, with the lake an easy quarter-mile walk away.

A few acres in surface area, this shallow lake has only a quarter of its surface free of aquatic plants. Most of the lake is filled with a heavy growth of the submerged plant, fanwort. This brushlike plant has tiny, white flowers which extend just above the water surface—a pretty sight in mid-summer. The other conspicuous plant, the white water lily, covers about two-thirds of the surface. A few watershields and pond weeds are also present.

Bur reed, buttonbush, alders, slippery elm and red maple rim much of the lake edge. One part of the lake abuts a steep slope where tall hemlocks and extensive rhododendron thickets provide an attractive backdrop. Large rocky outcrops on these slopes are of interest because of the extensive lichen growth evident there.

The outlet stream forms a broad, soggy seepage area filled mainly with sensitive fern, bur reed and sphagnum moss. Figure 5.17 presents a profile of plants typically found from shallow water to the moist margins of eutrophic lakes. Not all of the species depicted are found at Lake Lenape.

Some of the rooted aquatic plants found in eutrophic lakes are found in other standing water habitats, as well. Microscopic plants and mobile animals follow suit. Much of the following discussion applies especially to pond life.

Phytoplankton populations are diverse, with many kinds of unicellular and colonial green algae, diatoms, and blue-green algae present. Zooplankton diversity is equally great with various protozoan species, rotifers, and many types of crustaceans represented.

Periphyton, some as tiny as the plankton, use the extensive aquatic plant growth for attachment. Attached diatoms, protozoans, fungi, and bacteria are consumed by larger creatures including isopods, insect larvae and adults, and snails.

Using the quiet water are many active insects such as water boatmen, backswimmers, and diving beetles—all of which are capable of taking air in the form of a bubble as they dive towards the bottom. Whirligig beetles and water striders use their specialized niche, the surface film, here as in lentic habitats elsewhere.

The mud bottom of eutrophic lakes has a good bit of organic matter settling on it from above; therefore, it provides food and hiding places for many benthic animals. Insect larvae of species such as midges, craneflies, damselflies, dragonflies, and mayflies, flatworms, annelid worms, tiny clams and small crustaceans are sometimes present in large numbers.

On the other hand, the number of fish species diminishes as lakes fill with sediment and vegetation. Soon only a few stunted sunfish, pickerel, and bullheads remain.

However, extensive aquatic vegetation provides good habitat for other cold-blooded vertebrates, thereby enhancing the diversity and abundance of amphibians and reptiles. Table 5.1 lists the amphibians and reptiles of the Poconos and indicates the principal communities where each is found.

Lake Lenape presently has a sizable population of green and

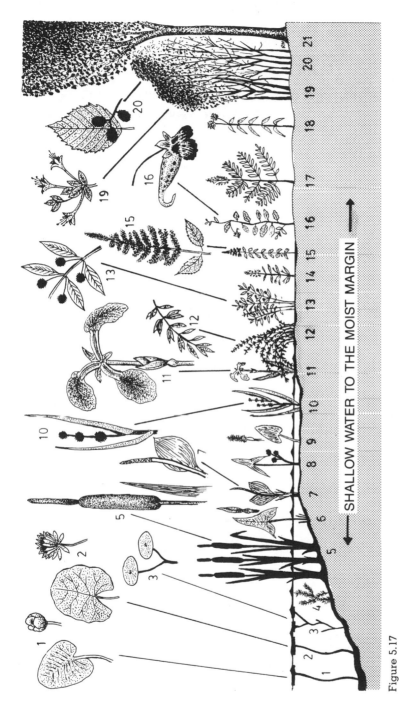

Figure 5.17
Common Plants of Pocono eutrophic lake margins. 1. Spatterdock. 2. White water lily. 3. Watershield. 4. Milfoil. 5. Broad-leaved cattail. 6. Arrow-arum. 7. Golden club. 8. Arrowhead. 9. Pickerel weed. 10. Bur reed. 11. Blue flag. 12. Water-willow. 13. Buttonbush. 14. Swamp candle. 15. Hardhack. 16. Jewelweed. 17. Royal Fern. 18. Swamp milkweed. 19. Swamp azalea. 20. Alder. 21. Red maple.

SHALLOW WATER TO THE MOIST MARGIN

Table 5.1.
Pocono Amphibians and Reptiles

Amphibians	Preferred habitat(s)
Eastern spadefoot*	Floodplain woods
Fowler's toad*	Floodplain sandy shores, lake shores
American toad	Widespread; woods, meadows, gardens, lawns
Gray treefrog	Woodland ponds, shrub swamps, wooded swamps
Northern spring peeper	Woodland ponds, shrub swamps, marshes, wet meadows
Boreal chorus frog*	Marshes, moist woods, ponds
Northern cricket frog*	Shrub swamps, ponds
Northern leopard frog	Ponds, marshes, wet meadows
Pickerel frog	Widespread; ponds, lakes, stream banks, marshes
Wood frog	Wooded swamps, moist woods
Green frog	Ponds, lakes, stream banks, swamps,
Bullfrog	Ponds, lakes, stream banks, marshes
Marbled salamander*	Woodland ponds
Jefferson salamander*	Woodland ponds
Spotted salamander*	Woodland ponds
Red-spotted newt	Widespread; ponds, lakes, marshes (terrestrial stage—moist woods)
Northern dusky salamander	Brooks, springs, seepage areas, small streams
Eastern red-backed salamander	Upland forests, wooded swamps
Slimy salamander	Upland forests, wooded swamps, hemlock ravines
Four-toed salamander	Sphagnum bogs, seepage areas
Northern spring salamander	Springs, brooks, small streams
Northern red salamander	Springs, brooks, small streams
Long-tailed salamander*	Seepage areas, rocky crevices near caves
Northern two-lined salamander	Brooks, seepage areas, moist woods

Table 5.1. (continued)   **155**

Reptiles	Preferred habitat(s)
Common snapping turtle	Widespread; all aquatic, semi-aquatic sites
Musk turtle	Rivers, sluggish streams, ponds, lakes
Spotted turtle*	Shallow lakes, ponds, wet meadows
Wood turtle	Swamps, moist woods, meadows
Bog turtle[†*]	Sphagnum bogs, swamps, wet meadows
Eastern box turtle	Upland woods, meadows
Eastern painted turtle	Ponds, lakes, slow streams
Map turtle*	Rivers, larger streams
Five-lined skink*	Moist woods, cutover woodlots
Northern red-bellied snake	Upland woods, forest edge
Northern brown snake	Fields, meadows, swamps, vacant lots
Northern water snake	Most aquatic, semi-aquatic sites
Eastern garter snake	Widespread; semi-aquatic to terrestrial sites
Eastern ribbon snake	Swamps, stream banks, bogs
Eastern hognose snake	Moist woods, forest edge
Eastern worm snake*	Primarily subterranean in moist woods
Northern ringneck snake	Wooded slopes, road cut banks
Northern black snake	Swamps, lowland forests
Smooth green snake	Meadows, fields, thickets
Black rat snake	Rocky hillsides in mature woods
Eastern milk snake	Widespread; semi-aquatic to terrestrial sites
Northern copperhead	Rocky upland forests, rock ledges
Timber rattlesnake	Mature upland forests

[†] = Endangered species
* = Rare, uncommon, or spotty distribution throughout the region

bullfrogs. In addition, Eastern painted turtles, northern water snakes, and garter snakes are common reptiles there.

Amphibians and reptiles are present with a comparable diversity and abundance in eutrophic lakes and ponds. Discussion concerning some of these animals common to both communities is presented in the section devoted to ponds.

Ponds

As a eutrophic lake continues to fill with sediment, the water becomes shallow enough so that rooted plants grow completely across the area and the quiet body of water evolves into a pond. Water temperature is fairly uniform throughout the pond, although water temperature does fluctuate as air temperature above the pond fluctuates. The amounts of O_2 and CO_2 dissolved in pond water are quite variable over a twenty-four-hour period. Extensive photosynthetic activity, which uses CO_2 and produces O_2, takes place only during daylight hours. Plant and animal respiration, which uses O_2 and

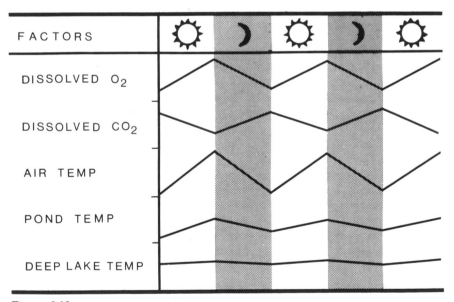

Figure 5.18
Abiotic factors of ponds. Amounts of dissolved gases (O_2 and CO_2) present in pond water tend to vary as photosynthesis occurs only during the day whereas plant and animal respiration is continuous throughout the twenty-four hours. Note that pond water temperature tends to fluctuate with air temperature changes, while the larger volume of water in a lake tends to lessen water temperature changes there.

produces CO_2, goes on day and night. These combined activities result in dramatic fluctuations in levels of these important gases. Figure 5.18 shows the typical pattern of those abiotic factors characteristic of ponds.

Ponds are readily accessible to naturalists and have been the focus of many scientific studies. As with lakes, ponds display considerable variation related to their successional stage as they evolve into other wetland communities. What follows is a description of principal inhabitants of a pond in the "middle stage" of succession.

Pond Plants

Many of the vascular plants found in eutrophic lakes, some of which are shown in Figure 5.17, are evident in ponds. Pickerel weed generally becomes most prominent as ponds accumulate more sediment. Its showy spike of purple flowers on a stalk with a single, broad, heart-shaped leaf makes this an easily recognized pond plant. Pond weeds, living up to their name, are submerged plants. Members of this largest family of truly aquatic plants have alternately arranged ribbonlike or threadlike leaves on the submerged stem. Small green or brownish flowers may emerge just above the water surface. Associated with pond weeds, other submerged plants such as milfoils, naids, and coontails often form dense beds. Finely branched leaves give these plants a brushlike appearance.

Pond surfaces, by midsummer, are frequently covered with a floating mat of duckweeds. These tiniest of all seed plants reproduce mainly by vegetative means. The plant body is only 0.1 to 0.2 inches long. Phytoplankton give pond water a greenish color but themselves are not readily evident. However, by late summer, some phytoplankton such as filamentous green algae and blue-green types may reach such high population levels that conspicuous green mats cover the pond surface.

Pond Animals

As is true with many pond plants, animals dwelling in ponds may also be seen in other aquatic habitats. In fact, the greater mobility of animals increases that likelihood.

Microscopic plankton, larger water fleas, and copepods are present as they are in lakes. With the greater number of rooted aquatic plants typical of ponds, it is not surprising that many animals and other plants live attached to the rooted aquatic plants. These periphyton, such as diatoms, green alae, fungi, hydras, insect larvae, and other tiny invertebrates, are abundant.

Other pond invertebrates live in or on the bottom sediments. Planarians, round and segmented worms, dipteran, dragonfly and damselfly nymphs, mayfly and beetle larvae, are common benthic representatives. Still other invertebrates move actively across the sediments and along submerged plant stems. Some, such as beetle larvae and adults, pond snails, caddisfly larvae (here encased in tubes composed of plant matter), are easily detected as they slowly move about.

Active animals such as diving beetles, backswimmers, and water boatmen should easily be observed as they move up and down through the water column. Utilizing the water film as they do in other quiet water settings are water striders and whirligig beetles (see Figure 5.8), and a smaller stouter relative of the water strider, the broad-shouldered water strider.

One last group of invertebrates should be mentioned. Bryozoa, moss animals, are tiny, hydralike individuals, which produce colonies anchored to submerged objects. By late summer, some of these colonies grow to grapefruit-sized gelatinous masses, sure to attract the attention of any pond visitor.

Pond fishes are not numerous or diverse. Most ponds will have a small population of bluegill and pumpkinseed sunfish. Sunfish nests are a conspicuous feature of pond and shallow lake edges. Males produce a nest in shallow water by creating a sediment-free depression on the bottom. After mating with one or several females, the male guards the developing young and aerates the nest with his swimming motions. Weedy areas of ponds provide habitat for pickerel. Bullheads and madtoms use their sensitive barbels to find prey in the muddy bottom.

Life in and out of Water

Ponds are ideal places to observe animals that spend part of their life in water and another part on land. The remaining animals considered in this discussion of pond life all share this trait.

Dragonflies and damselflies are conspicuous insects probably seen by every pond visitor. Figure 5.19 shows these closely related insects. These active aquatic nymphs stalk their prey among dense underwater vegetation or along the ponds bottom. Both types of nymphs have elaborate, hinged mouthparts, which extend rapidly to capture prey.

After an aquatic life of from one to as much as four years in some species, the nymph transforms into a winged adult in a final molt after emerging onto land.

It is interesting to watch male dragonflies establish territories

DRAGONFLY

DAMSELFLY

Figure 5.19
Two prominent pond insects.
Dragonflies have heavier
bodies and broader wings
than their close relatives,
damselflies. Dragonflies,
at rest, hold their wings
horizontally outward from the
body. Damselflies have
narrower wings, shown
extended for comparison,
normally folded over the
abdomen when the insects
are at rest.

around a pond. The male will visit the same perch time and time again and drive other males from the area. When a female appears, she is seized quickly by one of the resident males. While flying, the pair mates as the male grasps the female behind her head with his abdominal claspers. In turn, the female arches her abdomen to receive sperm from the male's second abdominal segment. In some species, the male liberates the mated female who soon begins hovering at the pond surface, dipping her abdomen repeatedly and releasing the fertilized eggs, which sink to the bottom. In other species, the male continues to clasp the female until she has laid all her eggs. Comparable mating and egg-laying behavior occur among damselflies.

Amphibians, as the name indicates, live both on land and in water, with the result that many types of frogs, toads, and salamanders frequent ponds. Many amphibians are well-camouflaged, alert to danger, secretive, often nocturnal, and, all in all, generally glimpsed only briefly as they slither or jump quickly out of sight. Reptiles such as turtles and water snakes also lead an amphibious life.

Although a bit more conspicuous, they are also alert and usually make their escape before more than a glance is obtained. Table 5.1 lists the principal amphibians and reptiles of the Poconos and indicates those commonly found in ponds.

Perhaps the amphibian one is most likely to observe in a pond is the red-spotted newt. This olive-drab salamander with a yellow underside and lateral rows of red spots lives in shallow water. It is active in daylight, as it slowly moves along the pond bottom in search of its prey. It consumes water fleas, copepods, mosquito larvae, frogs' eggs, and even small tadpoles.

A springtime visit to almost any Pocono pond should be rewarded with views of this animal's intricate mating ritual. The male newt slowly approaches the female and grasps her around the neck or front end with his large hindlegs. An embrace, which may last as long as an hour, will end as the male drags the female over previously deposited sperm packets. She is able to pick up the sperm packets with her everted anal vent. Shortly thereafter, the female deposits 200–400 internally fertilized eggs, each surrounded by a gelatinous coating and each attached singly to twigs and plants, near the pond bottom. Within two to four weeks, the young hatch into quarter-inch larvae with feathery gills. After about three months, the larvae undergo a pronounced metamorphosis. Gills atrophy as lungs develop, and skin color gradually changes from olive to red or red-orange. Then the red eft, as it is called, leaves the water to live in moist terrestrial habitats. Look for red efts as you hike along a wooded trail on a damp or rainy day.

After spending two or three years on land, the salamander once again enters a pond in late summer to live the rest of its life as the totally aquatic, adult newt. Only the conspicuous lateral red spots are reminders of its terrestrial existence.

Frogs and toads, as numerous as newts, are known more by their breeding choruses than from direct sightings. The official announcement of spring is the single, clear note issued by the one-inch long tree frog, the spring peeper, as the first warm rains stirs it from its hibernating place in leaf litter some distance from the pond. This event in late March is followed shortly thereafter by the high-pitched breeding trill of male American toads. The characteristic "banjo-plunk" of the green frog and the deep, vibrant bass notes, the "jug-o-rum" of our largest frog, the bullfrog, are familiar sounds as summer sets in.

Of the fewer reptiles dwelling in and near ponds, the eastern painted turtle and the northern water snake are candidates for easy detection. The most widespread turtle in North America, painted turtles are regularly seen basking on exposed rocks or logs and usually may be approached so as to detect the bright yellow spots on the head. The red markings along the edge of the shell are less noticeable.

Also soaking up the warm rays of the sun, water snakes tend to blend in with their background and may almost go undetected. They are adept at swimming and obtain most of their food—frogs, salamanders, fish, and crayfish—in the water. This snake has variable markings, usually reddish-brown against a brown or gray background. As is true with many snakes, the pattern becomes obscure as the animal ages. There are distinctive black half moon markings on the belly but it is not a good idea to verify this. Although nonpoisonous, this aggressive snake will bite if handled.

Ponds are numerous and accessible in the Poconos and visits to them will always be rewarded with fascinating glimpses of the diverse plants and animals which reside there.

Bogs

There may be some uncertainty about the designation of a certain type of lake or whether it may actually be a pond. But the idea of a "bog" carries with it a great deal more confusion and misunderstanding. There are many who have never visited a bog, but all have

Figure 5.20
Eastern painted turtle. A close-up view to show distinctive neck and shell markings. It is more commonly viewed at a distance as it basks on exposed logs and rocks.

heard stories about bogs and the big snakes, quicksand, and poisonous plants present there. The word bog is associated with words such as "bogyman" (a frightful, imaginary being) and "bogus" (false). The true nature of bogs and the truth or falsity of stories about bogs will be explored in the following discussion.

What *is* a bog? A bog is an area of blocked drainage with a cushionlike vegetation mat, which is able to grow out over the acidic and brown-tinted water. The mat is primarily composed of sphagnum moss mixed with specialized, acid-loving herbs and shrubs.

Development of Bogs

Following the glaciers' retreat, huge ice blocks were left behind throughout the Poconos. As the ice eventually melted, lakes—called kettle-hole lakes—were formed. In time, some of these lakes developed into the Poconos' rarest wetland community, the sphagnum or quaking bog.

Bogs are a characteristic successional feature of northern regions such as Canada and northern New England. The higher elevations of the Poconos produce conditions comparable to those of higher latitudes so that, on occasion, a bog develops.

Sphagnum moss is indeed the indicator plant and principal agent in the formation of a bog. The gray-green leaf color with pink or red growing tips differentiate this moss from its relatives. As Figure 5.21 illustrates, special cells enable sphagnum to absorb much water, as much as sixteen to eighteen times its own weight.

Bog Vegetation

Associated with sphagnum are many plant members of the heath family. In Pocono bogs, representatives such as leatherleaf, sheep laurel, bog laurel, bog rosemary, Labrador tea, and blueberry are all woody shrubs of the heath family. Most heaths have leathery, elliptical leaves with wax or dense hairs to cut water loss. Why, in a water-laden bog? The acidic waters of a bog cannot readily be absorbed, thus the heath's conservation of usable humidity is warranted. Scattered among the heaths are bog orchids, mostly short plants with spikes of small flowers. A visit to a bog in mid-summer will be the best time to see these uncommon relatives of the showy tropical beauties.

As the sphagnum mat and heaths advance over the open water, circulation is restricted even more than previously. Soon anaerobic conditions develop. As a result, the accumulating organic matter is only partially decomposed by bacteria. Rates of decomposition are slowed also by the cold climate. Soon peat has formed. As the pro-

BOX 5.2

Places to Observe ⎯⎯⎯⎯⎯⎯⎯⎯⎯⎯ 163
Standing Water
Communities

Shohola Waterfowl Management Area. State Game Lands 180 along Route 6, Shohola Falls.

Promised Land State Park. Conservation Island Trail, plus auto road around lake.

Gouldsboro State Park. Hiking trail (one mile) around lake.

Tobyhanna State Park. Hiking trail (five miles) around lake.

Brady's Lake. Pennsylvania Fish Commission facility off of Route 940 near Pocono Lake.

Lake Wallenpaupack (Figure 5.14), Bruce Lake, and Lake Lenape. See detailed descriptions in Chapter 5.

cess continues, peat releases humic acids that produce the brown-tinted water. It is these harsh conditions that make a bog a place for specialists, both plant and animal. Specialized bacteria thrive, such as anaerobic sulfur bacteria which generate hydrogen sulfide (H_2S). The rotten-eggs odor of this gas is noticeable to anyone who becomes a "bog trotter."

A careful walk onto the mat will convince one that "quaking bog" is an apt description. Shrubs and trees some yards away will quiver if one jumps up and down on the mat. Don't be too enthusiastic in those jumps—remember that there are several feet of water under the mat.

As bog development continues, small, irregularly shaped black spruce and the American larch make their appearance. The latter conifer is atypical of the group, since the distinctive clusters of one-inch gray-green needles drop in autumn after turning a bright orange-yellow. Numerous gray-green lichens grow abundantly on the trunks of both conifers. At the edge of the bog, a tall shrub, poison sumac, should be noted and then avoided. Figure 5.22 depicts this plant.

One last group of bog specialists is worthy of note. In the low-nutri-

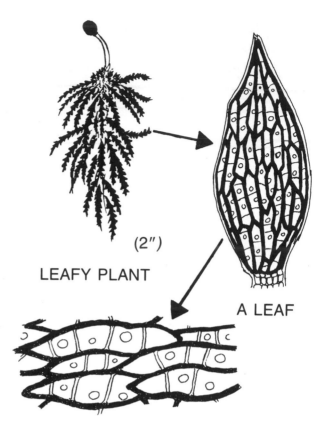

(2″)

LEAFY PLANT

A LEAF

SEVERAL CELLS

Figure 5.21
Sphagnum, at various enlargements. The dark areas
represent living photosynthetic cells, while the clear
areas with holes are large empty dead cells that
allow sphagnum to imbibe enormous quantities of
water.

ent environment, several plants have evolved a way of supplement-
ing their nutrient supply, especially the nitrogen and phosphorus
usually in limited supply in any aquatic habitat. These plants capture
and consume protein-rich animals—tiny animals to be sure, but
still they are turning the tables (trophic levels really). The pitcher
plant, with distinctive eight-inch tubular leaves, traps insects in the
water that accumulates at the bottom of the specialized leaf. The sundew, with its tiny rosette of spoon-shaped leaves, utilizes sticky secre-
tions on leaf hairs to trap tiny insects. Figure 5.22 presents a section

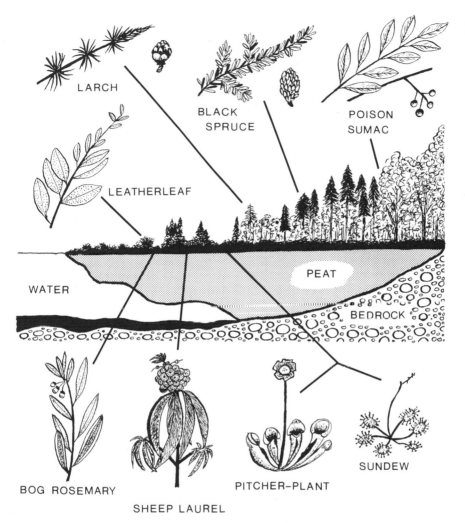

LARCH

BLACK
SPRUCE

POISON
SUMAC

LEATHERLEAF

WATER

PEAT

BEDROCK

BOG ROSEMARY

SHEEP LAUREL

PITCHER–PLANT

SUNDEW

Figure 5.22
Profile of a Pocono peat bog.

through a Pocono peat bog, highlighting these carnivorous plants and other typical bog plants. Table 5.2 lists plants common to Pocono bogs.

Bog Animals

More animals periodically visit bogs for feeding or breeding purposes than actually live there. The acidic, nutrient-poor waters permit only a few specialists to dwell there. Copepods, ciliate protozoans, and rotifers are the limited zooplankton which accompany the desmids and diatoms, the sparse phytoplankton representatives. A few water mites and scuds may be seen dwelling at the edge of the sphagnum mat.

Few fish species are represented in Pocono bogs. However, yellow perch and mud minnows, tolerant of harsh conditions, can be collected in bog waters.

Amphibians and reptiles are not as abundant here as they are in other wetland habitats. Green frogs, pickerel frogs, bullfrogs, spring peepers, and American toads breed here, but breeding choruses are not so boisterous as in marshes, swamps, and ponds. Four-toed salamanders may occasionally be found in the sphagnum mat. An en-

Table 5.2.
Common Plants of the Pocono Bogs

Community structure	Dominants	Associates	
Trees	Black spruce	Black gum	Red maple
	Larch	Gray birch	White pine
		Hemlock	Yellow birch
		Pitch pine	
Shrubs	Bog laurel	Black alder	
	Bog-rosemary	Common alder	
	Highbush blueberry	Labrador tea	
	Huckleberry	Poison sumac	
	Leatherleaf	Rhododendron	
	Sheep laurel	Swamp honeysuckle	
Herbs	Sphagnum moss	Wild calla	
	Pitcher plant	Royal fern	
	Sundew	Chain fern	
	Cranberry	Marsh fern	
	Cottongrass	Dwarf mistletoe	
	Various sedges	Water-willow	
	Various orchids	Other Herbs	

dangered reptile, Muhlenberg's turtle, now more commonly called the bog turtle, is as frequently found in bogs as in other sites, such as pasture land streams. Small (four inches maximum length) and secretive, bog turtles have distinctive orange (rarely, yellow) patches on either side of the head, which readily identify them. If discovered, this endangered reptile should not be molested or removed from its home. Other reptiles seen infrequently in bogs are musk turtles, snapping turtles, water snakes, and garter snakes.

Paths through bogs are used by white-tailed deer, cottontails and their rarer relative, the snowshoe hare, but browsed shrubs and fecal droppings may be the only signs of their presence. Muskrat use the open waterways and mink, their major predator, will be nearby, but rarely seen. Smaller mammals such as star-nosed moles, water shrews, short-tailed shrews, and the bog lemming have been trapped in Pocono bogs by researchers.

Value of Bogs
Bogs are valuable not only because of the unique array of plants and animals but also because they serve as natural flood control areas. When the famous hurricane Diane devastated the Poconos in the summer of 1955, many small bridges in Monroe County were washed away but the Bog Lane bridge south of Tannersville Bog held intact. Bogs are natural sponges. They soak up tremendous amounts of water and then release the pent-up stores to the surrounding streams, when drier conditions occur.

Because of the slow decay rates, pollen deposited thousands of years ago in bog sediments can be extracted and studied to aid our understanding of past vegetational patterns and paleoclimates.

Finally, bogs serve as the source of peat used by gardeners, and Pennsylvania ranks second in peat production in all of the United States. It would perhaps be wiser, in the long run, to preserve bogs as natural wildlife refuges and flood control regions.

Fortunately, a few Pocono bogs have been preserved through the efforts of local citizens with the aid of national conservation organizations. (See Box 5.3 for the location of two Pocono bogs.)

Marshes
A marsh usually has a lake or pond in its ancestry, but marshes are also formed by stream meanders and, especially in the Poconos, by beaver dams. Marsh soil is a dark muck, rich with decaying remains of earlier generations of vegetation. Since marshes are relatively shallow, dissolved oxygen content in the water is sufficient for aqua-

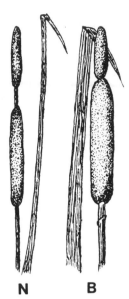

Figure 5.23
Cattails. The rarer narrow-leaved species (N) has a distinctive gap between the upper male flowers and the lower female flowers on the flower stalk. The broad-leaved cattail (B) lacks this feature.

N   **B**

tic plants rooted in the muck. Bacteria can also operate aerobically to break down organic remains. Thus the acidic conditions typical of bog development will not occur. Slow stream flow into the marsh provides additional oxygen-rich water.

Marsh Plants

Marshes are sometimes called "wet grasslands", which is somewhat a misnomer. It is true that an abundance of shallow, standing, or slow-moving water is present. However, many "grasses" are actually sedges and rushes, which closely resemble true grasses. Many sedges have a stem, triangular in cross section. For this reason, the mnemonic "sedges have edges" usually applies. Rushes, even more grasslike in appearance, have flowers borne in clusters near the tip of a round stem.

The plant that best characterizes the marsh is the cattail. Cattails are emergent plants, which flourish even as roots and lower parts of the stem are continuously submerged. (See Figure 5.23, which illustrates the distinctive features of the common broad-leaved cattail and its rarer narrow-leaved relative.)

Amidst the patches of cattails, numerous herbaceous plants will be found; and, where hummocks are formed as herbaceous growth continues, woody plants will take hold. Table 5.3 lists the common cattail marsh associates.

BOX 5.3

Places to See
Pocono Bogs

Tannersville Bog. A national natural landmark, this bog has a 350-foot boardwalk into the bog. Permission to visit the bog must be obtained from the staff of the Messing Nature Center, Stroudsburg, PA 18360. Phone 717-992-7334.

Lacawac Sanctuary. This 400-acre nature preserve is adjacent to Lake Wallenpaupack. A small sphagnum bog borders the picturesque fifty-acre lake that is the focal point of the preserve. The bog is not readily accessible by foot. Tours are sometimes given during the summer. Phone 717-689-9494 for information about hours and arrangements necessary for a visit.

Table 5.3.
Cattail Marsh Plants

Dominants	Associates	
Floating aquatic marsh plants		
Duckweed	Spatterdock	
Emergent semi-aquatic marsh plants		
Broad-leaved cattail	Purple loosestrife	Smartweed
Bur reed	Blue flag	Horsetail
Tussock sedge	Joe-pye weed	Arrow head
Bulrush	Jewelweed	Grasses, spp.
	Boneset	Other sedges
	Narrow-leaved cattail	Other rushes
	Pickerel weed	
Transitional plants on drier hummocks		
Buttonbush	Red maple	
Alder		
Chokeberry		
Blueberry		
Willow		

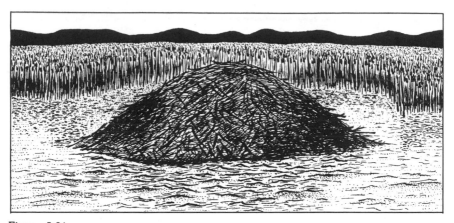

Figure 5.24
Muskrat lodge. The lodge, composed of cut-off cattails and other herbaceous plants, provides a sleeping chamber for one to as many as ten individuals. Beaver lodges are similar but are constructed of heavier, woody materials.

Marsh Animals

If cattails typify a marsh, so do muskrats. These aquatic rodents are well-equipped for swimming, with slightly webbed hind feet and a long, laterally compressed, almost hairless tail, which together serve as efficient oars and scull. Males possess two prominent scent glands, which produce a strong, musky odor, especially at breeding season, and give the species its common name.

In late summer, muskrats quickly build round houses of cattails and other plants in water not more than two feet deep. Where conditions do not permit lodge construction, muskrats dig burrows into the bank. These burrows lead to sleeping chambers above the high water mark. Figure 5.24 shows a muskrat lodge such as those frequently seen in Pocono marshes.

Chiefly vegetarian, muskrats mostly eat a variety of aquatic plants but will consume nearby field corn. Mussels, frogs, and fish are minor dietary items.

Since female muskrats may have three litters per year with five to six young per litter, populations may reach fifteen to twenty individuals per acre. Many predators including northern harriers, larger owls, snapping turtles, water snakes, weasels, raccoons, foxes, and, especially, mink help to control population levels of this rodent.

Most of the predators mentioned above are hard to find when one visits a marsh. Even smaller prey species which dwell among the marsh vegetation such as the shorttailed shrew, meadow vole, and deer mice are a rare sight.

Amphibians and reptiles found in or near other aquatic habitats are present also in marshes. Some species such as spring peepers, green frogs, bullfrogs, snapping turtles, and garter snakes may be more abundant here than elsewhere.

Decker Marsh, located alongside U. S. Route 6 about one mile east of Lake Wallenpaupack, is a wildlife refuge established by the Pennsylvania Game Commission. This is an accessible site for the study of marsh plants and animals. Other marshes are scattered throughout the Poconos. Most of these are in the natural areas of Delaware State Forest, in state game lands, and in state parks, especially Promised Land.

Swamps

If marshes are considered wet grasslands, then swamps may be thought of as wet woodlands. The shrubs, and the occasional tree, present on hummocks in a marsh eventually spread over the area —producing first a shrub swamp, then a wooded swamp. Shrubs such as buttonbush, blueberry, chokeberry, alders, and willows form dense thickets. Humans have difficulty in penetrating such dense thickets, but some animals make the attempt and are rewarded by a meal of ripe berries. Black bear are visitors to shrub swamps at berrytime. Cottontails and snowshoe hares live year-round amidst the tangled growth. White-tailed deer use the swamp for winter feeding yards.

Transformation to Wooded Swamp

The drier conditions created by shrub growth favor the invasion of more trees. In the Poconos, the trees that initiate the transformation from shrub swamp to wooded swamp are red maples, also appropriately called swamp maple. Black gum, yellow birch, swamp white oak, white ash, and an occasional hemlock and white pine are other species found in Pocono wooded swamps.

The dense shade and somewhat soggy soil permit a limited number of ground cover and understory species. Skunk cabbage with its broad, bright green leaves is so consistently present that it serves as an indicator plant of wooded swamps. Figure 5.25 shows the distinctive flower of skunk cabbage.

Other herbs and shrubs have adapted to the shady, moist condi-

Hood–
3-6"

Figure 5.25
Skunk cabbage. The distinctive
hooded, purple blossom is one of the
first signs of spring. The bright green
leaves appear shortly thereafter.
When bruised, the plant emits a
smelly, skunklike odor.

tions. Those herbs, shrubs, and trees typical of Pocono wooded swamps are listed in Table 5.4.

Wooded Swamp Animals

Some amphibians are more common in wet woods than in more aquatic habitats. These animals include several species of lungless salamanders. Most common is the red-backed salamander, which usually has a broad dorsal stripe of dark red. In some members of the population, the red stripe is replaced by a dark gray or black band, producing the "lead-backed" color phase. Closely related, the slimy salamander is found in the same places one discovers the red-backed salamander—that is, under logs, flat rocks, and forest litter. The jet- black slimy salamander has silvery-white flecks scattered over the back and sides. If one handles this animal, its common name will soon be evident as a sticky mucus is quickly released from skin glands. This defensive behavior protects the slimy salamander from some potential predators.

The frog species one is likely to encounter in wet woods is the wood frog. Easily recognized by its "black mask" (markings at and behind the eye region), wood frogs are among the earliest breeders in spring. The male's breeding call sounds more like a duck quacking than a frog croaking. Spring peepers, gray tree frogs, the related

Table 5.4.
Pocono Wooded Swamp Plants

Community structure	Dominants	Associates
Trees	Red maple	White ash
	Swamp white oak	Black gum
	Yellow birch	American elm
		Hemlock
		White pine
Shrubs	Spicebush	Alder
	Buttonbush	Swamp azalea
	Shadbush	Chokeberry
		Blueberry
		Viburnum spp.
Herbs	Skunk cabbage	Jack-in-the-pulpit
	Royal fern	False hellebore
	Cinnamon fern	Sensitive fern
		Gold thread

chorus and cricket frogs (uncommon and at the limits of their range in the Poconos), and the far-ranging American toad live in wooded swamps. Reptiles such as box and wood turtles and snakes, particularly garter, ribbon, and milk snakes, are present here.

Skunks, opossums, and raccoons are found in many habitats. These habitats include mature wooded swamps. If you search carefully during your visit, you may discover a raccoon or a family of 'possums, such as those shown in Figure 5.26, spending the daylight hours resting in the upper fork of an old tree.

Short-tailed shrews and star-nosed moles, smaller, secretive mammals, are common, if seldom seen, swamp dwellers.

Most Pocono swamps are located on public lands, especially state game lands near Shohola Falls, Tobyhanna and Camelback Mountain, Hickory Run and Promised Land State Park, and Stillwater and Buckhorn Natural Areas in Delaware State Forest.

One can reach a readily accessible wooded swamp by hiking

Figure 5.26
Opossum family. After a photograph, courtesy Carolina Biological Supply Co.

about one mile along the Blooming Grove 4-H Trail located in Delaware State Forest. A parking area is available west of Route 402, approximately two miles north of the Route 402–Interstate 84 junction. The trail starts at the Pennsylvania Power and Light Company utility easement, goes through a mixed oak forest and past a wet meadow, probably a beaver pond a few decades ago. The trail then reaches the wooded swamp, which has some good-sized yellow birch, red maple, and white ash. Several mature hemlocks and white pine are scattered among the hardwoods. Don't forget the insect repellent if you visit in summer!

Birds of Aquatic Communities

As discussed in Chapter 4, birds are the most mobile of all vertebrates, which makes the task of "pigeonholing" harder than the term

BOX 5.4

Places to Observe Wetlands

Shohola Waterfowl Management Area. State Game Lands 180 along Route 6, Shohola Falls.

Bruce Lake Natural Area. Panther Swamp Trail, off Egypt Meadows Trail. (See description for Bruce Lake in Chapter 5.)

Tobyhanna State Park. Trail along Jim Smith Run and aside of Bender Swamp; starts at Tobyhanna Lake Trail.

Decker Marsh. On State Game Lands 183 along Route 6 east of Hawley.

Delaware State Forest. Stillwater Natural Area, one mile west of Edgemere; Pennel Run Natural Area, two miles west of Twelve Mile Pond; Buckhorn Natural Area, one mile east of Pond Eddy; Pine Lake, two miles north of Greentown; Blooming Grove 4-H Trail (see description in Chapter 5).

Brady's Lake. Pennsylvania Fish Commission facility off of Route 940 near Pocono Lake.

usually implies. However, Table 4.1 indicates the habitats where a particular species of bird is most likely to be observed and, thus, should be of help to visitors attempting to verify a particular observation. Aquatic settings are ideal for observing varied wildlife including birds. Waterfowl and related species frequent many of the birding sites listed in Box 4.1. Even the smallest pond may serve as a brief resting place for migrating birds. The familiar Canada goose, in settings observed by many visitors, is shown in Figure 5.27.

An Abundance of Aquatic Communities

The Poconos have varied and accessible aquatic sites. The gradational and evolving nature of watercourse and wetland communities results in an amazing diversity of plants and animals.

Figure 5.27
Canada goose. A. Characteristic "black stocking" neck. B. Typical V-formation with High Point State Park (New Jersey) monument. C. As observed on water.

Since the distribution and abundance of biota is variable, it may at times be frustrating to be unable to put an identification label on a particular plant or animal that doesn't appear to be in the "right spot." Nevertheless, your visits will be amply rewarded as you experience the beauty and intricacy of these fascinating aquatic ecosystems.

CHAPTER 6

Roadside Natural History

"I often see flowers from a passing car / that
are gone before I can tell what they are."
—ROBERT FROST, "A Passing Glimpse"

Even if the Pocono visitor chooses not to hike into the bogs, swamps, or woodlands, he will still have an opportunity to see and learn some of the close-at-hand natural history—that of the roadsides. In fact, the average vacationer will probably see more of this kind of natural history than that of any other because of its proximity to human activity.

What Is an Ecotone?

An ecotone is a transition between two (or more) diverse communities. One might think of it as a tension zone or a juncture zone of linear extent and much narrower than the two adjoining communities. Hence, a roadside is such an ecotone between a road rubble strip and the adjoining fields or forests. Also in this category are power and utility line rights-of-way, junctures of fields and forests, and in a limited way, the edge between one's property and a neighbor's.

Several general features make these ecotones distinct from the "intact" communities of swamps, woodlands, and plantations. Because they are junctures, they are not wide. A narrow road border along a cornfield may be but a few feet wide; along an interstate highway the transition zone to an adjacent forest may be dozens of feet wide; and, along a utility line corridor, even wider. Although narrow, eco-

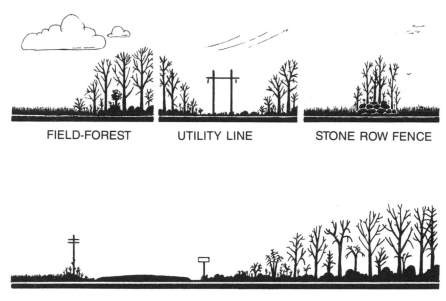

FIELD-FOREST   UTILITY LINE   STONE ROW FENCE

FIELD-ROADWAY-FOREST EDGE

Figure 6.1
Some common ecotone (edge) types. These edges typically have a greater variety
and density of plants and animals than their adjacent habitats.

tones typically harbor a diverse and dense flora and fauna, for in
these transition zones one finds species of both adjacent communities
as well as those of the transition zone. Such a tendency is called
edge effect. Such an effect is well-known to bird watchers, for it is at
these edges where one can find a large number of species in a short
time. Parts of ecotones typically have a disturbed soil, which encour-
ages a large number of the weed species, such as dandelion, black-
eyed Susan, Queen Anne's lace, etc. Hence, there is much similarity
in early abandoned fields and ecotones. In this chapter, all the plants
of roadsides, ecotones in general, abandoned fields, and "waste
places" are treated together.

While the term ecotone, as here applied, is appropriate, the term
is also used to describe the broad transition between major communities, as—for example—when the Mixed Oak forest of the Poconos

grades into the Northern Hardwoods. That band is more of a continuum, with a gradual blending.

Man, the Ecotone Creator

Wherever man settles, he creates ecotones. A "second home" in the Pocono forest has a small patch of cleared and maintained land surrounded by a forest. If the home is built in a field, trees are quickly planted to create an edge. If a home is built in the city, hedges and fences both define the property and establish an edge. It seems that humans are an edge-species; and, with the continuing development of roads, golf fairways, utility line corridors and the like, an increasing number of edges act to break up the continuum of the environment.

It is unfortunate that much roadside edge is "maintained" through chemical and mechanical means, for left to its own course, it generally would perpetuate itself in an interesting tangle of roadside weeds (or, wildflowers, or both, depending on how one defines them!).

One of the most successful ways of handling the wider and steeper roadside rights-of-way, and without having to resort to extensive control methods, has been the use of crown vetch.

Crown Vetch, a Special Case

Crown vetch is a perennial member of the bean family (legumes) that grows about one to two feet tall and produces a heavy set of pink-purplish flowers in an inflorescence, loosely described as a "crown." The genus name of the plant is *Coronilla*, in reference to its crown-like assemblage of flowers. It has been extensively planted by the Pennsylvania Department of Highways for slope control, and one cannot travel in the Poconos without seeing many fine stands of crown vetch.

Crown vetch is much used for several reasons. It produces attractive flowers through most of the summer. Its extensive and multi-branched root system helps stabilize the soil. As a spreading perennial legume, it needs virtually no maintenance. It is disease free, drought tolerant, and, if properly and densely grown, it essentially excludes other invading plants.

The only apparent liability of this otherwise utilitarian plant is that

Figure 6.2
Crown vetch. The tangled mat of weakly erect plants and their pink-purple flowering "crowns" are a common site along Pocono roadsides through the summer.

it is not evergreen; thus, the roadsides have a rather drab brown look through the winter months. During this period, it is flammable—hence not used on less accessible utility line corridors.

Several varieties of crown vetch are commercially available. The *Penngift* variety is most widely used in the Commonwealth. Much of the research on this interesting plant was done at the Pennsylvania State University.

Roadside Plants

What sort of list of plants would be appropriate for the Pocono roadsides? Ten, a hundred, a thousand? Ten is obviously too elementary. A thousand? That number would, quite probably, be close to the truth but demand exhaustive lists of grasses, sedges, and inconspicuous plants reserved for the professional. So, a compromise assemblage of plants one might commonly see along roadsides, rights-of-way, abandoned fields, and waste places, is included. The organization that follows is somewhat synthetic but quick and easy to use.

Woody Trees and Shrubs. Any edge will, in part, be a reflection of the forested area through which the open area has been cut. Hence, reference to the earlier Figures 3.2, 3.5, 3.8, 3.9, 3.10, 3.14, 3.17, 3.24, and 3.29 will be helpful in identifying the woody-edge species of the area of interest. Many of the abandoned-field woody plants, common to edges were illustrated in Figure 3.20. High on the list of edge

BOX 6.1

Where to See Crown Vetch

Newer, limited access roads (such as routes 9, 33, 80, 84, and 380) are often bordered with crown vetch. The planting is especially used at overpasses and on steep banks.

species are sassafras, gray birch, the aspens, and several varieties of sumac.

Woody Vines. The woody vines, illustrated in Figure 3.11, are common along the edges throughout the Poconos. Poison Ivy and Virginia creeper are most prevalent, although the introduced honeysuckle, a plant with opposite, entire, and simple leaves, is becoming more common.

Ferns. Some of the most common ferns of the Poconos were illustrated in Figure 3.22. On moist ground and along roadside ditches, the most common ferns are the sensitive, royal, and interrupted. Although all die back over the winter, the persistent reproductive stalks of the sensitive fern are easily identified throughout the year. On drier ground, the hayscented and brake (also called the bracken fern) are most common ferns, often forming large patches to the exclusion of most other plants. Occasionally, horsetails and clubmosses may be seen. If the roadside borders on a swamp, a rocky cliff, or a mature forest, some of the ferns common to those habitats may be close to the roadside.

Herbaceous Plants. The zenith of variety is reached with the roadside edge herbaceous plants, for this area harbors not only some of the native plants from adjoining habitats (Figures 3.12 and 3.13), but it is the site of most of the introduced plants, common weeds, and garden escapees. The plants range in size from the occasional colonies of the tall (twelve-foot) *Phragmites* reed to the tiny chickweeds; in looks, from the pretty black-eyed Susan to the ugly plaintain; and, in cost, from the allergy-causing ragweed to the innocuous yellow buttercups. Distribution patterns further compound the variety, for in one small locality a given wildflower may be very abundant but sparse elsewhere.

Many of the roadside plants are annuals—they reproduce each season by a new crop of seeds. By comparison, most of the wildflowers of the woodlands are perennial and, using stored food reserves of their underground parts, flower in the spring. Roadside flowers tend to flower later, and the summer and early fall seasons are most interesting for the Pocono roadside naturalist.

As an aid to the identification of roadside herbaceous plants, the visual approach is used in Figures 6.3–6.6; the illustrated plants, in turn, are grouped by color. Where features other than color are important, such as fruits, leaves, etc., these are highlighted. Because of the widespread nature of these roadside plants, the figures are applicable to much of the northeast.

Ecotone Animals

Since the varied environmental conditions of ecotones promote a diverse and abundant flora, especially wildflowers and other herbaceous plants, it is not surprising that an array of animals use these plants for food and shelter.

Invertebrate Dwellers of Ecotones

As in other communities, invertebrates are well-represented in ecotones, although frequently not as well-studied or provided with common names as are many plants and vertebrates. In summer, close examination of herbaceous matter should reveal invertebrates, particularly insects, so varied as to defy brief, meaningful descriptions.

A few such as the large brown "flying grasshopper," the grotesque praying mantis, and the superb mimic, the walking stick, are familiar to most country road walkers. Careful examination of flowers and soft herbaceous plant parts should reward the observer with glimpses of less well-known species. Beetles, caterpillarlike larvae, and adults with shiny, metallic-colored wing covers, are numerous. Japanese beetles, ladybird beetles, and weevils are just a few representatives of this large group of insects. Leafhoppers, bugs with piercing-sucking mouthparts, are abundant. As they feed, they exude "honeydew," actually surplus plant sap, which attracts ants and bees. A closely related insect, the spittlebug, attracts attention because of the white froth which the female makes on plant stems to cover her eggs. Other bugs, larger and more colorful, include squash bugs, stink bugs, and milkweed bugs. The latter, as the name suggests, are specific to one type of plant. The black and orange markings of these bugs as well as their presence on milkweed plants make identification easy. Also conspicuous because of their markings are bees and wasps. Since they are attracted to the same flowers and fruits

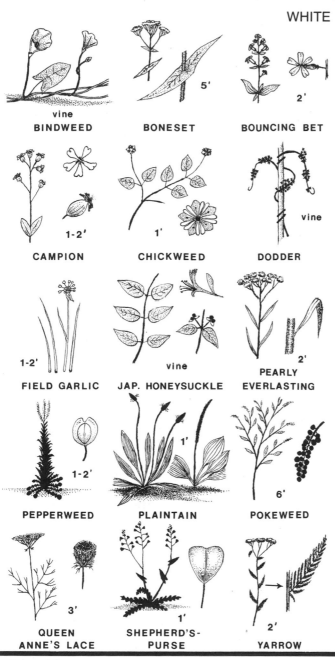

Figure 6.3
Common white roadside flowers. Heights are average for all figures. Colors may vary.

YELLOW

BLACK-EYED SUSAN

BUTTERCUP

BUTTER 'N EGGS

CINQUEFOIL

COLTSFOOT

DANDELION

EVENING PRIMROSE

FIELD DAISY

FLEABANE

GOLDENROD

HAWKWEED

MULLEIN

MUSTARD

STICKTIGHT

ST. JOHNSWORT

SWEET CLOVER

WILD PARSNIP

WOOD SORREL

Figure 6.4
Common yellow roadside flowers.

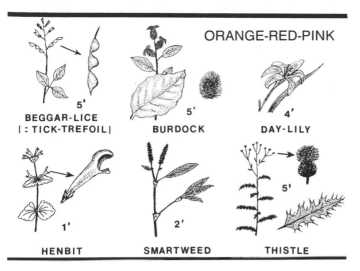

ORANGE-RED-PINK

BEGGAR-LICE
[: TICK-TREFOIL] 5'

BURDOCK 5'

DAY-LILY 4'

HENBIT 1'

SMARTWEED 2'

THISTLE 5'

BLUE-VIOLET

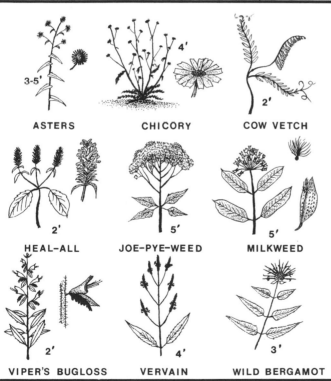

ASTERS 3-5'

CHICORY 4'

COW VETCH 2'

HEAL-ALL 2'

JOE-PYE-WEED 5'

MILKWEED 5'

VIPER'S BUGLOSS 2'

VERVAIN 4'

WILD BERGAMOT 3'

Figure 6.5
Common orange, red-pink, and blue-violet roadside flowers.

GREEN

COCKLEBUR 4'   DOCK 3'   FOXTAIL 2'

LAMBSQUARTER 2'   ORCHARD GRASS 2'   RAGWEED 4'

REED   SHEEP SORREL 1'   STINGING NETTLE 3'

Figure 6.6
Common green roadside flowers.

that attract human attention, most of us have become acquainted with these insects in a most painful manner. The large paper nest of the bald-faced hornet usually remains undetected until leaves fall in autumn, when it is sure to attract the attention of the ecotone traveler. Invertebrates other than insects are also well represented in ecotones. Spiders of various sizes and shapes, snails, slugs, sowbugs, centipedes, and millipedes will be spotted by the careful observer.

The invertebrate groups that attract the most interest of ecotone visitors are butterflies and moths. Butterflies, especially, are brightly colored, active in the daytime, slow moving, and can usually be approached closely enough to insure identification. Caterpillars are frequently as showy as the adults. Many caterpillars possess distinctive color markings, spines, and other features that make them an interesting discovery for the ecotone visitor. Moths tend to feed at night and are attracted to lights where a visitor can examine them close up. Here too, larvae are often conspicuous. One, the woollybear (the larva of the Isabella moth), is abundant in autumn. Although the orange band that separates the black front and hind ends does indeed vary in width, these variations are not the predictor of winter severity that myth suggests.

Two insect endeavors are sure to attract the attention of travelers. Tent caterpillars, in the spring, and webworms, in late summer and early fall, spin prominent silken thread nests in roadside and forest-edge trees. The familiar and ugly nests, along with the less familiar adult moths, are illustrated in Figure 6.7. Although the caterpillar tents are disfiguring, the damage in general is minimal. Removal and disposal is the simplest control method. A summary and comparison of the natural history of these two insects is included in Table 6.1

Vertebrate Ecotone Representatives

Numerous vertebrates also utilize the diverse flora of ecotones for food and shelter. Unlike most invertebrates, vertebrates show greater mobility and may exploit ecotones for brief periods before moving on to other habitats. Birds and mammals are the primary representatives seen here and, in fact, the more open conditions of ecotones may permit the visitor the best views of certain Pocono animals. As indicated earlier, birds are so mobile, widespread, and adaptable

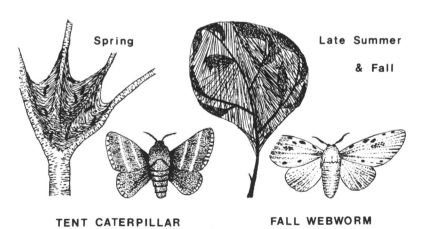

Spring

Late Summer

& Fall

TENT CATERPILLAR   **FALL WEBWORM**

Figure 6.7
Tent caterpillar and fall webworm. See also Table 6.1.

that they are considered separately in the book. Suffice it to state here, certain species such as American kestrel, kingbirds, robins, eastern bluebirds, chipping sparrows, and northern mockingbirds are conspicuous edge species.

Among mammals, woodchucks, striped skunks, opossums, raccoons, porcupines, eastern cottontails, and white-tailed deer are species one sees more often along roadsides than in more natural settings. Sadly, some of these observations are of dead animals usually killed at dusk or evening, times when many mammals are active. Occasionally the largest of Pocono mammals, the black bear, is sighted along roads. It, too, may have a sad fate as approximately forty black bears are reported as highway kills each year in the Poconos. Some of the smaller mammals such as shrews, moles, and mice are typical ecotone inhabitants, but their presence is often undetected until a dead roadside specimen is discovered.

In contrast, most amphibians and reptiles are uncommon along roadsides and other ecotones. Snakes are the exception here, as they use sunny sites for basking at certain seasons, mainly early spring and autumn. Species such as milk, garter, ringneck, red-bellied, and hognose snakes may be spotted on a sunny roadbank, grassy strip, or other open place. Snakes seek the warmth retained by paved roadways during cooler evenings and then, unfortunately, many are crushed by cars. Box and wood turtles also wander through open areas in midsummer. Rainy nights, especially in early spring, are a time when a slow drive on a country road may reveal frogs, toads, and salamanders moving to breeding sites.

Walks along country roads, powerline rights-of-way, and forest edges can be some of the most rewarding times for the Pocono visitor to get good views of animals generally only glimpsed in other habitats. The sad but frequent sight of a dead animal is also a reminder of just one of the many hazards facing wildlife. This sight, however, can be an impetus to the visitor to search more diligently for a view of a living representative of the species.

The Changing Natural History

The roadside flora and fauna is not static. As introduced species spread (deliberately, as with the case of *Penngift* crown vetch, or inadvertently, as with many of the weeds) they become part of the environment. In many cases, their presence goes almost unnoticed,

Table 6.1.
A Comparison of Two Common Nest (Tent) Building Insects along
Pocono Roadsides

Natural history features	Eastern tent caterpillar	Fall webworm
Season of nests	Spring to early summer	Late summer to fall
Nest location	Fork of branches	Tips of branches
Favored tree species	Wild cherry, poplar, apple, and other fruit trees	Black walnut, butternut, cherry, etc.
Overwintering stage	Eggs	Pupae encased in a cocoon
Generations per year	One	Two
Egg hatching and nest building	Early spring; caterpillars build nests in spring	Spring *and* summer (two generations); second cycle (*only*) of caterpillars builds nests in the late summer
Caterpillar description	Hairy and black with blue spots and brown and yellow lines	Hairy and pale yellow with brown or black spots
Adult moths	Tan; fore-wings have two pale lines	White-winged; fore-wings with dark spots
Damage and control	Minimal; remove and destroy nests	Ugly, but not serious; remove and destroy nests

while in others, like the spreading Japanese honeysuckle or the ubiquitous starling, they become a conspicuous part of the changing natural history. About a fourth of our eastern plants have been introduced, which suggests the changeable nature of "current" lists.

Additionally, many of the plants do hybridize, or cross; this fact adds both some changes to the plant composition and also, because of the blending effect, some frustration to the novice.

CHAPTER 7

Human Activity from Native Americans to Vacationers

"What!" said Tecumseh. "Sell land! As well
sell air and water. The Great Spirit gave
them in common to all."
—Quoted by John Collier, *The Indians of the
Americas*, 1947

Archaeologists believe that the first migrant hunters crossed from
Siberia into Alaska by way of an exposed Bering Sea land bridge.
This may have occurred about 15,000 years ago, although some
scholars argue for an even earlier entry. The Paleo-Indians gradually drifted south, and after the retreat of the Wisconsin glacier—about 13,000 B.C.—moved into northeastern Pennsylvania. There is some evidence that Paleo-Indians were here as early as
10,000 B.C.

The Paleo-Indian Period (circa 10,000–8000 B.C.)

An important archaeological excavation that promises to increase
our understanding of the earliest Pocono inhabitants is the Shawnee-
Minisink site, located on a river terrace at the confluence of Brodhead
Creek and the Delaware River in Monroe County. Fluted-type spear
points, sometimes called Eastern Clovis points after the town in New
Mexico of this distinctive spearpoint's discovery, were unearthed
at the site along with scrapers, knives, and other stone tools. Ra-
diocarbon dates obtained from the earliest levels of this site suggest a time from 9100 B.C. to 7300 B.C. for this Paleo-Indian

occupation. The excavations also revealed unidentifiable fish bones,
along with carbonized wild hawthorn pits that may be from the earliest time periods.

Paleo-Indians spent much time in hunting and gathering. Deer, elk, and caribou were important game, but many smaller mammals and birds were also killed. On very rare occasions, a group of cooperating hunters may have been fortunate enough to kill a mastodon, but no evidence for such activity exists in the East. Two mastodon fossils sites at Marshalls Creek unfortunately revealed no associated artifacts.

The Archaic Period (8000 B.C.-1000 B.C.)

During the long Archaic period a great variety of spearpoint types came into being. Many of these were hurled with the aid of spear throwers. Knives, scrapers, drills, and gravers were among the utilitarian implements chipped from fine-grained stones. Grooved axes, adzes, and an occasional gouge were the woodworking tools that enabled the people of Archaic times to cut down trees and make dugout canoes and wooden mortars and pestles. In addition to the latter, millingstones and mullers were used to grind nuts and seeds into flour and meal. Notched netsinkers attest to the use of fish nets, as well as bolas stones attached to a throwing device to entangle large marsh birds. The Archaic peoples doubtless made basket and bark containers, but none of these have survived.

Most of the vegetable food was eaten raw. Meats and fish were roasted over an open fire. Cooking in bark vessels or skin containers was possible with the immersion of fire-heated stones, but it was a laborious process. The end of the Archaic period ushered in the use of cooking pots made from steatite (or, soapstone). Steatite kettles could be placed directly over the fire because soapstone transmits heat and does not crack.

The Woodland Period (1000 B.C.-1570 A.D.)

This period, characterized by forests and animals like those of today, is the era of developed native American culture. It differs from earlier cultures due to three major shifts in tribal life which had developed gradually through the last few millennia of the Archaic period. These shifts were (1) a more settled village life, (2) the introduction of horticulture or gardening farming, and (3) more extensive use of ceramics.

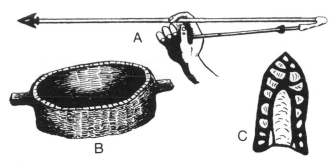

Figure 7.1
Native American artifacts
A. Spear thrower (atlatl). Developed during the Archaic
   Period, enabled the hunter to throw his spear farther
   and harder.
B. Soapstone (steatite) bowl. Characteristic of the Terminal
   Late Archaic Period, these vessels were used in cooking.
C. Fluted (Clovis) point. Best-known artifact of the
   Paleo-Indian Period, a small spearhead distinguished
   by a channel along one or both faces of the blade.

Many excavations on both sides of the upper Delaware River Valley have revealed stone tools relating to hunting, fishing, and food
processing activities. The bow and arrow were now the preferred
weapons of the chase. Fishnets weighted with notched stone net sink-
ers, and fencelike fish weirs, were the most commonly used methods
of gathering large numbers of fish, especially during the spring shad
runs. Traps and snares were also used, but evidence has not survived. Corn, beans, and a variety of squash grown in the gardens
now supplemented wild plant foods, roots, nuts, and berries. Clay
cooking pots were present in substantial numbers. Postmolds, or organic stains from houseposts once thrust into the ground, provide evidence for the outline of native American houses. Some of these bark
dwellings were oval, but others were round-ended longhouses with
an entrance on one of the long sides. One such house pattern discovered on the Miller Field site, on the New Jersey side of the Delaware
River, measured sixty by twenty feet. There were several partitions
within the house, and benches along one wall provided a place to sit
in the daytime and sleep at night. Such a house was occupied by an
extended family, all of whose members were related through the
women—a matrilineage. Gardens were usually located near the
house. A section of forest trees and shrubs had to be cut down and
burned so that sunlight might penetrate. Wood ash helped to fertilize

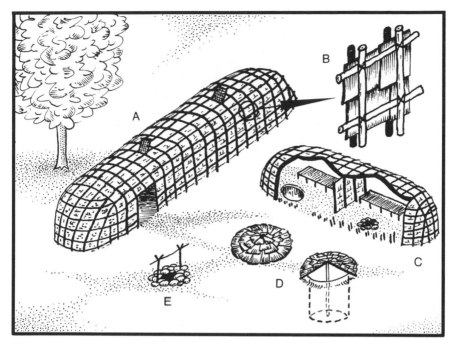

Figure 7.2
Bark-covered longhouse typical of the Woodland Period.
A. Exterior view.
B. Detail of construction technique for walls and roof.
C. Interior view with family compartments and cooking and storage areas.
D. Storage pit.
E. Open hearth and split.
Drawing modified from H. C. Kraft, in *The Minisink*, 1975.

the soil. Hoes made from chipped stone blades, or the shoulder blades of deer or elk, were attached to wooden handles and served to loosen the soil. Pointed sticks were used to plant the seeds. Corn, beans, and squash were the primary cultivated crops, but sunflower and some herbs may have been grown as well. It is not known if tobacco (*Nicotiana rustica*) was also grown here, but the Indians did smoke other aromatic leaves in clay tobacco pipes.

Lenape or Delaware

The native people who lived in the Pocono area in late prehistoric times were known as the Minisink. They were one of many bands that comprised the northern or Munsee-speaking Lenape tribe of native Americans. The Lenape, meaning "common" or "ordinary" people, were also called "Delaware" after the seventeenth century because so many of them resided along the Delaware River. The English were responsible for renaming this river to honor Sir Thomas West, Lord de la Warr, the first governor of Virginia colony.

Archaeological evidence suggests that the Lenape developed out of prehistoric native American cultures that had existed in Lenapehoking for many hundreds of years. Lenapehoking, the "Land of the Lenape" included all of New Jersey, eastern Pennsylvania, northern Delaware, and southeastern New York. By A.D. 1000, the Minisink bands of the Lenape were already well established in the upper Delaware River Valley. Their bark-covered longhouses and associated gardens were located along both sides of the river above the Delaware Water Gap.

The Delaware River and its tributaries provided these Minisink with an abundance of fish and freshwater mussels. The almost stone-free floodplains near the river were fertile, well-drained, and easy to work with simple digging sticks and stone hoes. Nearby woodlands and forests provided an abundance of saplings and bark for house construction, firewood, and nuts. Mast foods sustained turkeys, black bear, deer, elk, and other game animals. This diverse environment enabled the Minisink to hunt, fish, and gather an abundance of edible wild plant foods, while raising corn, beans, squash, and sunflowers in their gardens. The people were peaceful, their houses were dispersed and unfortified, and life was satisfying.

The coming of the white settlers in the seventeenth century changed the Minisink way of life in significant ways. European traders introduced iron axes, adzes, and brass kettles that simplified the native Americans' labors, and glass beads, mirrors, bangles, and other trinkets as well. Other European contributions had more disastrous effects. Epidemic diseases and alcohol decimated native populations and demoralized those who survived. Religious intolerance, suspicion, and greed proved to be major obstacles to the integration of native people into the new Euro-American way of life. The native Americans were shunned and pushed relentlessly westward. The Minisink in the Pocono-Kittatinny region managed to hold out longer than other Lenape bands, but, in the Treaty of Easton in 1758, they too were forced to relinquish their ancestral homelands in the upper Delaware River Valley. In time, most of these Minisink and other Munsee-speaking Lenape bands resettled in Ontario, Canada, where their descendants live today.

White People in a Native American World

In 1609, Henry Hudson entered the region now known as New York harbor. Shortly thereafter, Dutch merchant traders began to exchange items of European manufacture for the native Americans' beaver, otter, and martin pelts, and deer skins. Lumber, minerals, and other commodities were also exploited.

According to the legend of the Old Mine Road, seventeenth-century Dutch prospectors discovered copper in the Kittatinny Mountains at Pahaquarra on the New Jersey side of the Delaware River about ten miles north of the Delaware Water Gap. To transport the extracted copper, the Dutch miners allegedly constructed a 104-mile-long road from Pahaquarra to Esopus (now Kingston, New York), where the ore was transferred to ships bound for Holland. A bronze plaque along the Old Mine Road once proclaimed this road as "the oldest commercial highway in the nation."

In fact, there is no archaeological, historical, or cartographic evidence that this enterprise existed in the mid-seventeenth century. The early Dutch records are not specific, and the finding of "good and pure ore" in the region between Manhattan and the South River (Dutch name for the Delaware River) probably refers to the Navesink region in present-day Monmouth County, New Jersey, rather than the Neversink River area near Port Jervis in the upper Delaware River valley.

It is unlikely that the Dutch ever mined copper in the Pocono-Kittatinny region. The mineral outcroppings here are not pure copper, but a low grade cupric oxide. The seventeenth-century Dutch miners had no way of processing this mineral. Even if the Dutch did intend to remove this unprofitable ore-bearing rock, they would have done so at the peril of their lives. There were no fortifications and no garrisons to protect the Dutch in this hostile wilderness. The native Americans throughout Lenapehoking were deeply disturbed by the often brutal actions of the Dutch at New Amsterdam. In 1634, Director Willem Kieft ordered the massacre of an entire village of the Hackensack tribe at Pavonia (now Jersey City, New Jersey), and attacks were also carried out in other parts of the circum-Manhattan area. The Dutch had broken treaties, cheated the native Americans, and alienated most of them. In consequence, there was open hostility from about 1634 until the English captured New Netherland in 1664. Many Esopus, Tappan, Hackensack, Raritan, and other dispossessed tribal bands moved into the Minisink region. They would not have been favorably disposed to any Dutch miners in this area.

Cartographic evidence shows no road leading to the Pahaquarra mines until the mid-nineteenth century. The usual route of travel in the upper Delaware Valley was from Easton or Stroudsburg north along the Pennsylvania side to Flatbrook or Minisink Island, where crossings might be made. Alternatively, a road crossed from Blairstown, New Jersey over the Kittatinny Mountains to Millbrook and north. The surveyor, John Reading, visited the Pahaquarra area in 1719. He kept a meticulous diary but makes no mention of copper mines or of a mine road.

The earliest known native American-European contact in the Minisink region was by Captain Arent Schuyler. Although he later established one of the most profitable copper mines at Arlington, New Jersey, he was unaware of any copper in the Minisink region and made no mention of such ore in his official report. Indeed, every commercial operation of the Pahaquarra copper mines up to the twentieth century failed or went into bankruptcy.

Before William Penn's "Holy Experiment," human impact in the Poconos by native Americans and settlers was minimal. Since Pennsylvania was one of the last colonies to be settled, the region remained wilderness until pressure from European settlers caused an influx of native Americans from Maryland and the Carolinas.

Penn petitioned Charles II for land to establish a colony in the New World dedicated to political and religious freedom. A charter was granted March 4, 1681, and the first arrivals to "Penn's Woods" came with Captain John Smith later the same year. Shortly after William Penn himself arrived in October 1682, he initiated meetings with the Lenape. Under the famous "Treaty Elm" near the banks of the Delaware in southeastern Pennsylvania, pledges of everlasting faith and trust were made by Penn and Chief Tammany on behalf of their peoples.

The white population grew rapidly during the first sixty years of Pennsylvania colonial existence. By 1740, 100,000 Europeans of various nationalities were attracted to the colony. Most settled in the southeastern part of the colony, with Philadelphia alone having a population of 10,000. At that time four-fifths of present-day Pennsylvania was in native American territory. However, the native American population in 1740 was believed to be scarcely 5000 in contrast to the 15,000 estimated in 1600. The Kittatinny or Blue Mountain marked a dividing line between the scattered white settlements of the southeastern section of the colony and the more widely scattered native American villages throughout the rest of the territory.

Colonial Landscape

The first white settler on the Pennsylvania side of the Delaware north of the Blue Mountain was Nicholas DePuy (DePui). Records indicate that a "Nicklas Depue" acquired 300 acres of land from the "Indian owners" in 1727. As the monument in Shawnee, near the original site, indicates, Nicholas was a grandson of Nicholas DePuy, a Huguenot refugee from Artois, France, who had arrived in New Netherland in 1622. Shortly after DePuy purchased his land, he constructed a large stone mansion that became a conspicuous frontier landmark and a place of importance during the subsequent Indian Wars.

Tom Quick, Sr., settled in the vicinity of present-day Milford in 1733. His son, Tom, Jr., was to become the legendary "Avenger of the Delaware" who sought revenge for his father's killing by an Indian in 1756. Whether Tom was a buckskin hero or psychopathic killer was debated by the local populace even as a monument to father and son was being dedicated in Milford in August 1886. The monument still stands, and visitors to the borough may read the inscription to learn more about Tom Quick.

Another early settler, Daniel Brodhead, came—as did most immigrants at this time—from the north (Albany, New York in his case) and settled in 1736 in what is now Stroudsburg (then called Dansburg). He and other whites dwelt harmoniously with the Lenape, but when surveyors were sent by the Proprietors of Pennsylvania to survey the DePuy land, native American neighbors told the surveyors to "put up iron string and go home," as they promptly did. The harmonious conditions in the Upper Delaware Valley were soon to be shattered by events occurring in the southeastern part of Penn's colony.

Shortly after William Penn's death in 1718, Penn's three sons became Proprietors (1727). They held a council with Chief Nutimas of the Delawares and confronted him with a questionable deed intimating that land "as far as a man can go in a day and a half" had been sold to William Penn in 1686. After two more years of intense persuasion by the Proprietors, the Delaware agreed to a walk to take place in the autumn of 1737.

Prior to the walk, Thomas Penn searched for athletic woodsmen, and, after their selection, had them secretly blaze a trail through the woods. At daybreak, September 19, 1737, the "walkers" Edward Marshall, James Yates, and Solomon Jennings began the walk at Wrightstown, Bucks County. Late in the day, Jennings and two Delaware walkers quit, but by sunset Marshall and Yates were camped north of the Blue Mountain. The next day Yates fell from exhaustion shortly after the hike resumed and he too gave up. Yates died three days later. Marshall continued at a good pace that permitted him to either fall full-length upon the ground or drive his hatchet into a tree (depending upon which "eye-witness" account is consulted) at noon on the summit of Broad Mountain near Jim Thorpe, Carbon County —a "walk" of about sixty-five miles.

The Minisink complained, rightly so, that this was not the intent of the deed, if the deed itself was authentic. To add insult to injury, the surveyor's line was not drawn directly to the Delaware River to form the upper boundary of the land purchase. Instead, the line projected at right angles from the end point of the walk to a point near where the Lackawaxen enters the Delaware. The Minisink lost 1200 square miles of land and the Penns lost valuable allies with this knavery. The Delaware and Shawnee tribes were forced to move west; and the Upper Delaware Valley was soon to become a region of riots, war, and frontier massacres.

The Indian Wars (1754 –1763)

The global struggle between France and England was to have an impact on settlers in the Pocono frontier. Attack by the French and their allies, primarily warriors from Great Lakes tribes as well as some Delawares and Shawnees, resulted in the defeat of the British at Fort Necessity (Great Meadows) at Confluence, Pennsylvania, in 1754. This defeat, capped by Braddock's defeat at Fort Duquesne the next year, did little to rouse the settlers, who believed they were secure behind the Allegheny Mountains and protected by the Iroquois alliance that had been forged by the British. The massacre of settlers at Penn's Creek (Selinsgrove) in October 1755 changed the Pocono settlers' thoughts. It was feared, rightly so, that the unhappy Delawares and Shawnees who had recently been forced to leave their homes along the Delaware would join forces with the French.

Teedyuscong, "the War Trumpet of the Delawares," gathered his warriors and laid plans for a war of revenge. On November 24, 1755, the Moravian mission at Gnadenhutten (Weissport) was burned and eleven persons were killed. (Incidentally, Teedyuscong had been baptized at this mission five years earlier, and there is no evidence to prove that he took part in this massacre.) Additional attacks occurred at Brodhead Manor and, on the same day, December 11, 1755, the

Delawares massacred the Hoeth family near Gilbert. Settlers fled from the region to the safety of towns such as Nazareth, Easton, and Bethlehem.

Benjamin Franklin was authorized to supervise the construction of a line of forts on the northwestern side of the Kittatinny range. During the winter and spring of 1756, a line of forts was erected at strategic sites from Machipacong Island to the Lehigh River. These forts—Fort Hyndshaw (Bushkill), Fort DePuy (Shawnee), Fort Hamilton (Strouds-burg), Fort Norris (Kresgeville), Fort Allen (Weissport), and others on the New Jersey side—served as headquarters for soldiers and re-treats for settlers. The forts, except for the stockaded mansion of Nicholas DePuy at Shawnee, were insubstantial structures, and no evidence of their existence can be found today.

During fort construction, native American attacks were infrequent, but one attack is of note since it involved the Edward Marshall of "walking purchase" fame. Marshall's son had been killed in an ear-lier Indian uprising. The family then fled the frontier, only to return in 1756. The following year, the Delawares attacked the Marshall family home, shot a daughter, and killed and scalped Marshall's wife. Mar-shall, however, escaped this and other hazardous episodes and died a natural death.

After 1757, native American attacks were few. As a result of Iroquois pressure on the Delawares to make peace, a treaty was signed in Easton by Teedyuscong in October 1758. Peace lasted until 1763. During this lull in hostilities, settlers from Connecticut moved into the Wyoming Valley—land claimed by both Pennsylvania and Connecticut.

On April 19, 1763, Teedyuscong was burned to death while asleep in his cabin. The attackers were a band of warriors from the Iroquois Confederacy. The Delaware braves, angered at the death of their chief, broke the peace and again attacked white settlements. John Penn offered bounties for captured or scalped Indians. None of this blood money was ever paid, and the Indian uprising soon ended. Shortly thereafter, most of the Delawares joined their brothers in Ohio, eventually moving to Oklahoma and to Ontario, Canada, where many of them settled permanently.

The American Revolution and the Pocono Frontier (1774–1789)

With the beginning of the Revolution, the frontier was again exposed to attack, this time from the Iroquois. Shortly after war broke out in Massachusetts in April 1775, Pennsylvania officials mobilized the militia. Colonel Jacob Stroud stockaded his home (Stroudsburg) and renamed it Fort Penn.

In early July of 1778, Major John Butler and 400 Tory rangers, accompanied by about 700 Iroquois warriors, attacked settlements and forts in the Wyoming Valley. The awful massacre that followed probably caused more horror and outrage among American settlers than any other episode to the Revolutionary War. According to Major Butler's report, the Iroquois took 227 scalps. Most of the panic-stricken survivors fled in haste, some going downriver, others striking eastward through the Pocono wilds towards Fort Penn sixty miles away. Unguided and unguarded, many women and children wandered through a great swamp, known henceforth as the "Shades of Death." One account, probably exaggerated, indicated that as many as 200 persons died of exhaustion or starvation during this wild flight. (The Shades of Death hiking trail in Hickory Run State Park traverses some of this swamp.)

Additional attacks on settlers on the frontier prompted Congress to call for an expedition to punish the Iroquois. George Washington

SULLIVAN'S MARCH

Brinker's mill was the storehouse and advance post for the Sullivan expedition which left Easton June 18, 1779 to attack hostile Iroquois Indians.

Figure 7.3
Historical marker of Sullivan's march. Located at business route U. S. 209 in Sciota.

assigned the task to General John Sullivan. Early in 1779, Sullivan assembled his troops at Easton. Roadbuilding regiments were sent out to widen the Indian trail that led through the Poconos to the Susquehanna Valley. Sullivan set out on June 18, 1779, with 2500 men, 2000 horses, and many baggage wagons. They entered the Poconos at Wind Gap, took on provisions at Brinker's Mill (Sciota), and marched on to Tannersville near the foot of Big Pocono. Several hard days' marching took them across the Poconos and on to Wyoming by June 23rd. After a month's delay, Sullivan's troops moved north and joined forces with Brigadier-General James Clinton's regiments at Tioga Point. The combined army of 4000 men eventually destroyed forty Iroquois villages and burned stored foods, farmlands, and orchards as they moved through the heart of the Iroquois territory. By October, Sullivan was back in Easton and the Iroquois Confederacy never recovered as a major force in the Revolutionary War.

Small bands of Iroquois did continue attacks upon settlers and continental troops. Several battles were fought in the Minisink, the last being that at Raymondskill Falls. Here, a small group of militia were attacked and survivors retreated to an area along the Delaware shore still known today as "Death Eddy."

The British surrender at Yorktown, Virginia, on October 19, 1781, had no immediate effect on frontier warfare. As late as April 1782, native American warriors were assaulting Pocono settlers. Peace came to the frontier at about the same time that formal announcement of the end of the Revolutionary War was made in Congress on April 11, 1783.

The Pocono Frontier at the Turn of the Eighteenth Century

Prior to the Revolution, most settlers in the Pocono region were the Dutch, who came from New York via the Old Mine Road. Now the immigrants, chiefly Quakers and Pennsylvania Germans, came from the south. By 1800, present state borders were formed as native Americans gave up the last bits of land, and Pennsylvania's territorial disputes with Virginia, Maryland, New York, and Connecticut were finally settled. By now the colonial population had increased to 600,000, a six-fold increase since 1740.

Since fully 70 percent of the populace resided south and east of the Kittatinny Ridge, the Poconos remained mainly wilderness. As had the native Americans before them, the pioneers settled in the fertile stream valleys. Upland, forested areas remained relatively untouched although some lumbering had occurred. Even before the Revolutionary War, rugged frontiersmen such as the renowned Dan Skinner and his companions rode rafts of logs down the Delaware to Philadelphia.

In 1793, Antoine Dutot, a French refugee, arrived in the Delaware Water Gap region. Soon after, he purchased a large tract of land and made plans for a community he named Dutotsburg. In 1854, the townspeople renamed their town Delaware Water Gap. Other settlements likewise developed, so much so that the Commonwealth formed a new county. Thus, in 1798, Wayne County was created out of old Northampton County, which itself had been set off from Bucks County in 1752. (Later, Pike County would be formed from Wayne in 1814, and still later, Monroe in 1836 and Carbon in 1843.)

By the turn of the century, the old Minisink paths were being improved to serve as wagon roads. The roads from Easton to Milford and that from Easton to Wilkes-Barre promoted increased activity in the Poconos. Public stagecoaches used these roads and inns; taverns and settlements sprang up at convenient stopping places along the route.

Ferries at several spots along the Delaware provided important links in the expanding road system. One of the earliest ferries was established by Andrew Dingman in 1734 between his home (near present-day Dingmans Ferry, Pennsylvania) and Sandyston Township, New Jersey. The ferry remained in operation for 100 years, when it was replaced by a toll bridge. On various occasions, the ferry was put back in operation when floods destroyed the bridge.

The vast forests of the region were being exploited in a more systematic fashion. Milford, founded in 1796, soon became a prosperous lumbering center. Those logs not used to supply lumber for local settlements were rafted down the Lehigh and Delaware Rivers. The rafts were about 300 feet long, 40 feet wide, and loaded to about 8 feet deep. Each raft was navigated by about four men—the captain in the middle and three men manning the long oars fastened to the front and rear.

In 1799, Jacob Stroud established the community of Stroudsburg, which later became the county seat of Monroe County. The Stroud mansion now serves as the headquarters and museum of the county historical society.

Farms at this time were restricted to flatlands. Buckwheat and rye were principal crops, tolerant of thin soils and cool summers. Numerous grist mills processed the grains. Other crops were potatoes, corn, and oats. Cattle, sheep, and hogs supplemented the diet and pro- vided wool.

Growth during the Nineteenth Century

The canal period of American history touched the fringes of the Poconos. In 1828, the Delaware and Hudson Canal was completed with a terminus at Honesdale. The impetus for the development of this 108-mile long canal was to provide a means of transport for a newly recognized fuel, "black stones" (anthracite coal), to markets in growing eastern cities. The next year, an elaborate system of inclined planes and stationary engines was devised to haul coal over the Moosic Mountains from mines sixteen miles away in Carbondale to Honesdale. A locomotive engine was imported from England for use on this pioneer gravity railroad. The "Stourbridge Lion" made a trial run from Honesdale on August 8, 1829. This "first" for the western hemisphere was not an overwhelming success. The wooden rails did not adequately support the engine. After a few more trials, the "Lion" was abandoned to rust and vandals.

The building of railroads shortly followed the initial canal-building period. By 1870 railroads would displace canals as the major mode of transport. The Delaware, Lackawanna, and Western Railroad, in 1853, linked the coal fields to the eastern markets and promoted development of mining in the anthracite regions west of the Poconos. The Gravity Railroad of the Pennsylvania Coal Company, 1850–1885, brought coal to the D & H Canal at Hawley from mines near Pittston.

As rivers and canals had served previously, now railroads conveyed logs from the Poconos to urban centers. After the Civil War, lumbering began in earnest, and vast tracts of forest were cut with little thought of saving smaller trees. Hemlock and oak bark provided tannic acid for the developing tanning industry. Pitch, tar, turpentine, and rosin were extracted from conifers. Alas, the vast virgin forest would be gone by 1900.

The tanning industry developed as railroads provided transport for bark and hides. One of the earliest tanneries was built in Stroudsburg in 1822. Jay Gould began his business ventures with a tannery at Thornhurst near present-day Gouldsboro. In the decade of 1860–1870, Pocono tanneries produced over a million dollars worth of leather. The industry was short-lived, as the rapidly dwindling forests provided less and less bark for the tanning process.

As forest-based industries declined, other sources of income were sought. The clear streams and lakes were to provide a new "cash crop"—ice. Natural and man-made lakes would be the basis for this activity. Stillwater Lake, Tobyhanna Lake, Pocono Lake, Trout Lake, Saylor's Lake, and Lake Naomi were some of the major sources of ice.

Teams of horses dragged large sleds out onto the ice, where workers used special saws to cut the ice into blocks (see Figure 7.4). Sheds nearby, insulated with straw and sawdust, stored the ice. Railroad spurs were built to the icehouses and, twice daily in the summer, railroad cars loaded with ice headed for thousands of iceboxes in New York City and Philadelphia. The industry continued into the twentieth century. In 1927, the total ice harvest of the three largest ice companies of Monroe County was 169,000 tons.

Figure 7.4
Ice-cutting operation. Ice houses capable of storing 40,000 tons of ice decked the shores of many Pocono lakes. After an apparent woodcut in *The Pennsylvania Naturalist*.

Throughout the last half of the nineteenth century, various industries such as brick-making, bluestone quarrying, woolen mills, grist mills, etc., had their start, their growth, and their decline. A Monroe County peg factory, where wooden pegs were made to hold together the world's shoes, was reported to be the largest of its kind in the United States in 1868. A large glass factory—the Dorflinger Glass Works at White Mills, Wayne County—became, for a time, a center employing 3000 workers. There were attempts to mine clay and make bricks. The high-quality white clay found west of Saylorsburg attracted outside investors, including, reputedly, John Jacob Astor. Workers quarried limestone at a few sites for use in the tanning industry and as a source of fertilizer. Many lime kilns were constructed to supply lime. Some of these interesting stone structures are still evident today alongside country roads.

The wool industry flourished, as sheep flourished on slopes cleared during lumbering operations. The fast-flowing streams provided power for the mills. Most woolen mills were small-scale, short-lived operations. The remains of a mill and an historical marker relating the events of an endeavor by Joseph Brooks in 1825 appear along Dingmans Creek in G. W. Childs Park. One wool indus-

Figure 7.5
Lime kiln. Limestone was burned in a kiln to produce lime for farmers and tanners. After a photograph in *Monroe County—Historic Legacy*, 1980.

try adventure late in the century is worth telling. As a delightful account in *The Stroudsburg Daily Times* of May 18, 1898, relates it, a world's record was set by a Mister Thomas Kitson, proprietor of the Stroudsburg Woolen Mills. In the time of six hours and four minutes, a suit of clothes was made for Mr. Kitson from wool of sheep sheared earlier that morning. This topped the previous record, held in Scotland, by one hour and fifty-six minutes. The article noted that Mr. Kitson held a celebration dinner that evening with lamb as the main course!

Even the clear mountain stream water was bottled in bottles produced locally. Distinctive bottles encased in wickerwork came from the Stroudsburg Glass Company from 1876 to 1897. The crystal-clear water was also the basis for beer production. Near Raymondskill Falls, Remy Loreaux began producing beer in 1840. His brewery had the distinction of producing the first "bottled beer for home consumption in the U.S."

Throughout the nineteenth century many industries would come and go, but the industry that was to survive and sustain the region

Figure 7.6
Kittatinny House. Built in 1829 by Antoine Dutot. Sketch depicts the hotel as it appeared about 1900. After a photograph in *Monroe County—Historic Legacy*, 1980.

BOX 7.1

Places of Archaeological and Historical Interest

DePuy House. Built by first settler in region, Nicholas DePuy, now part of the Fred Waring estate, Shawnee-on-Delaware.

Dorflinger-Suydam Wildlife Sanctuary. Historic manor house and grounds. Proposed museum will feature glass from Dorflinger Glass Works. Off Route 6 in White Mills, north of Hawley.

Dutot School. Two-story brick schoolhouse now used as a museum with focus on Delaware Water Gap history. Delaware Water Gap village.

Grey Towers. French chateau-like ancestral home of former Governor Gifford Pinchot, maintained by USDA Forest Service as an ecology center and museum; the grounds include virgin white pine and hemlock forests. Milford.

Jim Thorpe. Historic canal and railroad center, once called Mauch Chunk. Asa Packer Mansion, St. Mark's Episcopal Church, a restored opera house and railroad station.

Lackawaxen Suspension Bridge. Designed by John Roebling (designer of the Brooklyn Bridge), the bridge was built 1846–1849; currently under restoration. Lackawaxen.

Millbrook Village. In Delaware Water Gap National Recreation Area on Old Mine Road in New Jersey, twelve miles north of I-80. Traditional crafts demonstrated in summer.

Monroe County Museum Association. Historical artifacts, country store. 537 Ann Street, Stroudsburg.

Octagon School (Jug Schoolhouse). One of four octagon-shaped stone schools built in Wayne County in the late 1830s. Just off Route 296, South Canaan Township.

Old Stone Mill. On Route 209, near Sciota. Built in 1800, has two large overshot wheels.

Pennsylvania Company Gravity Railroad Coach. A pioneer coach which operated on the gravity railroad, as cars were elevated to the summits of grades by water or steam power and then rolled down the track by means of gravity. Hawley.

BOX 7.1 (CONTINUED)

Pike County Historical Society. Indian artifacts, extensive regional history displays. Milford.

Pocono Indian Museum. Artifacts of the Delaware and of western tribes. Bushkill.

Quiet Valley Living Historical Museum. Numerous buildings of a Pennsylvania Dutch farm including a log house built in 1765, craft demonstrations. Off business Route 209, three-and-a-half miles south of Stroudsburg; follow signs another one-and-a-half miles.

Slateford Farm. Partial restoration of a typical farm of the mid- to late nineteenth century; buildings open seasonally with guides in period dress on duty. Off Route 611 south of the village of Delaware Water Gap in Delaware Water Gap National Recreation Area.

Stourbridge Lion. Full-scale replica of America's first locomotive, used in a trial three-mile run on August 8, 1829. West Park Street, Honesdale.

Stroud Community House. Mansion built in 1795, contains Monroe County Historical Society's collections. Ninth and Main Streets, Stroudsburg.

VanCampen Inn. In Delaware Water Gap National Recreation Area, five miles south of Peters Valley (New Jersey) on Old Mine Road. Restored stone house built around 1746.

Wayne County Historical Society. Built in 1860, the former office building of the Delaware and Hudson Canal Company now houses the collections and exhibits of the society, especially glass, blown and cut in local factories such as Dorflinger Glass Works. 810 Main Street, Honesdale.

was tourism. Stagecoach taverns turned into lodges, as travelers expressed interest in delaying their journeys. However, the enterprising Mr. Dutot is credited with constructing the first "resort," the Kittatinny House at the Delaware Water Gap, in 1829. The site was well-chosen, upstream from the gap on a plateau 180 feet above the river.

Through several ownerships, the lodge expanded until it could accommodate 500 guests. The famed resort burned to the ground on October 30, 1931. The expansion of railroads brought an increasing number of visitors and the need to develop more resorts. Hotel rates in the late nineteenth century varied from $3.50 to $4.50 per day or $10–$21 per week.

Artists and scholars found the region attractive. George Innes painted two oils of the Delaware Water Gap, and Currier and Ives made a lithograph of another Innes painting, entitled *View of the Delaware, "Water Gap" in the Distance.* On a sunny summer day, one might encounter Francis Stedman the poet, actor Joseph Jefferson, or the famed Sarah Bernhardt strolling the sidewalks in one of the fashionable resort towns. Charles S. Peirce spent his last years in Milford, with his genius in the fields of philosophy, mathematics, and cartography unrecognized by most of his neighbors.

Although augmented by summer visitors, the Poconos by the end of the nineteenth century remained a region of small- and medium-sized towns and villages, with small farms and pasture land scattered among the second-growth forests. By this time, most communities had replaced the log and wooden public buildings with stone and brick edifices. Churches, schools, and courthouses were a source of public pride. The Pocono region still retains many of the buildings constructed at the turn of the century; this is especially true of towns serving as county seats, such as Milford, Stroudsburg, and Honesdale. (See Box 7.1 for a list of places of archaeological and historical interest.)

The Twentieth Century

Tourism flourished in the early 1900s. Lodges extended further north onto the Pocono plateau to take advantage of the cooler elevations in the reforested tracts. Resort complexes were the rule as tourists sought more "active leisure." Tennis courts, golf courses, riding, and hiking trails were added to the lodges. These activities required large tracts of land, a condition considered significant in permitting reforestation to continue throughout much of the Poconos. Private hunting and fishing associations also preserved large tracts for their special needs. Various religious groups likewise purchased extensive acreage for use as vacation centers and religious retreats. Buck Hill Falls was the site of a lodge constructed by Quakers in 1901. Other religious group centers were established shortly thereafter—for example, Pocono Manor, Paradise Falls, and Lutherland. In sharp contrast to the peaceful uses envisioned for these vacation centers, the 20,000 acres of the Tobyhanna Military Reservation were first used in 1913 as an artillery training site. Artists and writers continued to be attracted to the region. Zane Grey wrote most of his novels while residing near Lackawaxen from 1905 to 1918.

A major development in the Poconos after World War I ended was the 1926 construction of dams across Wallenpaupack Creek near Hawley. Part of a hydroelectric project of the Pennsylvania Power and Light Company, Lake Wallenpaupack shortly became the prime recreational area in the northern Poconos.

The 1920 U.S. census revealed, for the first time in American history, the shift to a predominantly urban rather than rural population. The Poconos became even more of a vacation mecca for urban dwellers from surrounding regions. The development of better roads, coupled to the American love affair with the automobile, insured a continued influx of visitors.

The hard times of the Great Depression, followed by the sacrifices and travel restrictions demanded by World War II, meant fewer visitors for the Poconos. The Tobyhanna Military Reservation was used again, this time as a site of an air corps training field. Thousands of gliders—later to be used in the invasion of France—were stored there. In the fall of 1944, the reservation became a prisoner-of-war camp for about 200 German prisoners who were put to work harvesting crops in the summer and cutting ice in the winter.

After World War II, renewed prosperity and the eagerness of city dwellers to travel spurred a new period of prosperity for the Poconos. The 1950s and 1960s brought a new pattern of activities, as skiing boomed and second-home developments joined the summer lodges, church vacation centers, and honeymoon resorts.

Fortunately, at the time when Pocono lands increasingly fell victim to commercial ventures, the state was purchasing substantial tracts as state forests, game lands, and parks. The Federal Government started a land acquisition program in 1966 to preserve for public use some of the lands on either side of the Upper Delaware River that had been the home of the region's first inhabitants, the Lenape. This region, the Delaware Water Gap National Recreational Area, preserves for all of us many of the Poconos' most fascinating scenic and historic features.

In recent years, the seven counties which make up the Pocono-northeastern Pennsylvania region have cooperated to study the physical, social, and economic aspects of the region under the guidance of the Economic Development Council in order to develop comprehensive regional development plans. The impetus for such regional cooperation was the devastation brought by tropical storm Agnes, which struck the area in June 1972. Although most flood damage occurred in the Wyoming Valley, other areas of Northeastern Pennsylvania were affected. Tourism in the Poconos declined and dispersion of flood victims to adjacent areas put a strain on facilities there. The immense regional impact required a regional response.

The rural Pocono counties (Carbon, Monroe, Pike, and Wayne) and the urban counties (Lackawanna, Luzerne, and Schuylkill) have many ties through economic, social, educational, media, and health support institutions. It made good sense to utilize these interconnections as the basis for a flood recovery program and, later, for long-range plans and development strategies. A summary report, from the study "Northeastern Pennsylvania: Toward the Year 2000," states the hopes of the Economic Development Council succinctly: "In essence, the overall goal of this regional land use planning program is to promote the health, safety, and general welfare of the people of Northeastern Pennsylvania by planning for the most appropriate use of our natural and manmade resources."

People Pressures

The Poconos are best known throughout the country for their tourist activities. Over three-fourths of Pennsylvania's resorts are found in the Poconos. Department of Commerce figures revealed that in 1980 some eight million persons visited the four-county area of Carbon, Monroe, Pike, and Wayne with a total expenditure of $9.22 million. Tourism is the number one industry in the Poconos and the second largest industry in Pennsylvania. Attendance at popular state parks such as Hickory Run and Promised Land more than doubled in the last five years. One study projects that almost eighteen million persons will annually visit the four Pocono counties by the year 2000. After all, almost 50 percent of the United States population lives within six hours driving time of the Poconos. How to preserve the natural scenic beauty that attracts most visitors to the Poconos while at the same time accommodating an increasing number of tourists is indeed a challenge.

The Poconos are not only a desirable place to visit. The region is also experiencing an increase in residents. The 1980 United States census figures for the seven-county Pocono-northeast showed a population of 907,819, an increase of 3.9 percent over the 1970 population. This increase reversed a trend in declining population since 1930, when the population stood at 1,115,167.

In the decades following 1930, coal mines cut production or closed as oil replaced coal as a primary fuel. Other regional industries, such as lumbering, also dwindled. As jobs grew scarce, people moved from the area, and population continued to decline until about 1970. Now, however, Pike County is the fastest growing county in the state with a population increase of 54.6 percent in the decade of the seventies. Monroe County population increased 52.8 percent during the same period. Population analysts report that the largest influx of people in the Poconos from 1980 to 1982 involved persons sixty-five years and over and those between thirty-five and thirty-nine. Some people are choosing to live in the Poconos and commute to work in the urban areas of the Northeast. Others are making the Poconos their retirement site.

The Economic Development Council estimated that the number of second homes in Northeastern Pennsylvania will increase from 21,881 (in 1970) to 61,800 by 1985. As more homes are constructed, maintenance of sufficient good-quality water supplies becomes a challenge. Problems of stormwater runoff and increased volume of domestic sewage must be solved. Most soils of the Poconos are not suited for on-lot sewage disposal; nevertheless, more complex sewage systems are generally lacking in many second-home communities. The addition of nutrients to nearby lakes from improper sewage disposal practices accelerates the eutrophication process. Future construction should be permitted only where soils, topography, and hydrology allow. Figure 7.7 shows land use designations as suggested by officials of the Economic Development Council of Northeastern Pennsylvania.

Increasing numbers of attractions developed in recent years promote more tourism. A major auto race track, various theme parks, alpine water slides, more ski slopes, increased miles of cross-country and snowmobile trails, numerous festivals and week-end events— these are just some of the activities that bring more visitors to the Poconos. The issue of legalized gambling in the Poconos has been hotly debated in local town hall meetings, as well as on the floor of the state legislature. The complexion of the region could be dramatically altered if gambling on the Atlantic City scale were permitted. All

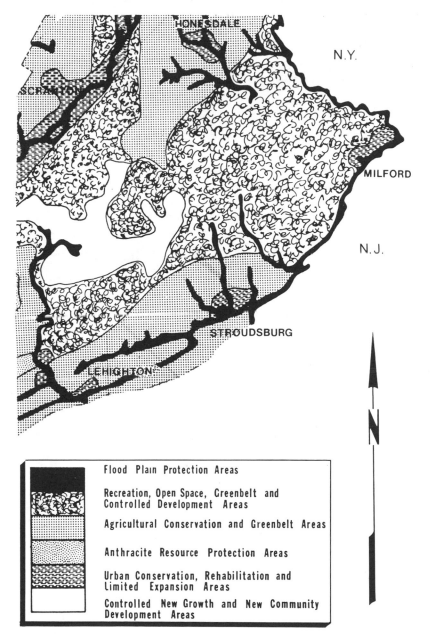

Figure 7.7
Land use policy areas of northeastern Pennsylvania. The rendering is a
possible policy area map based on natural suitabilities, existing land use
pattern, existing transport facilities, suggested option choices, and
strategy objectives. (Above map, slightly modified, reproduced from Figure
V-5 in *Northeastern Pennsylvania: Toward the Year 2000*, published in
1975; with permission from the EDCNP).

in all, "people pressures" will be a continuing challenge for planners and citizens of the region.

Natural Resource Management

Forests predominate the Pocono landscape. Pike County has 80 percent of its total land area classified as commercial forest. Significant stands of saw timber are found in Monroe, Pike, and Wayne Counties. Numerous saw mills and other forestry-related industries dot the region. Sound forest management, proper timber cutting, and extensive planting programs—now done on state-owned lands—are needed also on private lands to maintain the vast forested areas that are home to wildlife. Forests also retain water, cut down on erosion, and thus play a vital role in maintaining stream quality.

Agriculture is not extensive in the glaciated soils that predominate over much of the Poconos. Wayne County leads the region principally with dairy farms in the northern part of the county as the form of agriculture. Erosion and inadequate animal waste management are problems that need continued attention. The preservation of agricultural land and family farms has been aided in recent years by state legislation permitting townships to establish "agricultural areas." As with forests, the wise use and maintenance of agricultural lands will benefit wildlife—all of us, as well.

Over a thousand miles of streams and more than 30,000 acres in lakes are primary natural attractions of the Poconos. Fortunately, most Pocono waters are good quality, but this quality would be diminished by increased soil erosion, stormwater runoff, and improper sewage disposal. Citizens of the region must be alert to the potential dangers to surface and ground water supplies and demand responsible action by those involved.

One potential threat to the well-being of the Poconos, acid rain, is not generated locally. Acid precipitation is an increasingly important national and international problem. Rainfall in the Commonwealth is the most acidic in the nation, according to a 1984 study released by the U. S. Department of the Interior. Rainfall with a pH of 4.1 is common in the state. Vinegar has a pH of about 3. When industrial pollutants, especially sulfur and nitrogen oxides, get into the atmosphere, they undergo oxidation to sulfuric and nitric acid, the primary acids in acid rain. Increased acidity of the soil threatens the health of forests, whether by nutrient leaching, mobilization of toxic aluminum, or accumulation of heavy metals. In lakes, a lowering of pH (increasing acidity) produces an increase in dissolved aluminum, which is toxic to fish.

Studies by scientists of the Philadelphia Academy of Natural Sciences were conducted on thirty-seven natural lakes in Wayne and Pike Counties. There, they found conditions in many lakes to be better than those in lakes in the Adirondack Mountains of New York. The buffering capacity of the shales and sandstones of the Appalachian Ridges is not good, but it is superior to the granite and gneisses of the Adirondacks. However, lakes in the south-central part of Pike County have less buffering capacity and are thus of most concern. Lehigh University researchers recently conducted studies of 160 lakes in the Poconos and adjacent regions. Their report concludes that acidification is increasing, with 7.5 percent of the lakes classified as acidified and 70 percent sensitive to acidification.

The Pennsylvania Fish Commission is concerned about effects of acid precipitation on stocked trout streams. Recently officials designated several streams in the Poconos as "vulnerable to further acidification." Such important trout streams as the Tobyhanna, Bushkill, Saw, Shohola, Middle Branch, and Wallenpaupack Creek received this designation.

No single scapegoat should be sought as attempts are made to solve the problem. Certainly, legislation requiring industries to burn cleaner coal would be an important step. Use of renewable energy sources, conservation of fuel, and the development of technologies to reduce vehicle emissions and other ecologically sound practices are also essential if we hope to protect our forests, lakes, and streams in the Poconos and elsewhere.

Wildlife and fisheries are principal attractions for many who visit or reside in the Poconos. State game lands and forests provide ample hunting and fishing opportunities. Within these tracts, knowledgeable management should avoid some of the dilemmas faced in other Pocono regions. However, even these state-owned lands cannot escape water quality problems, if unwise practices occur on adjacent lands.

Maintaining a Delicate Balance

The objectives listed by the Economic Development Council in the summary report quoted earlier should be a great assistance to the citizens of the region as they plan to make the most appropriate use of their natural and man-made resources. Some of these objectives were mentioned in the previous discussion. Others of particular importance to the Poconos not mentioned previously include: to protect or enhance the natural beauty of roadsides, wetlands, and scenic vistas; to protect or enhance significant fish and wildlife habitat including deer wintering areas, waterfowl areas, and surface waters; to promote appropriate timber management of timber resources; to provide recreational opportunities to meet local and regional demands that do not cause significant harm to the environment, and to protect and enhance resources and areas that offer significant recreational opportunities. It is hoped that the Pocono populace will make use of these guidelines not only to insure their own long-term benefit, but also to preserve those natural wonders of the region so that future generations of visitors may explore and enjoy the Poconos.

CHAPTER 8 Delaware Water Gap National Recreation Area

> "We dined at Strouds and finding the after-
> noon to spare concluded to make use of it to
> visit the passage of the Delaware thro' the
> Blue Mountain at the break called the Water
> Gap which we were informed was often vis-
> ited as a great natural curiosity. . . . we
> walked on about a mile and a half from the
> Saw Mill till we came opposite to the
> narrowest pass of the water which is a place
> of singular curiosity and capable of much
> amusing research and observation. . . ."
> —JOSHUA GILPIN, *Journey to Bethlehem,*
> 1802

On September 1, 1965, Congress authorized the establishment of Delaware Water Gap National Recreation Area (DWGNRA) to "preserve
for public use a large and relatively unspoiled area along the river
boundary of Pennsylvania and New Jersey." The original area authorized consisted of 70,000 acres along both sides of the Delaware
River. A highly controversial aspect in the original plans for the recreation area was the proposed construction of a dam on the Delaware at Tocks Island, which would have formed a 12,000 acre reservoir. It is unlikely that a dam will be built in the foreseeable future,
since the Middle Delaware River, between Milford and the Delaware
Water Gap, was designated part of the National Wild and Scenic
Rivers System. About 7000 acres within the park boundaries are still

privately owned; thus they are not open to the public until they are acquired by the National Park Service.

Delaware Water Gap National Recreation Area includes land and facilities in four counties, Monroe, and Pike in Pennsylvania and Warren and Sussex in New Jersey, along a thirty-five-mile stretch of the Delaware River. Over millions of years, the river cut through the Kittatinny Ridge to produce the dramatic gap that has been a site of activity and inspiration for natives and visitors for centuries. Now the Delaware Water Gap serves as the southern boundary of the recreation area. The northern border of the park is near the meeting point for three states—New York, New Jersey, and Pennsylvania—at Port Jervis. (See Figure 8.1 for a map of DWGNRA, with locations of features mentioned in the remainder of this chapter.)

Starting Point

A good place to start your exploration of DWGNRA is the Kittatinny Point Visitor Center in New Jersey. This main visitor center, just off I-80, is open daily from 9:00 AM to 5:00 PM—from April through November, and weekends through the winter months. Here displays, a slide show, and helpful personnel will aid your orientation. Detailed park and hiking trail maps may be obtained at the station. From the Kittatinny Point Visitor Center, you may wish to explore the New Jersey side of the park by traveling along the River Road or, returning to I-80, you may take the toll bridge across the Delaware to explore the Pennsylvania portion of DWGNRA. Another visitor center, open from May 1 through October, is located at Dingmans Falls, a mile off of Route 209 just south of the Route 739 intersection, in the Dingmans Ferry area. Excellent natural history exhibits and an audiovisual program are located in the center.

Hikes in the Park

Visitors will find numerous trails in DWGNRA, including approximately 25 miles of the Appalachian Trail. This 2000-mile marked footpath extends from Mount Katahdin, Maine, to Mount Springer, Georgia. In Pennsylvania, a short distance south of the Delaware Water Gap, a 2.7 mile portion of the Appalachian Trail leads to the summit of Mt. Minsi. Walking time for this fairly steep trail, marked with white blazes, is one to two hours to the summit. Excellent views of the water gap reward the hiker. On the New Jersey side of the river, the Appalachian Trail can be picked up at Dunnfield Parking

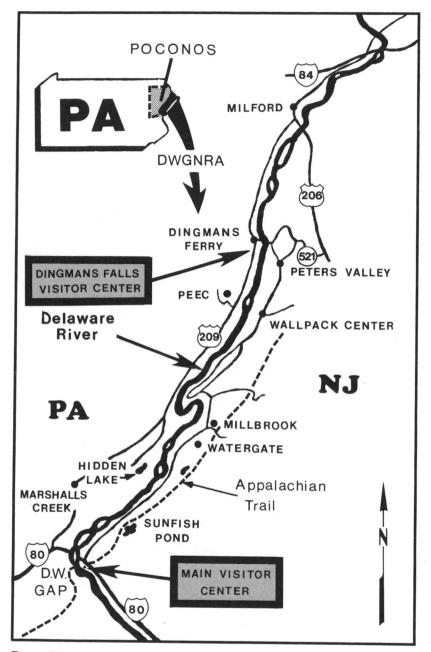

Figure 8.1
Delaware Water Gap National Recreation Area. Regional map indicating
locations and features discussed in text.

Area along I-80 across from the main visitor center. Two interesting hikes begin at the parking area. One is a 3.75-mile, gradual climb up the Kittatinny Ridge to Sunfish Pond. Walking time is four hours, round trip (white-blaze trail). The other hike, to Mt. Tammany, goes by way of a blue-blazed trail, which branches off of the Appalachian Trail from Dunnfield Parking Area. It's 2.5 miles to the summit. A one-mile trail, marked with red dots, begins at the New Jersey rest area east of Dunnfield Parking Area and ends at Mt. Tammany. Either way, the two- to three-hour round trip will have rewarded the hiker with vistas of the water gap. Children need supervision at the sum-

Figure 8.2
Silver Thread Falls.

mit, since dangerous precipices exist near the trail. The Appalachian Trail, as it runs along the ridge tops, is a good site for studying the chestnut oak forests characteristic of the ridges. Raccoon Ridge, on the Appalachian Trail, is a vantage point for observing migrating hawks. (See Box 4.3).

Shorter DWGNRA hikes can be taken that will provide visitors good opportunities to observe some of the plants and animals discussed in earlier chapters. The hike to Dingmans Falls and Silver Thread Falls (see Figure 8.2) is a good place to view large hemlocks, streamside vegetation, and rhododendron thickets. A self-guided nature trail around Hidden Lake reveals much about lake-side life and is a good place for bird-watching. The trails around Lake Lenape and the adjacent woods provide additional opportunities for easy hikes and good birding.

Environmental Education

Two facilities in DWGNRA have environmental education as a major focus. In New Jersey, Wallpack Valley Environmental Center, sponsored by the Eatontown, New Jersey, school district, is used primarily by students and teachers.

In Pennsylvania, the Pocono Environmental Educational Center (PEEC), off Route 209 a short distance north of Bushkill, has an extensive program of seminars, weekend courses, and field trips for school groups and others. A professional staff coordinates activities at the center. A four-mile loop trail (Tumbling Waters Trail), which starts at PEEC, is a rugged two- to three-hour hike available to interested visitors.

Historic Sites

In an area rich in history, it is fortunate that the National Park Service made an effort early in its development of DWGNRA to preserve significant sites for the edification of present and future generations.

Slateford Farm, off Route 611 south of the Water Gap, is the site of a restored ten-room house decorated with furniture and accessories of the nineteenth century. In summer, guides in period dress conduct tours. A slate quarry was part of the original farm holdings. An old shanty from the quarry operations was relocated to the farm property and slate-splitting demonstrations take place there seasonally.

Millbrook, New Jersey, had an origin typical of many villages, that is, as a gristmill site along a swift brook. The hamlet had its heyday in the late 1800s. In summer, craftsmen in village shops and inter-preters in houses and the school re-create those earlier days.

You may wish to take a rough ride on the Old Mine Road and trace the path taken by the earliest settlers to the Minisink three cen-turies ago. Along this road, south of Peters Valley, you'll see the Isaac VanCampen Inn, a Georgian stone house built about 1746. John Adams stayed there on his travels from Massachusetts to ses-sions of the Continental Congress in Philadelphia. The National Park Service restored the building.

On Your Own

There are varied recreational activities permitted in DWGNRA. Boat-ing on the Delaware River has been a favorite pursuit of many visi-tors to the region for decades. Canoeing has become increasingly popular and several suppliers rent, launch, and pick up canoes for those without their own. Fishing, hunting, picnicking, and even rock climbing are enjoyed by the two million annual visitors.

Landscape artists were attracted to the Water Gap as early as the 1800s. Today, Peters Valley in New Jersey is a center for artists and craftsmen. Interested persons may obtain information about galleries, craft fairs, and other artistic activities at visitor centers.

Figure 8.3
Canoes along the Delaware. The free-flowing Delaware River is an increasingly popular site for canoeing.

Although only limited camping is permitted in the recreation area (group, canoe beaching areas, Appalachian Trail sites), numerous private campgrounds and state parks located nearby permit visitors to engage in extended activities within DWGNRA.

Many proud townspeople claim their town is "the gateway to the Poconos." The Delaware Water Gap was, in fact, a gateway into the wilds of the Poconos for the earliest human visitors. There is still much to be said for using the recreation area as your gateway to learn more about the human and natural history of the Poconos.

APPENDIX A Sources of Further Information

Appalachian Mountain Club (Delaware Valley Chapter, 476 Kerr Ln., Springfield, PA 19064). Publishes a regional newsletter **Appalachian Foot Notes** for members.

Bureau of State Parks (P. O. Box 1467, Harrisburg, PA 17120). Various free publications on camping, cabins, special places, recreation, trails, and scenic rivers.

Carbon County Conservation District (P. O. Box 206, Courthouse, Jim Thorpe, PA 18229).

Citizens Advisory Council to the Department of Environmental Resources (P. O. Box 2357, 816 Executive House, Harrisburg, PA 17120).

Clean Air Council (1324 Locust St., Philadelphia, PA 19107). Publishes a quarterly newsletter **Fresh Air** for the general public.

Delaware River Basin Commission (25 Scotch Road, P. O. Box 360, Trenton, NJ 08603).

Delaware State Forest (Pennsylvania Bureau of Forestry, 474 Clearview Ln., Stroudsburg, PA 18360). Maps and information available about the Pocono forest lands.

Delaware Water Gap National Recreation Area (Superintendent, Bushkill, PA 18324). Newsletter: **Spanning the Gap.**

East Stroudsburg University (East Stroudsburg, PA 18301). Natural History Museum, Biology Department.

Economic Development Council of Northeastern Pennsylvania (P. O. Box 777, Avoca PA 18641). Organized to further social, economic, and physical development. Produces many useful maps, land use studies, and projections for the area.

Environmental Resources, Department of (DER, Fulton Building, P. O. Box 2063, Harrisburg, PA 17120).

Everhart Museum (Nay Aug Park, Scranton, PA 18510). Exhibits of interest in natural history, science, and art; Pennsylvania emphasis; fine exhibit of Dorflinger glass.

Governor's Energy Council (P. O. Box 8010, Harrisburg, PA 17105). Publishes a bimonthly newsletter **PENNENERGY** for the general public.

Hawk Mountain Sanctuary Association (Route 2, Kempton, PA 19529). Strong on conservation and education; offers a variety of short courses through Cedar Crest College; fall lectures and slide shows; exhibits; issues **Hawk Mountain News**.

Historical Society of Philadelphia (1300 Locust St., Philadelphia, PA 19107). Publishes **The Pennsylvania Magazine of History and Biography**.

Joint Legislative Conservation Committee (Box 254—Main Capitol, Harrisburg, PA 17120). **The Environmental Synopsis** is a monthly statewide newsletter for the general public.

Keystone Trails Association (R-252 Edgewood Ave., Duboistown, PA 17701). A quarterly statewide newsletter is distributed to its 1200 members.

Lacawac Sanctuary (P. O. Box 518, R. D. 1, Lake Ariel, PA 18436). A National Natural Landmark and National Historic Site owned by Nature Conservancy. Trails, nature walks, short courses, research; modest lodging available. Located just north of the western end of Lake Wallenpaupack.

Lackawanna County Regional Planning Commission (200 Adams Ave., Scranton, PA 18503).

Lake Wallenpaupack Water Shed Association, Inc. (Box 296, Colony Cove, Tafton, PA 18464). Newsletter.

Legislative Reference Bureau (647 Main Capitol Building, State and Third Sts., Harrisburg, PA 17120). The official weekly gazette, **Pennsylvania Bulletin**, covers current regulations, legislative documents, court rules, etc.; reports of the Department of Environmental Resources, the Fish Commission, Game Commission, etc., are applicable to environmental matters.

Lehigh River Restoration Association, Inc. (120 N. Ellsworth St., Allentown, PA 18103). Publishes an annual report for the region.

Luzerne County Conservation District (71 N. Market St., P. O. Box 148, Nanticoke, PA 18634). Newsletter **Environ** for the county.

Meesing Nature Center Five miles north of Marshalls Creek along Marshall Creek Road. Educational programs and nature trails.

Milford Reservation (Box 560, Milford, PA 18337). Unique energy-efficient building; program emphasis on energy conservation and environmental awareness.

Monroe County Conservation District (Box 2335A, R. D. 2, Stroudsburg, PA 18360). **Conservation Through Education Newsletter, Meesing Nature Center Newsletter**, and an annual report are issued.

Monroe County Historical Society (9th and Main Sts., Stroudsburg, PA 18360).

Monroe County Museum Association (537 Ann St., Stroudsburg, PA 18360).

Monroe County Recycling (R. D. 2, Box 2335A, Stroudsburg, PA 18360).

National Park Service (Upper Delaware Planning Team, Box 13, Milanville, PA 18443). The newsletter **Our Scenic Delaware** covers planning and progress on the Upper Delaware.

Nature Conservancy, The (Pennsylvania/New Jersey Office, 1218 Chestnut St., Room 1002, Philadelphia, PA 19107). Quarterly newsletter **Penn's Woods** for members.

New Jersey Outdoors Resource Guide (Resources Interpretive Service, CN402, Trenton, NJ 08625). Detailed listing of outdoor activities, addresses, groups, wildlife education programs, etc.

Northeastern Pennsylvania Environmental Council (P. O. Box 3113, Scranton, PA 18505-3113).

Pennsylvania Academy of Science The Academy's annual **Proceedings** (*Journal*, 1988–) may include scientific reports on the Poconos.

Pennsylvania Department of Transportation (Publication Sales Store, P. O. Box 134, Middletown, PA 17057). County highway maps.

Pennsylvania Environmental Council, Inc. (225 S. 15th St., Philadelphia, PA 19102). Statewide bimonthly **News and Views** for members.

Pennsylvania Fish Commission (3532 Walnut St., P. O. Box 1673, Harrisburg, PA 17105-1673). Issues charts, regulations, boating information, etc.; magazines: **Pennsylvania Angler** and **Boat Pennsylvania**; sponsors Pennsylvania League of Angling Youth.

Pennsylvania Forestry Association (310 E. Main St., Mechanicsburg, PA 17055). Bimonthly magazine, **Pennsylvania Forests**, covers local to statewide concerns.

Pennsylvania Game Commission (8000 Derry St., P. O. Box 1567, Harrisburg, PA 17105-1567). Active in conservation, education, research, management; publishes **Pennsylvania Game News** monthly.

Pennsylvania Geographical Society Issues newsletters and the journal **The Pennsylvania Geographer**.

Pennsylvania Historical and Museum Commission (Box 1026, Harrisburg, PA 17120). Publishes the quarterly **Pennsylvania Heritage and Pennsylvania Preservation**.

Pennsylvania Historical Association Publishes **Pennsylvania History**, with emphasis on the colonial period.

Pennsylvania Outdoors, Inc. (801 Oregon St., Oshkosk, WI 54901). Publishes the magazine **Pennsylvania Outdoors** seven times a year.

Pennsylvania Power and Light Company (Box 122, Hawley, PA 18428-0122). Information about Lake Wallenpaupack.

Pennsylvania Recreation and Park Society, Inc. (1831 London Road, Abington, PA 19001). Magazine: **Pennsylvania Recreation and Parks**.

Pennsylvania Travel Council (5403 Carlisle Pike, Mechanicsburg, PA 17055). Motel and hotel information.

Pennsylvania Wildlife Federation and the **Pennsylvania Federation of Sportsmen's Clubs** (1718 N. Second St., Harrisburg, PA 17102). Their magazine, **Pennsylvania Wildlife and Outdoor Digest**, issued bimonthly, covers a wide variety of environmental topics.

Pike County Historical Society (Milford, PA 18337).

Pocono Environmental Education Center (PEEC) (R. D. 1, Box 268, Dingmans Ferry, PA 18328). The largest residential environmental facility in North America, PEEC offers many short courses on natural history, botany, acid rain, nature photography, etc. Active and well-run, it is a key place for people interested in the natural history of the Poconos.

Pocono Indian Museum (Route 209, Bushkill, PA 18324). Commercial museum, which re-creates life of the Delaware Indians. Indian gift shop.

Pocono Mountain Audubon Chapter (Contact: National Audubon Society, 950 Third Avenue, New York, NY 10022).

Pocono Mountains Vacation Bureau, Inc. (1004 Main St., Stroudsburg, PA 18360). Information source for travel, recreation, promotions, etc.

Quiet Valley Living Historical Farm (Box 2495, R. D. 2, Stroudsburg, PA 18360). Fourteen buildings, museum, gift shop, tours; life and activities of the colonial period are re-created.

Sierra Club—Pennsylvania Chapter (R. D. 2, Box 183A, Newville, PA 17241). The Pennsylvania Chapter issues **Sierra Club Newsletter** bimonthly.

Society for Pennsylvania Archeology (American Indian Archeological Institute, Washington, CT 06793). The scholarly journal, **Pennsylvania Archeologist**, covers Pennsylvania, New Jersey, and other states.

Society of American Foresters, Pennsylvania Division (R. R. 1, Box 999, Franklin, NJ 07416). Quarterly magazine **Allegheny News** for members.

Soil Conservation Service, USDA (470 Sunrise Ave., Honesdale, PA 18431).

The State Book Store (Department of General Services, P. O. Box 1365, Harrisburg, PA 17125). For over-the-counter purchases and mail orders of official publications of the state.

Susquehanna River Tri-State Association (165 So. Franklin St., Wilkes-Barre, PA 18702). Quarterly newsletter **The Susquehanna**.

Tannersville Cranberry Bog Preserve Committee of Nature Conservancy (c/o Meesing Nature Center, R. D. 2, Box 2335-A, Stroudsburg, PA 18360). Issues **Bog Notes**.

This Week in the Poconos (Ed. offices: Pocono Pines, PA 18350). A 100-page magazine with a controlled complimentary distribution. The "This Week Forecasts" section is an excellent advisor on scheduled activities, including events of natural history interest. Includes a "Points of Interest" section that notes many features for naturalists.

Topographic and Geologic Survey (Pennsylvania Department of Environmental Resources, Harrisburg, PA 17120). Issues many technical reports and maps; **Pennsylvania Geology** is published bimonthly.

Travel Development, Bureau of (416 Forum Building, Harrisburg, PA 17120). Campground and travel information.

Trout Unlimited (Pennsylvania Council) (1563 W. Mountain Ave., South Williamsport, PA 17701). Newsletter: **Pennsylvania Trout**.

Wayne County Conservation District (Agricultural Service Center, 470 Sunrise Ave., Honesdale, PA 18431).

Wayne County Historical Society (810 Main St., Honesdale, PA 18431).

Wayne-Pike Audubon Society (Contact: National Audubon Society). Monthly newsletter.

Selected List of Pocono Area Maps

Area Street and Road Maps

A number of current, detailed maps by county, area, or city are available from Alfred B. Patton, Inc., Rte. 313 and Center St., Doylestown, PA 18901. Write for catalog and price list.

Forest Maps

Lull, W. H. 1968. **A Forest Atlas of the Northeast.** Northeastern Forest Experimental Station, Upper Darby, PA.

Delaware State Forest Map

Map of these areas open to public use. Includes contour lines. Free from District Forester, 474 Clearview Ln., Stroudsburg, PA 18360.

Geologic Maps

Atlas of Preliminary Geologic Quadrangle Maps of Pennsylvania. 1981. Pennsylvania Geological Survey, 4th Series, Map 61, 636 pp., by T. M. Berg and C. M. Dodge.

Fossil Collecting in Pennsylvania. 1969. Pennsylvania Geological Survey, 4th Series, General Geology Report 40, by D. M. Hoskins. Book includes sections of topographic maps appropriate to fossil study.

Geologic Map of Pennsylvania. 1980. Three sheets by T. M. Berg, W. E. Edmunds, A. R. Geyer, and others. Pennsylvania Geological Survey, 4th Series, Map 1, Scale 1:250,000.

Geology of the Appalachian Trail in Pennsylvania. 1983. Text and map of the 228-mile segment of trail in Pennsylvania, by J. Peter Wilshusen of the Pennsylvania Geological Survey. Available as **General Geology Report 74** from the State Book Store (P. O. Box 1365, Harrisburg, PA 17125).

Glacial Border Deposits of Late Wisconsin Age in Northeastern Pennsylvania. 1980. Map by G. H. Crowl and W. D. Sevon of the Department of Environmental Resources, Harrisburg. General Geology Report 71.

Rock Types of Pennsylvania. 1984. Map by T. M. Berg, W. D. Sevon, and R. Abel. Department of Environmental Resources, Harrisburg.

Highway Maps

Type 3 County General Highway Maps are 18″ × 24″ in black and white from PennDOT Publications Sales Store, P. O. Box 134, Middletown, PA 17057. Write for availability and prices.

Hydrographic Map

Maps of lakes that show depths, contours, dropoffs, etc., are available for some lakes. Write: Angler's Maps, Pennsylvania Fish Commission, P. O. Box 1673, Harrisburg, PA 17105-1673.

Land Resource Map of Pennsylvania

1967. Map by H. W. Higbee. A detailed multicolor map of the soil units and their evaluations for Pennsylvania. Published by the Pennsylvania State University, College of Agriculture, University Park, PA 16802.

Northeast PA Regional Map

A 24″ × 36″ multicolored map of northeastern PA printed on spunbonded Polyofefin. In addition to roads, towns, etc., it depicts public and leased lands open to the public for hunting and recreation. Contour intervals. $4.00 from Pennsylvania Game Commission, P. O. Box 1567, Harrisburg, PA 17105-1567.

Official Transportation Map (PA)

Prepared by the Department of Transportation. Free copies available from Travel Development Bureau, Pennsylvania Department of Commerce, Harrisburg, PA 17120 and local PennDOT offices.

Recreation/Camping

The Bureau of State Parks (P. O. Box 1467, Harrisburg, PA 17120) issues free information on camping, cabins, special places, recreational guides, trail guides, and scenic river systems. Write for information.

Slope, Base Geology, and Soil Maps

Northeastern Pennsylvania maps, by county, available from Economic Development Council of Northeastern Pennsylvania, P. O. Box 777, Avoca, PA 18641.

Sportsmen's Recreation Maps

Four-color 9″ × 15″ maps of each tract of Game Lands. Each map shows streams, roads, trails, and prominent land features. Brief narrative on game species. Order by Game Land Numbers at $0.50 each from Pennsylvania Game Commission.

Topographic Maps

For the Pocono area, many maps are available at local stationery and sporting goods stores. For an index to the maps available, write to Eastern Regional Map Distribution Center, U.S.G.S., 1200 Eads Road, Arlington, VA 22202.

Trout Fishing Map

A map of trout areas of the Northeast Section of Pennsylvania appeared as part of the 1984 issues (as a supplement) of the *Official Pennsylvania Guide to Wines and Liquors*. Write to the Pennsylvania Fish Commission, P. O. Box 1673, Harrisburg, PA 17105-1673.

Nomenclature

All **flowering plants** and vertebrates mentioned in the text, figures, or tables are included below. Section I converts common names to scientific names; section II, the reverse. The common names are those, in our opinion, generally used in eastern Pennsylvania and/or the larger naturalist community. Synonyms are generally not given. Scientific names (genus and species) are technical and presumably fixed —although they do change with new information and technologies. Spp. (the plural of species) is added where common names refer to any one of a number of similar species. Subspecies are not used in our lists, although specialists do recognize some subspecies in the same group, such as in the reptiles and amphibians.

I. Common Names to Scientific Names

Alder flycatcher	Empidonax alnorum
Alders	Alnus spp.
American beech	Fagus grandifolia
American black duck	Anas rubripes
American chestnut	Castanea dentata
American coot	Fulica americana
American crow	Corvus brachyrhynchos
American eel	Anquilla rostrara
American goldfinch	Carduelis tristis
American kestrel (Sparrow hawk)	Falco sparverius
American redstart	Setophaga ruticilla
American robin	Turdus migratorius

American shad	Alosa sapidissima
American toad	Bufo americanus
American tree sparrow	Spizella arborea
American widgeon	Mareca americana
American woodcock	Philohela minor
Arrow arum	Peltandra virginica
Arrow-wood	Viburnum dentatum
Arrowhead	Sagittaria spp.
Aspens	Populus spp.
Austrian pine	Pinus nigra
Bald eagle	Haliaeetus leucocephalus
Balsam fir	Abies balsamea
Bank swallow	Riparia riparia
Barn owl	Tyto alba
Barn swallow	Hirundo rustica
Barred owl	Strix varia
Basswood	Tilia americana
Beaver	Castor canadensis
Bedstraw	Galium spp.
Beech fern	Dryopteris phegopteris
Beechdrops	Epifagus virginiana
Beggar-lice (tick-trefoil)	Desmodium spp.
Bellwort	Uvularia spp.
Belted kingfisher	Megaceryle alcyon
Big brown bat	Eptesicus fuscus
Big-toothed aspen	Populus grandidentata
Bindweed	Convolvulus arvensis
Black alder	Alnus glutinosa
Black bear	Ursus americanus
Black cherry	Prunus serotina
Black crappie	Pomoxis nigromaculatus
Black gum	Nyssa sylvatica
Black locust	Robinia pseudoacacia
Black oak	Quercus velutina
Black rat snake	Elaphe obsoleta
Black spruce	Picea mariana
Black walnut	Juglans nigra
Black-and-white warbler	Mniotila varia
Black-billed cuckoo	Coccyzus erythropthalmus
Black-capped chickadee	Parus altricapillus
Black-eyed Susan	Rudbeckia serotina
Black-throated blue warbler	Dendroica caerulescens

Black-throated green warbler	Dendroica virens
Blackburnian warbler	Dendroica fusca
Blacknose dace	Rhinichthyes atratulus
Blackpoll warbler	Dendroica striata
Bladderwort	Utricularia vulgaris
Bloodroot	Sanguinaria canadensis
Blue flag	Iris versicolor
Blue jay	Cyanocitta cristata
Blue-gray gnatcatcher	Polioptila caerulea
Blue-winged teal	Anas dicors
Blue-winged warbler	Vermivora pinus
Blueberry	Vaccinium spp.
Bluegill	Lepomis macrochirus
Bluets	Houstonia spp.
Bobcat	Lynx rufus
Bobolink	Dolichonyx oryzivorus
Bog laurel	Kalmia polifolia
Bog rosemary	Andromeda glaucophylla
Bog turtle	Clemmys muhlenbergi
Boneset	Eupatorium perfoliatum
Boreal chorus frog	Pseudacris triseriata
Boreal redback vole	Clethrionomys gapperi
Bouncing bet	Saponaria officinalis
Bracken (Brake) fern	Pteridium aquilinum
Broad-leaved cattail	Typha latifolia
Broad-winged hawk	Buteo platypterus
Brook trout	Salvelinus fontinalis
Brown creeper	Certhia familiaris
Brown thrasher	Toxostoma rufum
Brown trout	Salmo trutta
Brown-headed cowbird	Molothrus ater
Bufflehead	Bucephala albeola
Bullfrog	Rana catesbeiana
Bullhead	Ictalurus spp.
Bulrushes	Scirpus spp.
Bur reed	Sparganium spp.
Burdock	Arctium minus
Butter 'n' eggs	Linaria vulgaris
Buttercups	Ranunculus spp.
Buttonbush	Cephalanthus occidentalis
Campion	Lynchis alba
Canada goose	Branta canadensis

Canada warbler	Wilsonia canadensis
Canada yew	Taxus canadensis
Cancerroot	Conopholis americana
Canvasback	Aythya valisineria
Cape May warbler	Dendroica tigrina
Carolina wren	Thryothorus ludovicianus
Catbrier	Smilax spp.
Cedar waxwing	Bombycilla cedorum
Cerulean warbler	Dendroica caerulea
Chain fern	Woodwardia virginica
Channel catfish	Ictalurus punctatus
Checkerberry	Gaultheria procumbens
Chestnut oak	Quercus prinus
Chestnut-sided warbler	Dendroica pensylvanica
Chickweed	Stellaria spp.
Chicory	Cichorium intybus
Chimney swift	Chaetura pelagica
Chipping sparrow	Spizella passerina
Choke cherry	Prunus virginiana
Chokeberry	Aronia spp.
Christmas fern	Polystichum acrostichoides
Cinnamon fern	Osmunda cinnamonea
Cinquefoil	Potentilla spp.
Cliff swallow	Petrochelidon pyrrhonota
Climbing fern	Lygodium palmatum
Closed gentian	Gentiana clausa
Club mosses	Lycopodium spp.
Cocklebur	Xanthium spp.
Coltsfoot	Tussilago farfara
Columbine	Aquilegia canadensis
Common alder	Alnus serrulata
Common elder	Sambucus canadensis
Common goldeneye	Bucephala clangula
Common grackle	Quiscalus quiscula
Common loon	Gavia immer
Common merganser	Mergus merganser
Common moorhen	Gallinula choropus
Common nighthawk	Chordeiles minor
Common redpoll	Carduelis flammea
Common shiner	Notropis cornutus
Common snapping turtle	Chelydra serpentina
Common snipe	Capella gallinago

Common yellowthroat	Geothlypis trichas
Coontails	Ceratophyllum spp.
Cooper's hawk	Accipiter cooperi
Corn lily	Clintonia borealis
Cottongrass	Eriophorum spp.
Cottonwood	Populus deltoides
Cow vetch	Vicia cracca
Cow-wheat	Melampyrum lineare
Coyote	Canis latrans
Cranberry	Vaccinium oxycoccos, macrocarpon
Creek chub	Semotilus atromaculatus
Crown vetch	Coronilla varia
Dandelion	Taraxacum spp.
Dark-eyed junco	Junco hyemalis
Day-lily	Hemerocallis fulva
Deer mouse	Peromyscus maniculatus
Deerberry	Vaccinium stamineum
Dock	Rumex spp.
Dodder	Cuscata spp.
Dogwoods	Cornus spp.
Douglas fir	Pseudotsuga menziesi
Downy woodpecker	Picoides pubescens
Duckweed	Lemna spp.
Dwarf mistletoe	Arceuthobium pusillum
Eastern bluebird	Sialia sialis
Eastern box turtle	Terrapene carolina
Eastern chipmunk	Tamias striatus
Eastern cottontail	Sylvilagus floridanus
Eastern garter snake	Thamnophis sirtalis
Eastern gray treefrog	Hyla versicolor
Eastern hognose snake	Heterodon platyrhinos
Eastern kingbird	Tyrannus tyrannus
Eastern meadowlark	Sturnella magna
Eastern milk snake	Lampropeltis triangulum
Eastern mole	Scalopus aquaticus
Eastern painted turtle	Chrysemys picta
Eastern phoebe	Sayornis phoebe
Eastern pipistrel	Pipistrellus subflavus
Eastern red-backed salamander	Plethodon cinereus
Eastern ribbon snake	Thamnophis sauritus
Eastern screech owl	Otus asio
Eastern spadefoot	Scaphiopus holbrooki

Eastern wood pewee	Contopus virens
Eastern wood rat	Neotoma floridana
Eastern worm snake	Carphophis amoenus
Elms	Ulmus spp.
European starling	Sturnus vulgaris
Evening grosbeak	Hesperiphona vespertina
Evening primrose	Oenothera biennis
Fallfish	Semotilus corporalis
False hellebore	Veratrum viride
False Solomon's-seal	Smilacina racemosa
Fanwort	Cabomba caroliniana
Field daisy	Chrysanthemum leucanthemum
Field garlic	Allium spp.
Field horsetail	Equisetum arvense
Field sparrow	Spizella pusilla
Fire cherry	Prunus pensylvanica
Fireweed	Erechtites hieracifolia
Fish crow	Corvus ossifragus
Five-lined skink	Eumeces fasciatus
Fleabane	Erigeron spp.
Flowering dogwood	Cornus florida
Fly-poison	Amianthium muscaetoxicum
Foamflower	Triarella cordifolia
Four-toed salamander	Hemidactylium scutatum
Fowler's toad	Bufo woodhousei
Fox grape	Vitis labrusca
Fox sparrow	Passerella iliaca
Foxtail	Setaria spp.
Fringed polygala	Polygala paucifolia
Geranium	Geranium spp.
Gold thread	Coptis groenlandica
Golden club	Orontium aquaticum
Golden eagle	Aquila chrysaetos
Golden-crowned kinglet	Regulus satrapa
Golden-winged warbler	Vermivora chrysoptera
Goldenrod	Solidago spp.
Grape fern	Botrychium spp.
Gray birch	Betula populifolia
Gray catbird	Dumetella carolinensis
Gray fox	Urocyon cinereoargenteus
Gray-cheeked thrush	Hylocichla minima
Great blue heron	Ardea herodias

Great crested flycatcher	Myiarchus crinitus
Great egret	Casmerodius albus
Great horned owl	Bubo virginianus
Great rhododendron (white laurel)	Rhododendron maximum
Greater yellowlegs	Tringa melanoleuca
Green frog	Rana clamitans
Green sunfish	Lepomis cyanellus
Green-backed heron	Butorides striatus
Green-winged teal	Anas carolinensis
Ground cedar	Lycopodium complanatum
Ground pine	Lycopodium obscurum
Hairy woodpecker	Picoides villosus
Hairy-tailed mole	Parasclops breweri
Hardhack	Spirea tomentosa
Hawkweed	Hieracium spp.
Hawthorn	Crataegus spp.
Hayscented fern	Dennstaedtia punctilobula
Heal-all	Prunella vulgaris
Hemlock	Tsuga canadensis
Henbit	Lamium spp.
Hepatica	Hepatica spp.
Hermit thrush	Hylocichla guttata
Herring gull	Larus argentatus
Highbush blueberry	Vaccinium corymbosum
Hoary bat	Lasiurus cinereus
Hobblebush	Viburnum alnifolium
Honeysuckle	Lonicera spp.
Hooded merganser	Lophodytes cucullatus
Hooded warbler	Wilsonia citrina
Hop hornbeam	Ostrya virginiana
Hornbeam	Carpinus caroliniana
Horned grebe	Podoceps auritus
Horned lark	Eremophila alpestris
Horsetails	Equisetum spp.
House finch	Carpodacus mexicanus
House mouse	Mus musculus
House sparrow	Passer domesticus
Huckleberry	Gaylussacia spp.
Indian pipe	Monotropa uniflora
Indigo bunting	Passerina cyanea
Interrupted fern	Osmunda claytoniana
Jack-in-the-pulpit	Arisaema triphyllum

Japanese honeysuckle	Lonicera japonica
Jefferson salamander	Ambystoma jeffersonianum
Jewelweed	Impatiens capensis
Joe-pye-weed	Eupatorium spp.
Killdeer	Charadrius vociferus
Labrador tea	Ledum groenlandicum
Lambsquarter	Chenopodium album
Larch	Larix laricina
Large-leaved holly	Ilex montana
Largemouth bass	Micropterus salmoides
Least flycatcher	Empidonax minimus
Least sandpiper	Erolia minutilla
Least shrew	Cryptotis parva
Leatherleaf	Chamaedaphne calyculata
Lesser scaup	Aythya affinis
Lesser yellowlegs	Tringa flavipes
Little brown bat	Myotis lucifugus
Long-eared owl	Asio otus
Long-tailed salamander	Eurycea longicauda
Longnose dace	Rhinichthyes cataractae
Longtail shrew	Sorex dispar
Longtail weasel	Mustela frenata
Louisiana waterthrush	Seiurus motacilla
Madtom	Noturus insignis
Magnolia warbler	Dendroica magnolia
Mallard	Anas platyrhynchos
Map turtle	Graptemys geographica
Mapleleaf viburnum	Viburnum acerifolium
Marbled salamander	Ambystoma opacum
Marsh fern	Dryopteris thelypteris
Marsh wren	Cistothorus palustris
Masked shrew	Sorex cinereus
Mayapple	Podophyllum peltatum
Meadow jumping mouse	Zapus hudsonius
Meadow vole	Microtus pennsylvanicus
Meadowrue	Thalictrum spp.
Meadowsweet	Spirea spp.
Milfoil	Myriophyllum spp.
Milkweed	Asclepias syriaca
Mink	Mustela vison
Mints	Mentha spp.
Moccasin flower	Cypripedium spp.

Mountain azalea	Rhododendron spp.
Mountain laurel	Kalmia latifolia
Mourning dove	Zenaida macroura
Mud minnow	Umbra pygmaea
Mud-plantain	Heteranthera spp.
Mullein	Verbascum thapsus
Musk turtle	Sternotherus odoratus
Muskellunge	Esox masquinongy
Muskrat	Ondatra zibethica
Mustards	Brassica spp.
Mute swan	Cygnus olor
Naiads	Najas spp.
Narrow-leaved cattail	Typha angustifolia
Narrow-leaved milkweed	Asclepias spp.
Nashville warbler	Vermivora ruficapilla
Nettles	Urtica spp.
Northern black snake	Coluber constrictor
Northern brown snake	Storeria dekayi
Northern cardinal	Cardinalis cardinalis
Northern copperhead	Agkistrodon contortrix
Northern cricket frog	Acris crepitans
Northern dusky salamander	Desmognathus fuscus
Northern flicker	Colaptes auratus
Northern flying squirrel	Glaucomys sabrinus
Northern goshawk	Accipiter gentilis
Northern harrier (marsh hawk)	Circus cyaneus
Northern house wren	Troglodytes aedon
Northern leopard frog	Rana pipiens
Northern mockingbird	Mimus polyglottos
Northern oriole	Icterus galbula
Northern parula	Parula americana
Northern pintail	Anas acuta
Northern red salamander	Pseudotriton ruber
Northern red-bellied snake	Storeria occipitomaculata
Northern ringneck snake	Diadophis punctatus
Northern saw-whet owl	Aegolius acadicus
Northern spring peeper	Hyla crucifer
Northern spring salamander	Gyrinophilus porphyriticus
Northern two-lined salamander	Eurycea bislineata
Northern water shrew	Sorex palustris
Northern waterthrush	Seiurus noveboracensis
Norway rat	Rattus norvegicus

Norway spruce	Picea abies
Opossum	Didelphis virginia
Orchard grass	Dactylis glomerata
Orchard oriole	Icterus spurius
Osprey	Pandion haliaetus
Otter	Lutra canadensis
Ovenbird	Seiurus aurocapillus
Palm warbler	Dendroica palmarum
Partridge berry	Mitchella repens
Pearly everlasting	Anaphalis margaritacea
Pectoral sandpiper	Calidris melanotos
Pepperweed	Lepidium campestre
Peregrine falcon	Falco peregrinus
Persimmon	Diospyros virginiana
Phlox	Phlox spp.
Phragmites reed	Phragmites communis
Pickerel	Esox spp.
Pickerel frog	Rana palustris
Pickerel weed	Pontederia cordata
Pied-billed grebe	Podilymbus podiceps
Pileated woodpecker	Dryocopus pileatus
Pine vole	Pitymys pinetorum
Pine siskin	Carduelis pinus
Pinesap	Monotropa hypopithys
Pitch pine	Pinus rigida
Pitcher plant	Sarracenia purpurea
Poison ivy	Rhus radicans
Poison sumac	Rhus vernix
Pokeweed	Phytolacca americana
Polypody fern	Polypodium virginianum
Pond weeds	Potomogeton spp.
Porcupine	Erethizon dorsatum
Prairie warbler	Dendroica discolor
Prickly pear catcus	Opuntia spp.
Pumpkinseed	Lepomis gibbosus
Purple finch	Carpodacus purpureus
Purple loosestrife	Lythrum salicaria
Purple martin	Progne subis
Quaking aspen	Populus tremuloides
Queen Anne's lace	Daucus carota
Raccoon	Procyon lotor
Ragweed	Ambrosia spp.

Rainbow trout	Salmo gairdneri
Red bat	Lasiurus borealis
Red cedar	Juniperus virginiana
Red fox	Vulpes fulva
Red maple	Acer rubrum
Red oak	Quercus rubra
Red pine	Pinus resinosa
Red squirrel	Tamiasciurus hudsonicus
Red-bellied woodpecker	Centurus carolinus
Red-breasted nuthatch	Sitta canadensis
Red-eyed vireo	Vireo olivaceus
Red-shouldered hawk	Buteo lineatus
Red-spotted newt	Notophthalmus viridescens
Red-tailed hawk	Buteo jamaicensis
Red-winged blackbird	Agelaius phoeniccus
Rhodora	Rhododendron canadense
Ring-billed gull	Larus delawarensis
Ring-necked duck	Aythya collaris
Ring-necked pheasant	Phasianus colchicus
River birch	Betula nigra
River weeds	Podostemum spp.
Rock bass	Ambloplites ruprestris
Rock dove	Columbia livia
Rock (yellow nose) vole	Microtus chrotorrhinus
Rose-breasted grosbeak	Pheucticus ludovicianus
Rough-legged hawk	Buteo lagopus
Rough-winged swallow	Stelgidopteryx ruficollis
Royal fern	Osmunda regalis
Ruby-crowned kinglet	Regulus calendula
Ruby-throated hummingbird	Archilochus colubris
Rue-anemone	Anemonella thalictroides
Ruffed grouse	Bonasa umbellus
Rufous-sided towhee	Pipilo erythrophthalmus
Rusty blackbird	Euphagus carolinus
Sarsaparilla	Aralia spp.
Sassafras	Sassafras albidum
Savannah sparrow	Passerculus sandwichensis
Saxifrage	Saxifraga spp.
Scarlet oak	Quercus coccinea
Scarlet tanager	Piranga olivacea
Scotch pine	Pinus sylvestris
Scrub oak	Quercus ilicifolia

Sensitive fern	Onoclea sensibilis
Shadbush (Juneberry)	Amelanchier spp.
Shagbark hickory	Carya ovata
Sharp-shinned hawk	Accipiter striatus
Sheep laurel	Kalima angustifolia
Sheep sorrel	Rumex acetosella
Shepherd's purse	Capsella bursa-pastoris
Shield fern (Marginal)	Dryopteris marginalis
Shining clubmoss	Lycopodium lucidulum
Shinleaf	Pyrola spp.
Short-eared owl	Asio flammeus
Short-tailed shrew	Blarina brevicauda
Shorttail weasel	Mustela erminea
Silky dogwood	Cornus amomum
Silver maple	Acer saccharinum
Silver-haired bat	Lasionycteris noctivagans
Skunk cabbage	Symplocarpus foetidus
Slimy salamander	Plethodon glutinosus
Slippery elm	Ulmus rubra
Smallmouth bass	Micropterus dolomieu
Smartweed	Polygonum spp.
Smoky shrew	Sorex fumeus
Smooth green snake	Opheodrys vernalis
Smooth sumac	Rhus glabra
Snow bunting	Plectrophenax nivalis
Snow goose	Chen caerulescens
Snowshoe hare	Lepus americanus
Snowy egret	Egretta thula
Solitary sandpiper	Tringa solitaria
Solitary vireo	Vireo solitarius
Solomon's-seal	Polygonatum spp.
Song sparrow	Melospiza melodia
Southern bog lemming	Synaptomys cooperi
Southern flying squirrel	Glaucomys volans
Spatterdock	Nuphar spp.
Spicebush	Lindera benzoin
Spottail shiner	Notropis hudsonius
Spotted salamander	Ambystoma maculatum
Spotted sandpiper	Actitus macularia
Spotted turtle	Clemmys guttata
Spotted wintergreen	Chimaphila maculata
Spreading dogbane	Apocynum androsaemifolium

Spring beauty	Clatonia virginica
St. Johns-wort	Hypericum spp.
Staghorn sumac	Rhus typhina
Star-nosed mole	Condylura cristata
Starflower	Trientalis borealis
Sticktight	Bidens spp.
Stinging nettle	Urtica spp.
Striped maple	Acer pennsylvanicum
Striped skunk	Mephitis mephitis
Sugar maple	Acer saccharum
Sumac	Rhus spp.
Sundew	Drosera rotundifolia
Swainson's thrush	Catharus ustulatus
Swamp azalea	Rhododendron viscosum
Swamp candle	Lysimachia terrestris
Swamp milkweed	Asclepias incarnata
Swamp sparrow	Melospiza georgiana
Swamp white oak	Quercus bicolor
Sweet birch	Betula lenta
Sweet clover	Melilotus officinalis
Sweet fern	Comptonia peregrina
Sycamore	Platanus occidentalis
Tennessee warbler	Vermivora peregrina
Tessellated darter	Etheostoma olmstedi
Thistles	Cirsium spp.
Timber rattlesnake	Crotalus horridus
Trailing arbutus	Epigaea repens
Tree swallow	Iridoprocne bicolor
Trout-lily	Erythronium americanum
Tufted titmouse	Parus bicolor
Tulip tree	Liriodendron tulipifera
Turkey vulture	Cathartes aura
Veery	Hylocichla fuscescens
Vervain	Verbena hastata
Vesper sparrow	Pooecetes gramineus
Violets	Viola spp.
Viper's bugloss	Echium vulgare
Virginia creeper	Parthenocissus quinquefolia
Walleye	Stizostedion vitreum
Warbling vireo	Vireo gilvus
Water pipit	Anthus spinoletta
Water-willow	Decadon verticellatus

Watercress	Nasturtium officinale
Watershield	Brasenia schreberi
White ash	Fraxinus americana
White oak	Quercus alba
White pine	Pinus strobus
White spruce	Picea glauca
White sucker	Catostomus commersonii
White water lily	Nymphaea odorata
White-breasted nuthatch	Sitta carolinensis
White-crowned sparrow	Zonotrichia leucophrys
White-footed mouse	Peromyscus leucopus
White-tailed deer	Odocoileus virginianus
White-throated sparrow	Zonotrichia albicollis
Whorled loosestrife	Lysimachia quadrifolia
Wild bergamot	Monarda fistulosa
Wild calla	Calla palustris
Wild celery	Vallisneria americana
Wild ginger	Asarum canadense
Wild grape	Vitis aestivalis
Wild indigo	Baptisia tinctoria
Wild lily-of-the-valley	Maiathemum canadense
Wild parsnip	Pastinaca sativa
Wild strawberry	Fragaria virginiana
Wild turkey	Meleagris gallopavo
Willows	Salix spp.
Wilson's warbler	Wilsonia pusilla
Winter wren	Troglodytes troglodytes
Wintergreen	Pyrola spp.
Witch hazel	Hamamelis virginiana
Wood duck	Aix sponsa
Wood frog	Rana sylvatica
Wood sorrel	Oxalis spp.
Wood thrush	Hylocichla mustelina
Wood turtle	Clemmys insculpta
Woodchuck	Marmota monax
Woodland jumping mouse	Napaeozapus insignis
Worm-eating warbler	Helmitheros vermivorus
Yarrow	Achillea millefolium
Yellow birch	Betula lutea
Yellow lady's-slipper	Cypripedium calceolus
Yellow perch	Perca flavescens
Yellow warbler	Dendroica petechia

Yellow-bellied sapsucker	Sphyrapicus varius
Yellow-billed cuckoo	Coccyzus americanus
Yellow-rumped warbler	Dendroica coronata
Yellow-throated vireo	Vireo flavifrons

II. Scientific Names to Common Names

Abies balsamea	Balsam fir
Accipiter cooperi	Cooper's hawk
Accipter gentilis	Northern goshawk
Accipter striatus	Sharp-shinned hawk
Acer pennsylvanicum	Striped maple
Acer rubrum	Red maple
Acer saccharinum	Silver maple
Acer saccharum	Sugar maple
Achillea millefolium	Yarrow
Acris crepitans	Northern cricket frog
Actitus macularia	Spotted sandpiper
Aegolius acadicus	Northern saw-whet owl
Agelaius phoeniceus	Red-winged blackbird
Agkistrodon contortrix	Northern copperhead
Aix sponsa	Wood duck
Allium spp.	Field garlic
Alnus glutinosa	Black alder
Alnus serrulata	Common alder
Alnus spp.	Alders
Alosa sapidissima	American shad
Ambloplites ruprestris	Rock bass
Ambrosia spp.	Ragweed
Ambystoma jeffersonianum	Jefferson salamander
Ambystoma maculatum	Spotted salamander
Ambystoma opacum	Marbled salamander
Amelanchier spp.	Shadbush (Juneberry)
Amianthium muscaetoxicum	Fly-poison
Anaphalis margaritacea	Pearly everlasting
Anas acuta	Northern pintail
Anas carolinensis	Green-winged teal
Anas dicors	Blue-winged teal
Anas platyrhynchos	Mallard
Anas rubripes	American black duck
Andromeda glaucophylla	Bog rosemary
Anemonella thalictroides	Rue-anemone
Anquilla rostrara	American eel

Anthus spinoletta	Water pipit
Apocynum androsaemifolium	Spreading dogbane
Aquila chrysaetos	Golden eagle
Aquilegia canadensis	Columbine
Aralia spp.	Sarsaparilla
Arceuthobium pusillum	Dwarf mistletoe
Archilochus colubris	Ruby-throated hummingbird
Arctium minus	Burdock
Ardea herodias	Great blue heron
Arisaema triphyllum	Jack-in-the-pulpit
Aronia spp.	Chokeberry
Asarum canadense	Wild ginger
Asclepias incarnata	Swamp milkweed
Asclepias spp.	Narrow-leaved milkweed
Asclepias syriaca	Milkweed
Asio flammeus	Short-eared owl
Asio otus	Long-eared owl
Aythya affinis	Lesser scaup
Aythya collaris	Ring-necked duck
Aythya valisineria	Canvasback
Baptisia tinctoria	Wild indigo
Betula lenta	Sweet birch
Betula lutea	Yellow birch
Betula nigra	River birch
Betula populifolia	Gray birch
Bidens spp.	Sticktight
Blarina brevicauda	Short-tailed shrew
Bombycilla cedorum	Cedar waxwing
Bonasa umbellus	Ruffed grouse
Botrychium spp.	Grape fern
Branta canadensis	Canada goose
Brasenia schreberi	Watershield
Brassica spp.	Mustards
Bubo virginianus	Great horned owl
Bucephala albeola	Bufflehead
Bucephala clangula	Common goldeneye
Bufo americanus	American toad
Bufo woodhousei	Fowler's toad
Buteo jamaicensis	Red-tailed hawk
Buteo lagopus	Rough-legged hawk
Buteo lineatus	Red-shouldered hawk
Buteo platypterus	Broad-winged hawk

Butorides striatus	Green-backed heron
Cabomba caroliniana	Fanwort
Calidris melanotos	Pectoral sandpiper
Calla palustris	Wild calla
Canis latrans	Coyote
Capella gallinago	Common snipe
Capsella bursa-pastoris	Shepherd's purse
Cardinalis cardinalis	Northern cardinal
Carduelis flammea	Common redpoll
Carduelis pinus	Pine siskin
Carduelis tristis	American goldfinch
Carphophis amoenus	Eastern worm snake
Carpinus caroliniana	Hornbeam
Carpodacus mexicanus	House finch
Carpodacus purpureus	Purple finch
Carya ovata	Shagbark hickory
Casmerodius albus	Great egret
Castanea dentata	American chestnut
Castor canadensis	Beaver
Cathartes aura	Turkey vulture
Catharus ustulatus	Swainson's thrush
Catostomus commersonii	White sucker
Centurus carolinus	Red-bellied woodpecker
Cephalanthus occidentalis	Buttonbush
Ceratophyllum spp.	Coontails
Certhia familiaris	Brown creeper
Chaetura pelagica	Chimney swift
Chamaedaphne calyculata	Leatherleaf
Charadrius vociferus	Killdeer
Chelydra serpentina	Common snapping turtle
Chen caerulescens	Snow goose
Chenopodium album	Lambsquarter
Chimaphila maculata	Spotted wintergreen
Chordeiles minor	Common nighthawk
Chrysanthemum leucanthemum	Field daisy
Chrysemys picta	Eastern painted turtle
Cichorium intybus	Chicory
Circus cyaneus	Northern harrier (marsh hawk)
Cirsium spp.	Thistles
Cistothorus palustris	Marsh wren
Clatonia virginica	Spring beauty
Clemmys guttata	Spotted turtle

Clemmys insculpta	Wood turtle
Clemmys muhlenbergi	Bog turtle
Clethrionomys gapperi	Boreal redback vole
Clintonia borealis	Corn lily
Coccyzus americanus	Yellow-billed cuckoo
Coccyzus erythropthalmus	Black-billed cuckoo
Colaptes auratus	Northern flicker
Coluber constrictor	Northern black snake
Columbia livia	Rock dove
Comptonia peregrina	Sweet fern
Condylura cristata	Star-nosed mole
Conopholis americana	Cancerroot
Contopus virens	Eastern wood pewee
Convolvulus arvensis	Bindweed
Coptis groenlandica	Gold thread
Cornus amomum	Silky dogwood
Cornus florida	Flowering dogwood
Cornus spp.	Dogwoods
Coronilla varia	Crown vetch
Corvus brachyrhynchos	American crow
Corvus ossifragus	Fish crow
Crataegus spp.	Hawthorn
Crotalus horridus	Timber rattlesnake
Cryptotis parva	Least shrew
Cuscata spp.	Dodder
Cyanocitta cristata	Blue jay
Cygnus olor	Mute swan
Cypripedium calceolus	Yellow lady's-slipper
Cypripedium spp.	Moccasin flower
Dactylis glomerata	Orchard grass
Daucus carota	Queen Anne's lace
Decadon verticellatus	Water-willow
Dendroica caerulea	Cerulean warbler
Dendroica caerulescens	Black-throated blue warbler
Dendroica coronata	Yellow-rumped warbler
Dendroica discolor	Prairie warbler
Dendroica fusca	Blackburnian warbler
Dendroica magnolia	Magnolia warbler
Dendroica palmarum	Palm warbler
Dendroica pensylvanica	Chestnut-sided warbler
Dendroica petechia	Yellow warbler
Dendroica striata	Blackpoll warbler

Dendroica tigrina	Cape May warbler
Dendroica virens	Black-throated green warbler
Dennstaedtia punctilobula	Hay-scented fern
Desmodium spp.	Beggar-lice (tick-trefoil)
Desmognathus fuscus	Northern dusky salamander
Diadophis punctatus	Northern ringneck snake
Didelphis virginia	Opossum
Diospyros virginiana	Persimmon
Dolichonyx oryzivorus	Bobolink
Drosera rotundifolia	Sundew
Dryocopus pileatus	Pileated woodpecker
Dryopteris marginalis	Shield fern (Marginal)
Dryopteris phegopteris	Beech fern
Dryopteris thelypteris	Marsh fern
Dumetella carolinensis	Gray catbird
Echium vulgare	Viper's bugloss
Egretta thula	Snowy egret
Elaphe obsoleta	Black rat snake
Empidonax alnorum	Alder flycatcher
Empidonax minimus	Least flycatcher
Epifagus virginiana	Beechdrops
Epigaea repens	Trailing arbutus
Eptesicus fuscus	Big brown bat
Equisetum arvense	Field horsetail
Equisetum spp.	Horsetails
Erechtites hieracifolia	Fireweed
Eremophila alpestris	Horned lark
Erethizon dorsatum	Porcupine
Erigeron spp.	Fleabane
Eriophorum spp.	Cottongrass
Erolia minutilla	Least sandpiper
Erythronium americanum	Trout-lily
Esox masquinongy	Muskellunge
Esox spp.	Pickerel
Etheostoma olmstedi	Tessellated darter
Eumeces fasciatus	Five-lined skink
Eupatorium perfoliatum	Boneset
Eupatorium spp.	Joe-pye-weed
Euphagus carolinus	Rusty blackbird
Eurycea bislineata	Northern two-lined salamander
Eurycea longicauda	Long-tailed salamander
Fagus grandifolia	American beech

Falco peregrinus	Peregrine falcon
Falco sparverius	American kestrel (Sparrow hawk)
Fragaria virginiana	Wild strawberry
Fraxinus americana	White ash
Fulica americana	American coot
Galium spp.	Bedstraw
Gallinula choropus	Common moorhen
Gaultheria procumbens	Checkerberry
Gavia immer	Common loon
Gaylussacia spp.	Huckleberry
Gentiana clausa	Closed gentian
Geothlypis trichas	Common yellowthroat
Geranium spp.	Geranium
Glaucomys sabrinus	Northern flying squirrel
Glaucomys volans	Southern flying squirrel
Graptemys geographica	Map turtle
Gyrinophilus porphyriticus	Northern spring salamander
Haliaeetus leucocephalus	Bald eagle
Hamamelis virginiana	Witch hazel
Helmitheros vermivorus	Worm-eating warbler
Hemerocallis fulva	Day-lily
Hemidactylium scutatum	Four-toed salamander
Hepatica spp.	Hepatica
Hesperiphona vespertina	Evening grosbeak
Heteranthera spp.	Mud-plantain
Heterodon platyrhinos	Eastern hognose snake
Hieracium spp.	Hawkweed
Hirundo rustica	Barn swallow
Houstonia spp.	Bluets
Hyla crucifer	Northern spring peeper
Hyla versicolor	Eastern gray treefrog
Hylocichla fuscescens	Veery
Hylocichla guttata	Hermit thrush
Hylocichla minima	Gray-cheeked thrush
Hylocichla mustelina	Wood thrush
Hypericum spp.	St. Johns-wort
Ictalurus punctatus	Channel catfish
Ictalurus spp.	Bullhead
Icterus galbula	Northern oriole
Icterus spurius	Orchard oriole
Ilex montana	Large-leaved holly
Impatiens capensis	Jewelweed

Iridoprocne bicolor	Tree swallow
Iris versicolor	Blue flag
Juglans nigra	Black walnut
Junco hyemalis	Dark-eyed junco
Juniperus virginiana	Red cedar
Kalima angustifolia	Sheep laurel
Kalmia latifolia	Mountain laurel
Kalmia polifolia	Bog laurel
Lamium spp.	Henbit
Lampropeltis triangulum	Eastern milk snake
Larix laricina	Larch
Larus argentatus	Herring gull
Larus delawarensis	Ring-billed gull
Lasionycteris noctivagans	Silver-haired bat
Lasiurus borealis	Red bat
Lasiurus cinereus	Hoary bat
Ledum groenlandicum	Labrador tea
Lemna spp.	Duckweed
Lepidium campestre	Pepperweed
Lepomis cyanellus	Green sunfish
Lepomis gibbosus	Pumpkinseed
Lepomis macrochirus	Bluegill
Lepus americanus	Snowshoe hare
Linaria vulgaris	Butter 'n eggs
Lindera benzoin	Spicebush
Liriodendron tulipifera	Tulip tree
Lonicera japonica	Japanese honeysuckle
Lonicera spp.	Honeysuckle
Lophodytes cucullatus	Hooded merganser
Lutra canadensis	Otter
Lycopodium complanatum	Ground cedar
Lycopodium lucidulum	Shining clubmoss
Lycopodium obscurum	Ground pine
Lycopodium spp.	Club mosses
Lygodium palmatum	Climbing fern
Lynchis alba	Campion
Lynx rufus	Bobcat
Lysimachia quadrifolia	Whorled loosestrife
Lysimachia terrestris	Swamp candle
Lythrum salicaria	Purple loosestrife
Maiathemum canadense	Wild lily-of-the-valley
Mareca americana	American widgeon

Marmota monax	Woodchuck
Megaceryle alcyon	Belted kingfisher
Melampyrum lineare	Cow-wheat
Meleagris gallopavo	Wild turkey
Melilotus officinalis	Sweet clover
Melospiza georgiana	Swamp sparrow
Melospiza melodia	Song sparrow
Mentha spp.	Mints
Mephitis mephitis	Striped skunk
Mergus merganser	Common merganser
Micropterus dolomieu	Smallmouth bass
Micropterus salmoides	Largemouth bass
Microtus chrotorrhinus	Rock (yellow nose) vole
Microtus pennsylvanicus	Meadow vole
Mimus polyglottos	Northern mockingbird
Mitchella repens	Partridge berry
Mniotila varia	Black-and-White warbler
Molothrus ater	Brown-headed cowbird
Monarda fistulosa	Wild bergamot
Monotropa hypopithys	Pinesap
Monotropa uniflora	Indian pipe
Mus musculus	House mouse
Mustela erminea	Shorttail weasel
Mustela frenata	Longtail weasel
Mustela vison	Mink
Myiarchus crinitus	Great crested flycatcher
Myotis lucifugus	Little brown bat
Myriophyllum spp.	Milfoil
Najas spp.	Naiads
Napaeozapus insignis	Woodland jumping mouse
Nasturtium officinale	Watercress
Neotoma floridana	Eastern wood rat
Notophthalmus viridescens	Red-spotted newt
Notropis cornutus	Common shiner
Notropis hudsonius	Spottail shiner
Noturus insignis	Madtom
Nuphar spp.	Spatterdock
Nymphaea odorata	White water lily
Nyssa sylvatica	Black gum
Odocoileus virginianus	White-tailed deer
Oenothera biennis	Evening primrose
Ondatra zibethica	Muskrat

Onoclea sensibilis	Sensitive fern	
Opheodrys vernalis	Smooth green snake	
Opuntia spp.	Prickly pear cactus	
Orontium aquaticum	Golden club	
Osmunda cinnamonea	Cinnamon fern	
Osmunda claytoniana	Interrupted fern	
Osmunda regalis	Royal fern	
Ostrya virginiana	Hop hornbeam	
Otus asio	Eastern screech owl	
Oxalis spp.	Wood sorrel	
Pandion haliaetus	Osprey	
Parasclops breweri	Hairy-tailed mole	
Parthenocissus quinquefolia	Virginia creeper	
Parula americana	Northern parula	
Parus altricapillus	Black-capped chickadee	
Parus bicolor	Tufted titmouse	
Passer domesticus	House sparrow	
Passerculus sandwichensis	Savannah sparrow	
Passerella iliaca	Fox sparrow	
Passerina cyanea	Indigo bunting	
Pastinaca sativa	Wild parsnip	
Peltandra virginica	Arrow arum	
Perca flavescens	Yellow perch	
Peromyscus leucopus	White-footed mouse	
Peromyscus maniculatus	Deer mouse	
Petrochelidon pyrrhonota	Cliff swallow	
Phasianus colchicus	Ring-necked pheasant	
Pheucticus ludovicianus	Rose-breasted grosbeak	
Philohela minor	American woodcock	
Phlox spp.	Phlox	
Phragmites communis	Phragmites reed	
Phytolacca americana	Pokeweed	
Picea abies	Norway spruce	
Picea glauca	White spruce	
Picea mariana	Black spruce	
Picoides pubescens	Downy woodpecker	
Picoides villosus	Hairy woodpecker	
Pinus nigra	Austrian pine	
Pinus resinosa	Red pine	
Pinus rigida	Pitch pine	
Pinus strobus	White pine	
Pinus sylvestris	Scotch pine	

Pipilo erythrophthalmus	Rufous-sided towhee
Pipistrellus subflavus	Eastern pipistrel
Piranga olivacea	Scarlet tanager
Pitymys pinetorum	Pine vole
Platanus occidentalis	Sycamore
Plectrophenax nivalis	Snow bunting
Plethodon cinereus	Eastern red-backed salamander
Plethodon glutinosus	Slimy salamander
Podilymbus podiceps	Pied-billed grebe
Podoceps auritus	Horned grebe
Podophyllum peltatum	Mayapple
Podostemum spp.	River weeds
Polioptila caerulea	Blue-gray gnatcatcher
Polygala paucifolia	Fringed polygala
Polygonatum spp.	Solomon's-seal
Polygonum spp.	Smartweed
Polypodium virginianum	Polypody fern
Polystichum acrostichoides	Christmas fern
Pomoxis nigromaculatus	Black crappie
Pontederia cordata	Pickerel weed
Pooecetes gramineus	Vesper sparrow
Populus deltoides	Cottonwood
Populus grandidentata	Big-toothed aspen
Populus spp.	Aspens
Populus tremuloides	Quaking aspen
Potentilla spp.	Cinquefoil
Potomogeton spp.	Pond weeds
Procyon lotor	Raccoon
Progne subis	Purple martin
Prunella vulgaris	Heal-all
Prunus pensylvanica	Fire cherry
Prunus serotina	Black cherry
Prunus virginiana	Choke cherry
Pseudacris triseriata	Boreal chorus frog
Pseudotriton ruber	Northern red salamander
Pseudotsuga menziesi	Douglas fir
Pteridium aquilinum	Bracken (Brake) fern
Pyrola spp.	Shinleaf
Pyrola spp.	Wintergreen
Quercus alba	White oak
Quercus bicolor	Swamp white oak
Quercus coccinea	Scarlet oak

Quercus ilicifolia	Scrub oak
Quercus prinus	Chestnut oak
Quercus rubra	Red oak
Quercus velutina	Black oak
Quiscalus quiscula	Common grackle
Rana catesbeiana	Bullfrog
Rana clamitans	Green frog
Rana palustris	Pickerel frog
Rana pipiens	Northern leopard frog
Rana sylvatica	Wood frog
Ranunculus spp.	Buttercups
Rattus norvegicus	Norway rat
Regulus calendula	Ruby-crowned kinglet
Regulus satrapa	Golden-crowned kinglet
Rhinichthyes atratulus	Blacknose dace
Rhinichthyes cataractae	Longnose dace
Rhododendron canadense	Rhodora
Rhododendron maximum	Great Rhododendron (white laurel)
Rhododendron spp.	Mountain azalea
Rhododendron viscosum	Swamp azalea
Rhus glabra	Smooth sumac
Rhus radicans	Poison ivy
Rhus spp.	Sumac
Rhus typhina	Staghorn sumac
Rhus vernix	Poison sumac
Riparia riparia	Bank swallow
Robinia pseudoacacia	Black locust
Rudbeckia serotina	Black-eyed Susan
Rumex acetosella	Sheep sorrel
Rumex spp.	Dock
Sagittaria spp.	Arrowhead
Salix spp.	Willows
Salmo gairdneri	Rainbow trout
Salmo trutta	Brown trout
Salvelinus fontinalis	Brook trout
Sambucus canadensis	Common elder
Sanguinaria canadensis	Bloodroot
Saponaria officinalis	Bouncing bet
Sarracenia purpurea	Pitcher plant
Sassafras albidum	Sassafras
Saxifraga spp.	Saxifrage
Savornis phoebe	Eastern phoebe

Scalopus aquaticus	Eastern mole
Scaphiopus holbrooki	Eastern spadefoot
Scirpus spp.	Bulrushes
Seiurus aurocapillus	Ovenbird
Seiurus motacilla	Louisiana waterthrush
Seiurus noveboracensis	Northern waterthrush
Semotilus atromaculatus	Creek chub
Semotilus corporalis	Fallfish
Setaria spp.	Foxtail
Setophaga ruticilla	American redstart
Sialia sialis	Eastern bluebird
Sitta canadensis	Red-breasted nuthatch
Sitta carolinensis	White-breasted nuthatch
Smilacina racemosa	False Solomon's-seal
Smilax spp.	Catbrier
Solidago spp.	Goldenrod
Sorex cinereus	Masked shrew
Sorex dispar	Longtail shrew
Sorex fumeus	Smoky shrew
Sorex palustris	Northern water shrew
Sparganium spp.	Bur-reed
Sphyrapicus varius	Yellow-bellied sapsucker
Spirea spp.	Meadowsweet
Spirea tomentosa	Hardhack
Spizella arborea	American tree sparrow
Spizella passerina	Chipping sparrow
Spizella pusilla	Field sparrow
Stelgidopteryx ruficollis	Rough-winged swallow
Stellaria spp.	Chickweed
Sternotherus odoratus	Musk turtle
Stizostedion vitreum	Walleye
Storeria dekayi	Northern brown snake
Storeria occipitomaculata	Northern red-bellied snake
Strix varia	Barred owl
Sturnella magna	Eastern meadowlark
Sturnus vulgaris	European starling
Sylvilagus floridanus	Eastern cottontail
Symplocarpus foetidus	Skunk cabbage
Synaptomys cooperi	Southern bog lemming
Tamias striatus	Eastern chipmunk
Tamiasciurus hudsonicus	Red squirrel
Taraxacum spp.	Dandelion

Taxus canadensis	Canada yew
Terrapene carolina	Eastern box turtle
Thalictrum spp.	Meadowrue
Thamnophis sauritus	Eastern ribbon snake
Thamnophis sirtalis	Eastern garter snake
Thryothorus ludovicianus	Carolina wren
Tilia americana	Basswood
Toxostoma rufum	Brown thrasher
Triarella cordifolia	Foamflower
Trientalis borealis	Starflower
Tringa flavipes	Lesser yellowlegs
Tringa melanoleuca	Greater yellowlegs
Tringa solitaria	Solitary sandpiper
Troglodytes aedon	Northern house wren
Troglodytes troglodytes	Winter wren
Tsuga candensis	Hemlock
Turdus migratorius	American robin
Tussilago farfara	Coltsfoot
Typha angustifolia	Narrow-leaved cattail
Typha latifolia	Broad-leaved cattail
Tyrannus tyrannus	Eastern kingbird
Tyto alba	Barn owl
Ulmus rubra	Slippery elm
Ulmus spp.	Elms
Umbra pygmaea	Mud minnow
Urocyon cinereoargenteus	Gray fox
Ursus americanus	Black bear
Urtica spp.	Nettles
Urtica spp.	Stinging nettle
Utricularia vulgaris	Bladderwort
Uvularia spp.	Bellwort
Vaccinium corymbosum	Highbush blueberry
Vaccinium oxycoccos, macrocarpon	Cranberry
Vaccinium spp.	Blueberry
Vaccinium stamineum	Deerberry
Vallisneria americana	Wild celery
Veratrum viride	False hellebore
Verbascum thapsus	Mullein
Verbena hastata	Vervain
Vermivora chrysoptera	Golden-winged warbler
Vermivora peregrina	Tennessee warbler
Vermivora pinus	Blue-winged warbler

Vermivora ruficapilla	Nashville warbler
Viburnum acerifolium	Mapleleaf viburnum
Viburnum alnifolium	Hobblebush
Viburnum dentatum	Arrow-wood
Vicia cracca	Cow vetch
Viola spp.	Violets
Vireo flavifrons	Yellow-throated vireo
Vireo gilvus	Warbling vireo
Vireo olivaceus	Red-eyed vireo
Vireo solitarius	Solitary vireo
Vitis aestivalis	Wild grape
Vitis labrusca	Fox grape
Vulpes fulva	Red fox
Wilsonia canadensis	Canada warbler
Wilsonia citrina	Hooded warbler
Wilsonia pusilla	Wilson's warbler
Woodwardia virginica	Chain fern
Xanthium spp.	Cocklebur
Zapus hudsonius	Meadow jumping mouse
Zenaida macroura	Mourning dove
Zonotrichia albicollis	White-throated sparrow
Zonotrichia leucophrys	White-crowned sparrow

Selected Readings and Source Material

Naturalist's Guides

These books describe communities of plants and animals over a wide geographic range and stress the interactions of organisms and the non-living environment. Color photographs are employed for identification purposes. Range maps and brief descriptions are provided for a wide variety of dominant plants and animals.

Lawrence, S., and B. Gross. 1984. *The Audubon Society Field Guide to the Natural Places of the Mid-Atlantic States: Inland*. New York: Pantheon Books.

Niering, W. A. 1985. *Wetlands*. New York: Alfred A. Knopf, Inc.

Sutton, A., and M. Sutton. 1985. *Eastern Forests*. New York: Alfred A. Knopf, Inc.

Field Guides

These volumes are more compact and portable. Various schemes are used to aid the user to identify a particular plant or animal. The Peterson series uses illustrations with diagnostic features highlighted to aid in identification. The Audubon series utilizes color photographs as identification aids. Both series typically include habitat notes, ranges, and related species. The Golden Nature Guides, published by Golden Press, are designed for the beginner. These guides provide color illustrations to selected species typically found over a wide geographic range, along with brief habitat notes, unusual features, etc.

Peterson Series

Burt, W. H., and R. P. Grossenheider. 1976. *A Field Guide to the Mammals*. 3rd ed. Boston: Houghton Mifflin Co.

Cobb, B. 1963. *A Field Guide to the Ferns and Their Related Families of Northeastern and Central North America*. Boston: Houghton Mifflin Co.

Conant, R. 1975. *A Field Guide to the Reptiles and Amphibians of the United States and Canada East of the 100th Meridian*. Boston: Houghton Mifflin Co.

Murie, O. J. 1954. *A Field Guide to Animal Tracks*. Boston: Houghton Mifflin Co.

Peterson, R. T. 1980. *A Field Guide to the Birds*. Boston: Houghton Mifflin Co.

Peterson, R. T., and M. McKenny. 1968. *A Field Guide to Wildflowers of Northeastern and North-Central North America*. Boston: Houghton Mifflin Co.

Petrides, G. A. 1972. *A Field Guide to Trees and Shrubs*. Boston: Houghton Mifflin Co.

Audubon Series

Behler, J. L., and F. W. King. 1979. *The Audubon Society Field Guide to North American Reptiles and Amphibians*. New York: Alfred A. Knopf, Inc.

Bull, J., and J. Farrand, Jr. 1977. *The Audubon Society Field Guide to North American Birds: Eastern Region*. New York: Alfred A. Knopf, Inc.

Whitaker, J. O., Jr. 1980. *The Audubon Society Field Guide to North American Mammals*. New York: Alfred A. Knopf, Inc.

Golden Nature Guides

Martin, A. C. 1972. *Weeds*. New York: Golden Press.

Reid, G. K., and G. S. Fichter. 1967. *Pond Life*. New York: Golden Press.

Shuttleworth, F. S., and H. S. Zim. 1967. *Non-Flowering Plants*. New York: Golden Press.

Identification Manuals

Cooper, E. L. 1983. *Fishes of Pennsylvania and the Northeastern States*. University Park: The Pennsylvania State University Press.

Ditmer, W. P. 1980. *Pennsylvania Weeds*. Harrisburg: Commonwealth of Pennsylvania Department of Agriculture.

Edmondson, W. T., ed. 1959. *Fresh-water Biology*. 2d ed. New York: John Wiley.

Fernald, M. L. 1950. *Gray's Manual of Botany*. 8th ed. New York: American Book Co.

Gleason, H. A. 1952. *The New Britton and Brown Illustrated Flora of the Northeastern United States and Adjacent Canada*. 3 vols. New York: New York Botanical Garden.

Gleason, H. A., and A. Cronquist. 1963. *Manual of Vascular Plants of Northeastern United States and Adjacent Canada*. Princeton, NJ: D. Van Nostrand.

Grimm, W. C. 1952. *The Shrubs of Pennsylvania*. Harrisburg: The Stackpole Press Co.

Harlow, W. M., and E. S. Harrar. 1958. *Textbook of Dendrology*. New
York: McGraw-Hill Book Co.

Illick, J. S. 1923. *Pennsylvania Trees*. Harrisburg: Pennsylvania Department of Forestry.

Magee, D. W. 1981. *Freshwater Wetlands: A Guide to Common Indicator Plants of the Northeast*. Amherst: The University of Massachusetts Press.

Rickett, H. W. 1965. *Flowers of the United States: The Northeastern States*. Vols. I and II. New York: McGraw-Hill Book Co.

Smith, A. H. 1963. *The Mushroom Hunter's Field Guide*. Rev. ed. Ann Arbor: University of Michigan Press.

General References

Brooks, M. 1965. *The Applachians*. Boston: Houghton Mifflin.

Harding, J. J., ed. 1986. *Marsh, Meadow, Mountain, Natural Places of the Delaware Valley*. Philadelphia: Temple University Press.

Knepp, T. A. 1966. *The Poconos: A Handbook and Guide to Pennsylvania's Vacation Land*. Stroudsburg, PA: T. Knepp.

Milne, L. J., M. Milne, and the editors of Time-Life Books. 1967. *The Mountains*. Rev. ed., Life Nature Library. New York: Time-Life Books.

Smith, R. L. 1980. *Ecology and Field Biology*. 3rd ed. New York: Harper and Row.

Tyson, C. B. 1982. *The Poconos*. Union City, NJ: William H. Wise and Co., Inc.

Chapter 1: Pocono Patterns

Clapham, W. B., Jr. 1983. *Natural Ecosystems*. 2nd ed. New York: Macmillan.

Grimm, W. C., and R. Whitebread. 1952. *Mammal Survey of Northeastern Pennsylvania*. Harrisburg: Pennsylvania Game Commission.

McCormick, J. 1959. *The Living Forest*. New York: Harper and Brothers.

Shafer, R. 1980. Natural history of the Poconos. *The Pennsylvania Naturalist* 2(6):24–27, 36–37.

Chapter 2: Geological Forces that Shaped the Poconos

Berg, T. M., W. D. Sevon, et al. 1975–8. Geology and Mineral Resources of the Brodheadsville, Hickory Run, Blakeslee, Christmans, Pohopoco Mountain, Tobyhanna, Buck Hill Falls, Pocono

Pines, Mount Pocono, and Skytop Quadrangles. *Atlases* 214a, 204c, 204d, 204a, 204b, 195a, 195b, 194c, 194d, and 205a apply. Harrisburg: Commonwealth of Pennsylvania Bureau of Topographic and Geologic Survey.

Berkheiser, S. W. 1984. Summary of the slate industry in Pennsylvania, 1983. *Pennsylvania Geology* 15(1):10–13.

Carswell, L. D., and O. B. Lloyd. 1979. *Geology and Groundwater Resources of Monroe County, Pennsylvania. Water Resources Report 47.* Harrisburg: Commonwealth of Pennsylvania Bureau of Topographic and Geologic Survey.

Crowl, G. H., and W. D. Sevon. 1980. *Glacial Deposits of Late Wisconsinan Age in Northeastern Pennsylvania.* General Geology Report 71. Harrisburg: Commonwealth of Pennsylvania Bureau of Topographic and Geologic Survey.

Geyer, A. R. 1969. Hickory Run State Park–Hickory Run Boulder Field. *Penn. Geol. Surv.*, 4th Ser., Park Guide 2.

Geyer, A. R., and W. H. Bolles. 1979, 1987. *Outstanding Scenic Geological Features of Pennsylvania.* Environmental Geology Report 7, parts 1 and 2. Harrisburg: Commonwealth of Pennsylvania Bureau of Topographic and Geologic Survey.

Geyer, A. R., and D. M. Snyder. 1983. Waterfalls in Pennsylvania. *Pennsylvania Geology* 14(5):2–5.

Hoskins, D. M., J. D. Inners, and J. A. Harper. 1984. *Fossil Collecting in Pennsylvania.* General Geology Report 40. Harrisburg: Commonwealth of Pennsylvania Bureau of Topographic and Geologic Survey.

Hoskins, D. M. n.d. *Common Fossils of Pennsylvania.* Educational Series No. 2. Harrisburg: Commonwealth of Pennsylvania Bureau of Topographic and Geologic Survey.

Majumdar, S. K., and E. W. Miller, eds. 1983. *Pennsylvania Coal: Resources, Technology, and Utilization.* Easton: The Pennsylvania Academy of Science.

Shepps, V. C. 1962. *Pennsylvania and the Ice Age.* Harrisburg: Commonwealth of Pennsylvania Bureau of Topographic and Geologic Survey.

Subitsky, S., ed. 1969. *Geology of Selected Areas of New Jersey and Eastern Pennsylvania.* New Brunswick, NJ: Rutgers University Press.

Willard, B. 1962. *Pennsylvania Geology Summarized.* Harrisburg: Commonwealth of Pennsylvania Topographic and Geologic Survey.

Wilshusen, J. P. 1983. *Geology of the Appalachian Trail in Pennsyl-*

vania. Harrisburg: Commonwealth of Pennsylvania Bureau of Topographic and Geologic Survey.

Wolfe, P. 1977. *The Geology and Landscapes of New Jersey*. New York: Crane, Russak and Co.

Chapter 3: Pocono Forests

Braun, E. L. 1950. *Deciduous Forests of Eastern North America*. New York: Hafner Publishing Co.

Ceres, A. F. 1962. *Pennsylvania's Flaming Foliage*. Harrisburg: Commonwealth of Pennsylvania Travel Development Bureau.

Day, G. M. 1953. The Indian as an ecological factor in the Northeastern Forest. *Ecology* 34:329–346.

Donahue, W. H. 1954. Some plant communities in the anthracite region of northeastern Pennsylvania. *The American Midland Naturalist* 51(1):203–231.

Eyre, F. H., ed. 1980. *Forest Cover Types of the United States and Canada*. Washington, D.C.: Society of American Foresters.

Gleason, H., and A. Cronquist. 1964. *The Natural Geography of Plants*. New York: Columbia University Press.

Hassinger, J. D. n.d. *Wildlife Management on Pennsylvania State Forest Lands*. Harrisburg: Bureau of Forestry.

Nichols, G. E. 1935. The hemlock-white pine-hardwood region of eastern North America. *Ecology* 16:403–422.

Niering, W. A. 1950. A preliminary survey of the vascular flora of Pike and Monroe Counties, Pennsylvania. M.S. thesis, The Pennsylvania State University, University Park, PA.

Niering, W. A. 1953. The past and present vegetation of High Point State Park, NJ. *Ecological Monographs* 23:127–148.

Robichaud, B., and M. F. Buell. 1973. *Vegetation of New Jersey*. New Brunswick, NJ: Rutgers University Press.

Wherry, E. T., Fogg, J. M., and H. A. Wahl. 1979. *Atlas of the Flora of Pennsylvania*. Philadelphia: The Morris Arboretum of the University of Pennsylvania.

Chapter 4: Animals of Pocono Forests

Alt, G. L. 1982. Reproductive biology of Pennsylvania's black bears. *Pa. Game News* 53(2):9–15.

Alt, G. L. 1986. 1985 bear season results. *Pa. Game News* 57(4):20–22.

Alt, G. L. 1987. Characteristics of bear cubs at birth. *Pa. Game News* 58(1):10–13.

Boyle, W. J., Jr. 1986. *A Guide to Bird Finding in New Jersey*. New Brunswick, NJ: Rutgers University Press.

Doutt, J. K., Heppenstall, C. A., and J. E. Guilday. 1977. *Mammals of Pennsylvania*. 4th ed. Harrisburg: Pennsylvania Game Commission.

Forbes, S. E., Land, L. M., Liscinsky, S. A., and H. A. Roberts. 1979. *The White-tailed Deer in Pennsylvania*. Harrisburg: Pennsylvania Game Commission.

Gerardi, M. H., and J. K. Grimm. 1979. *The History, Biology, Damage and Control of the Gypsy Moth Portheria dispar (L)*. Cranbury, NJ: Associated University Presses.

Giles, J. 1986. Pennsylvania bobcat roundup. *Pa. Game News* 57(9):17–20.

Grimm, W. C., and R. Whitebread. 1952. *Mammal Survey of Northeastern Pennsylvania*. Harrisburg: Pennsylvania Game Commission.

Halma, J. R. 1973. Bird species diversity and foliage height diversity correlations in a Pocono deciduous forest. *Proc. Pa. Acad. Sci.* 47:97–98.

Harrison, H. H. 1950. *Pennsylvania Reptiles and Amphibians*. 2nd ed. Harrisburg: Pennsylvania Fish Commission.

Heintzelman, D. S. 1976. *A Guide to Eastern Hawk Watching*. University Park: Pennsylvania State University Press.

Leck, C. F. 1975. *Birds of New Jersey: Their Habits and Habitats*. New Brunswick, NJ: Rutgers University Press.

Mitchell, B. 1983. Eagles across the state. *Pa. Game News* 54(12):7–13.

Nichols, J. O. 1980. *The Gypsy Moth*. Harrisburg: Pennsylvania Department of Environmental Resources.

Street, P. B. Birds of the Pocono Mountains, 1890–1954. *Cassinia* 41(1954):3–76.

Street, P. B. Birds of the Pocono Mountains, 1955–1975. *Cassinia* 55(1974–75):3–16.

Wakeley, J. S., and L. D. Wakeley. 1984. *Birds of Pennsylvania: Natural History and Conservation*. Harrisburg: Pennsylvania Game Commission.

Chapter 5: Watercourse and Wetland Communities

Amos, W. H. 1967. *The Life of the Pond (Our Living World of Nature)*. New York: McGraw-Hill Book Co.

Barker, J. L. 1978. *Characteristics of Pennsylvania Recreational Lakes*. Harrisburg: Pennsylvania Department of Environmental Resources in cooperation with U.S. Geological Survey.

Cameron, C. C. 1970. *Peat Deposits of Northeastern Pennsylvania.* Geol. Survey Bulletin 1317-A, Washington, D.C.

Clark, K. 1981. Red-spotted newt. *The Conservationist* 36(2):19–21.

Edgerton, C. D. 1969. Peat bog investigations in northeastern Pennsylvania. *Pennsylvania Geol. Surv. Bull.* IC-65.

Fables, D., and S. Fables. 1958. Descent to a boreal swamp. *Audubon Magazine* 60:206–208.

Goodwin, R. H., and W. A. Niering. 1975. *Inland Wetlands of the United States.* Natural History Theme Studies, No. 2. Washington, D.C.: National Park Service.

Halma, J. R. 1980. The dominant vascular flora of the Tannersville Bog, Monroe Co. *Proc. Pa. Acad. Sci.* 54:39–42.

Hammer, D. A. 1971. The durable snapping turtle. *Natural History* 80(6):58–65.

Hodge, W. H. 1981. Where a heavy body is likely to sink. *Audubon* 83(5):98–111.

Johnson, C. W. 1985. *Bogs of the Northeast.* Hanover, NH, and London: University Press of New England.

Letcher, G. 1985. *Canoeing the Delaware River. A Guide to the River and Shore.* New Brunswick, NJ: Rutgers University Press.

McMillan, V. 1984. Dragonfly monopoly. *Natural History* 93(7):32–39.

Niering, W. A. 1957. The Cranberry Bog area: A "natural" for wildlife. *Pa. Game News* 28(5):21–22.

Niering, W. A. 1966. *The Life of the Marsh: The North American Wetlands (Our Living World of Nature).* New York: McGraw-Hill Book Co.

Palmer, T. 1980. *Rivers of Pennsylvania.* University Park: The Pennsylvania State University Press.

Usinger, R. L. 1967. *The Life of Rivers and Streams (Our Living World of Nature).* New York: McGraw-Hill Book Co.

Chapter 6: Roadside Natural History

Batten, L. A. 1972. Breeding bird species diversity in relation of increasing urbanisation. *Bird Study* 19(3):157–166.

Burgess, R. L., and D. M. Sharp, eds. 1981. *Forest Island Dynamics in Man-Dominated Landscapes.* New York: Springer-Verlag.

Ditmer, W. P. 1980. *Pennsylvania Weeds.* Harrisburg: Commonwealth of Pennsylvania Department of Agriculture.

Egler, F. E., and S. R. Foote. 1975. *The Plight of the Right-of-way Domain Victim of Vandalism.* Mt. Kisco, NY: Future Media Services.

Harper, J. C. n.d. *Crown Vetch for Erosion Control and Beautifi-*

cation. Special Circular 161. University Park: The Pennsylvania State University.

Leck, C. 1973. Highways and the birdlife of New Jersey. *N.J. Nature News.* 28(2):70–71.

Niering, W. A. 1958. Principles of sound right-of-way vegetation management. *Economic Botany* 12(2):140–144.

Odum, E. P. 1969. The strategy of ecosystem development. *Science* 164:262–269.

Page, N. M., and R. E. Weaver, Jr. 1975. *Wild Plants in the City.* New York: Quadrangle/The New York Times Book Co.

Chapter 7: Human Activity from Native Americans to Vacationers

Appel, J. C. The Pocono forests and the military movements of 1779. *Pennsylvania Heritage* 8(3):19–22.

Appel, J. C. et al. 1976. *History of Monroe County, Pennsylvania 1725–1976.* East Stroudsburg, PA: Pocono Hospital Auxillary.

Baron, J., Karish, J., and E. Johnson. 1985. *Acidic Atmospheric Deposition in Delaware Water Gap National Recreation Area.* Milford, PA: National Park Service.

Bertland, D. N., P. M. Valence, and R. J. Woodling. 1975. *The Minisink, A Chronicle of One of America's First and Last Frontiers.* Stroudsburg, PA: Four-County Task Force on the Tocks Island Dam Project.

Bradt, P. T., and M. B. Berg. 1983. Preliminary survey of Pocono mountain lakes to determine sensitivity to acid deposition. *Proc. Pa. Acad. Sci.* 57:190–194.

Bradt, P. T. et al. 1986. Biology and chemistry of three Pennsylvania lakes: Responses to acid precipitation. *Water, Air, and Soil Pollution* 30:505–513.

Brewster, W. 1954. *The Pennsylvania and New York Frontier. History of from 1720 to the Close of the Revolution.* Philadelphia: George S. MacManus Co.

Gilpin, J. 1922. Journey to Bethlehem (an 1802 account). *The Pennsylvania Magazine of History and Biography* 46:15–38, 122–153.

Goodrich, P. G. 1880. *History of Wayne County.* Honesdale, PA: Haines and Beardsley.

Guide to the Historical Markers of Pennsylvania, 4th ed. 1975. Harrisburg: Pennsylvania Historical and Museum Commission.

Historic Pennsylvania Leaflets. Nos. 1, 24, 26, 31, 40, 41. Harrisburg: Pennsylvania Historical and Museum Commission.

Hunter, W. A. 1960. *Forts on the Pennsylvania Frontier, 1753–1758.* Harrisburg: Pennsylvania Historical and Museum Commission.

Impact of Second Home Development on Northeastern Pennsylvania. 1976. Prepared by Economic Development Council of Northeastern Pennsylvania, Avoca, PA.

Keller, R. B. 1927. *History of Monroe County, Pennsylvania.* Stroudsburg, PA: The Monroe Publishing Co.

Kent, B. C. 1980. *Discovering Pennsylvania's Archeological Heritage.* Harrisburg: Pennsylvania Historical and Museum Commission.

Kinsey, W. F., III. 1983. Eastern Pennsylvania prehistory: a review. *Pennsylvania History* 50(2):69–108.

Kraft, H. C. 1981. The Historic Minisink settlements: an investigation into a prehistoric and early historic site in Sussex County, New Jersey. Elizabeth, NJ: Archaeo-Historic Research.

Kraft, H. C. 1986. *The Lenape.* Collections of the New Jersey Historical Society, Vol. 21. Newark, NJ: New Jersey Historical Society.

Majumdar, S. K., F. J. Brenner, and A. F. Rhoads. 1986. *Endangered and Threatened Species Programs in Pennsylvania and Other States: Causes, Issues and Management.* Easton, PA: The Pennsylvania Academy of Science.

Mathews, A. 1886. *History of Wayne, Pike and Monroe Counties, Pennsylvania.* Philadelphia: R. T. Peck and Co.

Monroe County-Historic Legacy. 1980. Stroudsburg, PA: Monroe County Planning Commission.

Northeastern Pennsylvania: Toward the Year 2000. Summary Report. 1975. Prepared by Economic Development Council of Northeastern Pennsylvania, Avoca, PA.

Resource Conservation and Development. 1981. Prepared by the Pocono-Northeast Resource Conservation and Development Council, Blakeslee, PA.

Sipe, C. H. 1927. *The Indian Chiefs of Pennsylvania.* Butler, PA: The Ziegler Printing Co.

Wallace, P. A. 1981. *Indians in Pennsylvania.* Rev. ed. Harrisburg: Historical and Museum Commission.

Weslager, C. A. 1972. *The Delaware Indians, A History.* New Brunswick, NJ: Rutgers University Press.

Witthoft, J. 1967. *The American Indian as Hunter.* Harrisburg: Pennsylvania Historical and Museum Commission.

Chapter 8: Delaware Water Gap National Recreation Area

Fulcomer, K., and R. Corbett. 1981. *The Delaware River. A Resource and Guidebook to the River and the Valley.* Springfield, VA: Seneca Press.

Harding, J. J., ed. 1986. *Marsh, Meadow, Mountain, Natural Places of the Delaware Valley.* Philadelphia: Temple University Press.

Menzies, E. 1966. *Before the Water.* New Brunswick, NJ: Rutgers University Press.

Subitsky, S., ed. 1969. *Geology of Selected Areas of New Jersey and Eastern Pennsylvania.* New Brunswick, NJ: Rutgers University Press.

Additional Readings

Albert, R. C. 1988. *Damming the Delaware.* University Park: Pennsylvania State University Press.

Davlin, R. 1988. Cultures clash amid boom (pt. 1 of 5). *The Morning Call,* July 3, pp. A1, A4, A6–A8.

Hayden, A. H. 1989. The eastern coyote revisited. *Pa. Game News* 60(4):12–15.

Lowry, T., and T. Mutchler. 1988. Police stretched thin, crime getting more violent (p. 4 of 5). *The Morning Call,* July 6, pp. A1, B12.

McPhee, J. 1983. *In Suspect Terrain.* New York: Farrar Straus Giroux.

Orenstein, R. H. 1988. Region's wild growth is taking its toll (pt. 3 of 5). *The Morning Call,* July 5, pp. A1, A4.

Salter, R. 1988. Long Pond. *The Morning Call,* July 5, pp. D1, D2.

Wittman, B. 1988. Dawn of change found region woefully unprepared (pt. 2 of 5). *The Morning Call,* July 4, pp. A1–A4.

Wittman, B. 1988. Hard-sell, high-volume resort industry is booming (pt. 5 of 5). *The Morning Call,* July 7, pp. A1, A4.

Index